ETHNIC AND RACIAL CONSCIOUSNESS

By the same author:

The Coloured Quarter
West African City
White and Coloured
The Policeman in the Community
Roles
Race Relations
Racial Minorities
Police–Community Relations
The Race Concept (with Jonathan Harwood)
The Idea of Race
Racial and Ethnic Competition
Promoting Racial Harmony
Investigating Robbery
Racial Theories
Racial Consciousness
Discrimination
International Action against Racial Discrimination

Ethnic and Racial Consciousness

Michael Banton

2nd Edition

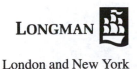

LONGMAN

London and New York

Addison Wesley Longman Limited,
Edinburgh Gate, Harlow,
Essex CM20 2JE, England
and Associated Companies throughout the world.

Published in the United States of America
by Addison Wesley Longman Inc., New York

First edition published 1988
This edition first published 1997

ISBN 0 582 29911 X PPR

British Library Cataloguing-in-Publication Data

A catalogue record for this book is
available from the British Library

Library of Congress Cataloging-in-Publication Data

Banton, Michael P.
    Ethnic and racial consciousness/Michael Banton.
      p.   cm.
    Includes bibliographical references and index.
    ISBN 0–582–29911–X (pbk.)
    1. Ethnicity.   2. Ethnic relations.   3. Race relations–
–Philosophy.   I. Title.
    GN495.6.B364   1997
    305.8–dc20

96-28506
CIP

Set in Times
Produced through Longman Malaysia, LSP

CONTENTS

LIST OF FIGURES AND TABLES

CHAPTER 1

Introduction

Armed conflicts have recently threatened the future of a series of multinational and multi-ethnic states. In some of them an ethnic dimension has been paramount, as in the former Yugoslavia and in Rwanda and Burundi; elsewhere the ethnic dimension has overlapped with political or religious dimensions, as in the Sudan, Kashmir, Tibet, and Chiapas in Mexico. According to the UN *Report on the World Social Situation* for 1993, there were in the years 1989–90 thirty-three armed conflicts that had each led to more than a thousand casualties. Just one was between nation-states, all the rest were between ethnic, religious or other groups within one and the same state. The calculation omitted smaller armed and all unarmed conflicts; it took no account of relations in Belgium, Fiji, Kenya, Malaysia, Moldova, Nigeria, Quebec, Spain, Transcaucasia, and so on. There have been continuing struggles in these places which many writers a hundred years ago would have called 'wars of races' because the word 'race' was then often used interchangeably with 'nation' or 'people'. Now they would be called ethnic conflicts.

In parts of Bosnia many people lived alongside others of a different ethnic origin for generations with very little consciousness of this difference. Then hostilities broke out elsewhere and spread to their localities. Inspired by beliefs about the importance of ethnic difference, terrible atrocities were committed. Trust was destroyed; people no longer felt safe with neighbours of different ethnicity. Why should conflict have escalated? After all, many countries have been populated by a series of immigrant groups, like the Angles, Saxons and Normans in England, and they have grown together. The number of distinctive languages spoken in the world continually diminishes as ethnic groups dissolve. Ethnic differences do not cause conflict, but conflict can make people much more conscious of ethnic difference if the conflicts follow the lines of ethnic division.

Conflicts can be managed by wise statesmanship, aided, sometimes, by international oversight. The Federal Republic of Yugoslavia was created after the First World War in such an operation; it was a unit big enough to be divided more recently into separate states. Czechoslovakia was created at the same time and has since undergone a 'velvet divorce' to create the separate states of the Czech Republic and Slovakia (though very many Czechs and Slovaks regret the split and did not believe it necessary). In other instances, like the

Lebanon, division is not possible; the chief causes of the conflicts between the ethno-religious groups in that small country have lain outside its frontiers in the tension between Israel and its Arab neighbours. South Africa is large enough for division, but the supporters of the new government there would regard partition as a terrible failure. They believe they can reverse earlier trends and create a non-racial society.

Sometimes ethnic relations within states are affected by changes in the relations between states. The fall of the Berlin wall on 9 November 1989 marked a major change of this kind. The reduction in tension between East and West removed forces which had been suppressing ethnic tensions in the East. The most notable of the succeeding events was Croatia's precipitate declaration of independence on 25 June 1991, followed by waves of 'ethnic cleansing' in the former Yugoslavia. Further east came the ethnic conflicts in Georgia, Armenia-Azerbaijan, Tadjikistan, Kazakhstan, Chechnya, and other republics whose boundaries had been drawn in Moscow with little regard for the ethnic geography. One consequence of the weakening of state controls was a flood of asylum-seekers, many of whom moved to Europe; in Germany some of them became subject to fierce attack in 1992–3. Hostility spilled over onto settled immigrants as well, but in general the ending of the Cold War did not bring ethnic conflicts to the surface in the West to the same extent as in the East.

Modes of discourse

Before trying to explain the presence or absence of ethnic conflict, it is prudent to pause over the nature of the task itself. The people who have been involved in the conflicts identify themselves as Serbs, Croats, Muslims, Hutu, Tutsi, and so on. They use proper names (in the technical sense of that expression). Serbs may say that they are caught up in a struggle with the Croats or the Muslims. They do not say that they are party to an ethnic, national, religious or racial struggle. It is a commentator from outside who imposes a definition of the nature of the struggle by adding an adjective of this kind. That is the operation over which the reader should pause because it introduces some complex issues.

Some Serbs may feel that they are Serbs, and not be bothered about the nature of Serb-ness. Others may believe that Serbs constitute a nation and that certain consequences follow from this presumed fact. An observer who decides that, because of their sentiments of belonging in a group, both groups display a national consciousness, must employ abstract criteria which ought also to help decide what sort of group consciousness is displayed by Hutu and Tutsi in Rwanda, or Unionist and Republican in Northern Ireland. That is the theory. The practice is not so systematic, because these issues are still quite new.

There are several ways of describing differences commonly called 'ethnic', or several modes of discourse. This book distinguishes the practical language of everyday life from the theoretical language being developed for the purposes of social science. Practical language is adapted to the circumstances of the locality and the tasks in hand. It is generalized and refined in the classifications elaborated for use in population censuses. It is refined further in the legal language fashioned to enable courts to decide how the law is to be applied in particular circumstances. Social scientists have to generalize in a different way. They seek to explain the nature and causes of conflict and to this end have to sort out and classify its forms. While the words used in the practical language of their own societies may be serviceable, they may also be of limited application or introduce bias. If social scientists are to develop criteria which can be used consistently in all regions of the world for deciding whether a conflict is to be accounted ethnic, national, religious or racial, or some combination of these characteristics, they must not take over the perceptions of those who have an interest in the outcomes of the struggles.

Tremendous advances in knowledge have been achieved since the 1940s in the physical and biological sciences. There have also been great advances in the social sciences, but they have been less obvious because many of them have passed into the language of everyday life. Advances in physical and biological science often entail the coining of new terms with precise significations; parallel advances in the social sciences are more likely to entail the revision of everyday language in order to give familiar words more precise meanings. An example of a new vocabulary which falls somewhere in between the two is that developed for use with computers; it includes some new words and some familiar ones with restricted meanings (like icon, cursor, default, file, format, menu, and so on). Someone starting with a computer can learn this vocabulary as an addition to that of everyday language. People interested in what social scientists have discovered about the nature and causes of ethnic conflict have to do more than this; they must be prepared to reconsider the ways they have been thinking about this subject and to engage with the attempt to construct a more systematic vocabulary as a necessary part of the enterprise.

Relations in Bosnia furnish an illustration of the need to go beyond the vocabulary of the parties. Elsewhere the name 'Muslim' is used to identify the followers of a religion, but in Bosnia it has been adopted to distinguish a class of persons who say they are neither Serbs nor Croats and who have adopted as the name for their group that of a religion practised by their ancestors, although many who now call themselves Muslims do not practise it in any orthodox manner. Their group was defined primarily by its opposition to the other groups. Members of all three groups spoke the same language with only small variations, while in some localities they had lived together in communities with little regard for group differentiation. Many in the wider Muslim world saw the Bosnian Muslims (as they have seen the Chechens) as co-religionists persecuted because of their faith by persons opposed to any Muslim presence in Europe. They were ready to come to their aid; so it was to the group's advantage if its representatives emphasized the religious as well as the ethnic dimension to their shared identity.

Parallels can be drawn in the case of Jews, Sikhs and Rastafarians. What sort of group do Jews constitute? Judaism is a religion but some of those who consider themselves Jews reject it. Since the foundation of the state of Israel in 1948 Jewishness has acquired a national dimension, while there have been people (both Gentile and Jewish) who have maintained that Jews are a race (depending sometimes upon the way that word is defined). The English courts have readily accepted that Jews are a good example of an ethnic group; they have also been asked to consider whether, for the purposes of the Race Relations Act 1976, Sikhs and Rastafarians constitute ethnic as well as religious groups. Judges in the House of Lords elaborated a set of criteria to define an ethnic group, but they could have taken a shorter route. There are Jewish and Sikh atheists who may suffer discrimination because others regard them as Jews and Sikhs. There are converts to both religions who are not of the same descent as most of their co-religionists. This shows that though most members belong to both a religious and an ethnic group, some belong to one alone. While the boundaries of the two groups overlap, the ethnic group is the larger. Rastafarianism, however, is purely a faith. It makes no sense at present to imagine a Rastafarian atheist or a Muslim atheist, proving that Rastafarians and Muslims (outside Bosnia) are not ethnic groups even if Rastafarian and Muslim individuals belong to ethnic groups because they are also, say, Jamaicans or Bengalis.

The sources of group consciousness

One of the lessons learned from the study of ethnic relations since the 1940s is that the features of such groups are not the expressions of innate characters. Ethnic, national, religious, racial and similar groups are continually changing as their members react to new circumstances and assess the opportunities they present. The complexities can be reduced a little by dividing them into those of structure, process and consciousness. Group formation is influenced by the structure of social institutions which may make it easier for individuals to come together in some forms of association than others (e.g. in many societies anyone can form a religious group because faith is thought to belong in the field of private life). Group formation is also influenced by the processes of change affecting the society, many of which can be observed in the changes in individual lives and in the relations between generations. Changes are brought about by

the way individuals perceive their circumstances, but their perceptions are at the same time conditioned by their social environment.
Thus the triangular web of structure, process and consciousness is
built out of interactions between its constituent parts.

One task for social scientists is to identify the factors which make
conflict more or less likely, how they interact, and what, if anything,
makes ethnic conflict distinctive. There is much for them to learn
from the absence of conflict. In some countries significant numbers
of people believe that to get what they want they have to change the
societies in which they live. But in other countries much of the
opposition to governments is that of political parties which want
office to make only small changes to the way in which the state is
run. Their supporters are people whose most pressing concerns are to
repay the mortgages on their houses, to clothe their children, save for
the family holidays, or with the progress of the local football team.
The Western industrial countries could not now be drawn into
international conflicts as easily as they were in 1870, 1914 and 1939.
Their populations feel that they have too much to lose and that
modern warfare is too terrible.

To explain the potentialities for ethnic conflict, it is necessary to
proceed step by step, setting out explicitly the various relevant
factors even if some of them appear self-evident. This starts in
Chapter 4, but before getting to the starting line some preparation is
needed. No reader of this book will begin it with a completely open
mind; every reader will have their own ideas about the nature of
ethnic and racial relations. So the book has, in Chapter 2, to review
these ideas and point out some of their peculiarities. In Chapter 3 it
has to explain where these ideas have come from. After this
preparation it can try to order the relevant factors.

The most difficult problems centre on the relations between the
individual and society. Obviously, individuals are fashioned by the
societies in which they grow up. Equally obviously, societies are
composed of, and changed by, their individual members. Since any
attempt to list all the ways in which the individual and society
interact would soon become deadly boring, a discussion has to be
selective. Chapter 4 maintains that some groups exist in a state of
almost continual mobilization, so that their members display a high
level of group consciousness. Other groups are coalitions whose
members usually manage to come together when the group's
interests are threatened, but are full of internal tensions. Most groups
have their rebels. The internal dynamics of a group are affected by
its external relations and in turn decide how the group will respond
to those relations.

Chapter 5 moves on to describe some of these external relations.
The events of history are often influenced by contingencies that could
not be predicted, like assassinations and the peculiarities of individuals in positions of power; this is why the social scientist can account
only for the potentialities of situations for conflict or harmony.

Chapters 6 and 7 attempt this, showing the ways in which societies can be organized so as to point individuals either towards conflict or in the opposite direction.

The first edition of this book in 1988 set out to explain how it was that many humans came to think of themselves and others as belonging in races. This second edition generalizes the argument to contend that racial consciousness is only one form of group consciousness. Though some features of racial consciousness, like doctrines of racial inequality, are found only in connection with inherited physical differences, most are shared with consciousness of ethnic origin. Many are shared with consciousness of gender, sexual orientation, social class, age, disability and other salient social characteristics. The underlying argument is therefore that ethnic and racial relations can be understood better if they are seen as examples of more general social processes (even if no full discussion of all these processes can be offered here). If this is borne in mind it may be easier to appreciate why some humans feel themselves to be members of ethnic and racial groups, and why such a feeling can vary in strength from one individual and one situation to another.

This edition includes a new chapter on the international oversight of state policies concerning ethnic relations. International action can be of two kinds, remedial and preventive. The UN protection force UNPROFOR in the former Yugoslavia was an ill-fated example of the former; it was sent in by the Security Council to keep the peace when there was no peace to keep. The prospects for remedial action are rarely encouraging, which makes it all the more important to reinforce procedures for preventive action, either by the UN or by regional organizations. The prospects for preventive action depend upon the accuracy with which the causes of conflict have been diagnosed. Those causes have to be analysed at both the level of the individual and that of the state.

CHAPTER 2

Naming groups

Anyone who takes a walk in London, New York or other major cities will see people of a different skin colour, people who may be classified as Asian, black, Chinese, Indian, white, etc. Some people may be difficult to classify. A person who reflects upon this will become aware of at least two things. First, that there is a social process by which individuals are assigned to categories of this sort, even though there is often doubt about the best names for the categories and about the boundaries to be drawn between one category and another. Second, that people's consciousness of such differences varies according to circumstances. A passenger may not remember whether the bus-driver who took the fare two hours previously was black or white, because colour does not signify very much in the relationship between a bus-driver and a passenger. But if that same person's sister had brought home a new boyfriend the previous week, would remember whether the boyfriend was black, Asian or white, and a lot more about him, because a relationship that may lead to marriage has important consequences for the kinsfolk of the parties. To cite another example, I remember being invited to lunch at the home of a professor in California. He and his family prepared to say grace. The language was strange and I thought, 'It must be Hebrew. These people must be Jews.' Nothing had happened before to make me perceive them as Jewish. Circumstances can also operate to make individuals classify themselves. Many young children must have come home from school and asked their parents why their home did not have a Christmas tree, as other children in their class did. When the parents explained that Christmas trees were for Christians and that they did not have one because they were Jews (or Muslims), the children may have become more conscious of being Jewish (or Muslim) than before.

The doubts about the correct name for a social category highlight certain features in the process of classification. Up to the 1970s, the British usually classified other people as either white or coloured. They were unsure about the classification of dark-skinned Medi-terranean people, showing that there was a doubt about where the boundary between white and coloured was to be drawn. The scientific procedure would be to define the category first and then to choose a name for it, but in social life the availability of a name often leads people to recognize a category. Now whites have a greater awareness of the differences between minority ethnic groups. Those from the Indian subcontinent are likely to be called Asians, and then divided by their national origin into Indians, Pakistanis, Bangladeshis, Sri Lankans, and so on, though the people themselves may prefer to be named by their religion (Hindu, Muslim or Sikh). To call people Asians is to classify them by their geographical origin; to call them Indians is to classify them by their presumed national origin; to call them coloured is to classify them by their appearance. Some individuals are not easily classified. If, say, children have an Indian mother and an English father, are they to be assigned to the same category as their mother, their father or to a separate category, either of persons of mixed origin or of intermediate appearance? The answer has to depend upon the purpose for which a classification is employed.

Just as it can be difficult to classify some individuals, so it can be difficult to decide by what criteria a group has been constituted. Jews are unquestionably a group of some sort, but, people dispute about whether they are a religious, racial, or ethnic group, or some combination of all three. Something similar can be said about the English. Many white people in Britain distinguish between themselves as English and all other groups. Some accept that there are other people appropriately called black British but question whether there are or can be black English. Yet if a mixed group of young men from London went to Glasgow to support a London football team they might well all count themselves and be counted English over against the supporters of the Scottish side. Popular consciousness adapts to circumstances.

A study of a multiracial nursery school in Sweden found that the teachers grouped the children according to the languages spoken in their homes. All the Latin American children – Argentinian, Bolivian, Chilean, Uruguayan, etc. – were put in one class and were referred to as 'the Spanish children'. There were five African children who all, unlike the Latin American children, spoke and understood Swedish well. They were placed in a Swedish-speaking class and referred to as Swedish children. The teachers knew that the Chilean children were not Spanish, and that the Nigerian children were not Swedish, but for the day-to-day running of the nursery that was less important than classification by language (Ehn 1986: 29–30). When, for convenience, larger ethnic categories are created in this way, people may not be conscious of their inaccuracies. A study of a town in north-west Ontario, Canada, found that there were residents often referred to as Ukrainians. This category included Poles, Romanians, Russians and Yugoslavs. It was called Ukrainian because, apparently, Ukrainians were the most numerous of what appeared to others a category of relatively similar people. Finns gave their name to a Scandinavian category and Chinese to an East Asian category (see Figure 2.1). The anthropologist who carried out this study (Stymeist, 1975: 50) heard someone in a bar addressed as 'Uke'. Instead of

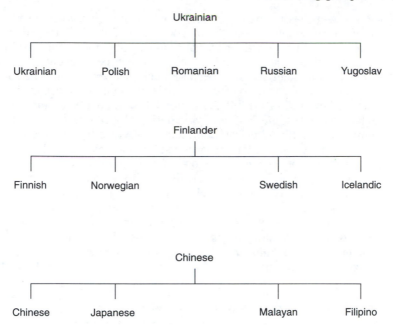

Figure 2.1 **Ethnic categorization in an Ontario town**

treating this name as simply a basis for interpersonal relations, as everyone else did, he asked the man if he was actually a Ukrainian. The answer was yes. The anthropologist then asked, in apparent innocence, 'What part of the Ukraine did your family come from?' and got the reply 'They didn't. They came from Poland. I'm a Polack.' The man was willing to be taken for a Ukrainian because that was the local convention. The local people were not interested in what they saw as the finer details of differentiation in a faraway land. It is in this way that ethnic identities are redefined in new situations.

Practical language

The classifications that people use in everyday life are fashioned to that purpose and can be internally inconsistent without causing difficulties because people use that part of the classificatory system which is appropriate to the circumstances and do not have to defend the system as a whole. Thus it is practical to group the children in the Swedish nursery according to their home languages. When people are joking with one another in a Canadian bar it is convenient to aggregate members of the smaller minorities into regional groups. However, anyone who has to compile a table of population statistics needs to work with a logically consistent scheme. Everyone must be classified by country of birth, or country of father's birth, or by country of mother's birth, or by nationality, or by appearance, or by self-assignation. Practical considerations sometimes prevent the use of a fully consistent scheme, because such a scheme would be too large and complicated for many people to administer accurately. Consider how, in 1990, Table 2.1 divided the US population into five 'racial' categories; the first two were defined by colour, the third by origin in the North American continent subdivided by ethnic group, the fourth by Asian and Pacific origin subdivided by national origin; the fifth was a residual category. Then there was a separate classification: Non-Hispanic/Hispanic, with the former subdivided to identify three different national origins plus a residual category. A Hispanic-origin person could be of any 'race'. It was a table constructed on multiple criteria to provide the sort of information most likely to be wanted, that is, about the size of the groups in which members of the US public are most likely to be interested.

Figure 2.2 reproduces the ethnic origin question in the United

Table 2.1 **Race and Hispanic origin for the United States, 1990**

Race		
All persons	248,709,873	100.0
White	199,686,070	80.3
Black	29,986,060	12.1
American Indian, Eskimo or Aleut	1,959,234	0.8
American Indian	1,878,285	0.8
Eskimo	57,152	0.0
Aleut	23,797	0.0
Asian or Pacific Islander	7,273,662	2.9
Chinese	1,645,472	0.7
Filipino	1,406,770	0.6
Japanese	847,562	0.3
Asian Indian	815,447	0.3
Korean	798,849	0.3
Vietnamese	614,547	0.2
Hawaiian	211,041	0.1
Samoan	62,964	0.0
Guamian	49,345	0.0
Other Asian or Pacific Islander	821,692	0.3
Other race	9,904,847	3.9
Hispanic origin	22,354,059	9.0
Mexican	13,494,938	5.4
Puerto Rican	2,727,754	1.1
Cuban	1,043,932	0.4
Other Hispanic	5,086,435	2.0
Not of Hispanic origin	226,355,814	91.0

Source: US Bureau of the Census, copied from UN document E/CN.4/ 1995/78/Add.1

11	Ethnic group	Person No. 1	Person No. 2

Please tick the appropriate box

Person No. 1
- White ☐ 0
- Black-Caribbean ☐ 1
- Black-African ☐ 2
- Black-Other ☐
  please describe

- Indian ☐ 3
- Pakistani ☐ 4
- Bangladeshi ☐ 5
- Chinese ☐ 6
- Any other ethnic group ☐
  please describe

Person No. 2
- White ☐ 0
- Black-Caribbean ☐ 1
- Black-African ☐ 2
- Black-Other ☐
  please describe

- Indian ☐ 3
- Pakistani ☐ 4
- Bangladeshi ☐ 5
- Chinese ☐ 6
- Any other ethnic group ☐
  please describe

If the person is descended from more than one ethnic or racial group, please tick the group to which the person considers he/she belongs, or tick the 'Any other ethnic group' box and describe the person's ancestry in the space provided.

Figure 2.2 **The ethnic question in the United Kingdom census, 1991 (source: UK Census Office)**

4	Race	Person No. 1	Person No. 2

Fill ONE circle for the race that the person considers himself/herself to be.

Person No. 1
- ○ White
- ○ Black or Negro
- ○ Indian (Amer.) (Print the name of the enrolled or principal tribe.)
- ○ Eskimo
- ○ Aleut

Asian or Pacific Islander
- ○ Chinese ○ Japanese
- ○ Filipino ○ Asian Indian
- ○ Hawaiian ○ Samoan
- ○ Korean ○ Guamanian
- ○ Vietnamese ○ Other API
- ○ Other race (Print race)

Person No. 2
- ○ White
- ○ Black or Negro
- ○ Indian (Amer.) (Print the name of the enrolled or principal tribe.)
- ○ Eskimo
- ○ Aleut

Asian or Pacific Islander
- ○ Chinese ○ Japanese
- ○ Filipino ○ Asian Indian
- ○ Hawaiian ○ Samoan
- ○ Korean ○ Guamanian
- ○ Vietnamese ○ Other API
- ○ Other race (Print race)

If **Indian (Amer.)**, print the name of the enrolled or principal tribe.

If **Other Asian or Pacific Islander (API)**, print one group, for example: Hmong, Fijian, Laotian, Thai, Tongon, Pakistani, Cambodian, and so on.

If **Other race**, print race

4. Fill ONE circle for the race each person considers himself/herself to be.

If you fill the **Indian (Amer.)** circle, print the name of the tribe or tribes in which the person is enrolled. If the person is not enrolled in a tribe, print the name of the principal tribe(s).

If you fill the **Other API** circle [under **Asian or Pacific Islander (API)**], only print the name of the group to which the person belongs. For example, the **Other API** category includes persons who identify as Burmese, Fijian, Hmong, Indonesian, Laotian, Bangladeshi, Pakistani, Tongan, Thai, Cambodian, Sri Lankan, and so on.

If you fill the **Other race** circle, be sure to print the name of the race.

If the person considers himself/herself to be **White, Black or Negro, Eskimo or Aleut, fill one circle only. Please do not print the race in the boxes.**

The **Black or Negro** category also includes persons who identify as African-American, Afro-American, Haitian, Jamaican, West Indian, Nigerian, and so on.

All persons, regardless of citizenship status, should answer this question.

Figure 2.3 **The race question in the United States census, 1990 (with thanks to the US Census Bureau)**

Table 2.2 **United Kingdom population by ethnic group, 1991**

All ethnic groups	54,889,000	100.0
White	51,874,000	94.5
Ethnic minority groups	3,015,000	5.5
Black groups	891,000	1.6
Caribbean	500,000	0.9
African	212,000	0.4
Other	178,000	0.3
Indian	84,000	1.5
Pakistani	477,000	0.9
Bangladeshi	163,000	0.3
Chinese	157,000	0.3
Other groups		
Asian	198,000	0.4
Non-Asian	290,000	0.5

Kingdom's 1991 population census. Table 2.2 displays the information it yielded (figures to the nearest thousand). The same categories are now being employed for the purposes of ethnic monitoring. When the police in Britain arrest people they now have to record their ethnic origin, ascertaining with which category they identify themselves. This will cause irritation to those who identify themselves in ways for which the classification does not allow, and thus generate pressure for modification of the categories to be used in the census of 2001. Many persons in the South Asian parental generation would sooner be classified by religion; their children may before long object to being classified by their parents' country of origin, and they too may prefer to be accounted Hindus, Muslims or Sikhs even if they follow these religions no more devoutly than most British people follow theirs. Others may want a category 'Black British' or one that represents an identity intermediate between black and white.

As a further example of the utility of distinguishing between the practical language of everyday life and the theoretical language needed for purposes of analysis, consider the situation in Northern Ireland. For several centuries most members of the population have aligned themselves in two groups, often called Catholics and Protestants. Most of the conflict is political, about whether the 'six counties' should be part of the United Kingdom or of the Republic of Ireland. There are political differences within the Protestant group and among Catholics, some of whom are content that Northern Ireland should remain within the United Kingdom. Differences in religious belief help keep the two groups apart (for example, through separate schools), and it is very common in everyday life for everyone to be classified as either Catholic or Protestant even if they practise neither faith or have no faith. Religious leaders on both sides condemn the way that religion is represented as if it were the cause of the conflict. On average, the socio-economic status of the Protestants is slightly higher, so the opposition between the two groups has several dimensions to it (politics, religion, social status, etc.). This example illustrates two principal points.

The first is the distinction between categories and groups. *A category is a class defined by the categorizer*, as when persons earning wages of more than x and less than y are made a category for purposes of taxation. They are not a social group. *A social group is constituted by the relations between its members*; they are conscious of belonging to it, and identify themselves with it in varying degrees. This distinction is often ignored, both by sociologists and by others, who use 'group' when 'category' would be more accurate. (On occasion I follow this looser practice rather than make the text more difficult for the reader.) The importance of the distinction is that something extra is needed to make a category into a social group. Groups are created by processes of assignment, both self-assignment and the actions of others in categorizing persons as parties to relationships that confer rights and define obligations towards fellow-members (such as expectations of solidarity). Sometimes people come together on a temporary basis and form an aggregate rather than a group, as at election time; the percentage of the vote secured by a political party changes from one election to another and parties are created or dissolved as groups and aggregates form new coalitions or change their allegiances. All social groups, in varying degree, have a similar potentiality for change, particularly when membership is purely voluntary. Racial and ethnic groups are often distinctive in that other people assign individuals to membership and allow very little freedom of choice, so that they appear to be permanent and involuntary units.

The second principal point concerns the naming of groups. To call the opposed units in Northern Ireland Catholic and Protestant groups is a double simplification. Neither is a homogeneous group, and for some purposes they are really categories rather than groups. In so far as they are groups it is not the kind of church that people attend that maintains their identification but *the structure of political opposition*. So it is often more accurate to refer to Republicans and Unionists. It is always important to watch out for possible misrepresentation when groups are named, for, as an old saying had it, if you can give a dog a bad name, you can hang it.

The doubts about what are the best names for groups, and where the boundaries are to be drawn, show that the groups people recognize in everyday life are often multidimensional. The English constitute a recognizable unit in respect of nationality, religion, language and culture, but the distinctions between them and some other peoples are not clear-cut. The English share United Kingdom citizenship with the Welsh, Scots and Northern Irish, and this tends to obscure their nationality; they are not all members of the Church of England; their pronunciation may be distinctive, but they share their language with others in North America, Australia, New Zealand, South Africa, etc. In their own country the English are an ethnic majority.

There are also minority groups which are likewise distinctive on several dimensions, chiefly of appearance, but sometimes of religion, language and culture as well. Another way of representing this is to see group boundaries as a series of circles. Sometimes these coincide so that two boundaries are congruent; for example a circle around the Sikhs as an ethnic group would be almost the same as one round them as a religious group. Some circles overlap. Thus nearly all Bangladeshis are Muslims, but the category 'Muslim' includes people from other national and ethnic groups as well. A circle around the people who speak 'BBC English' would overlap one round people classed as 'Church of England', and most of it would come within a circle delimiting people of English nationality. Any particular set of individuals is likely to consist of persons who share attributes with many but not all members of the set. In the practical language of ordinary life people have to simplify. They are apt to assume that English people will be of 'white' appearance, have grown up in England, will speak in a particular way, profess Christianity, and so on. Such assumptions underly what may be called folk classifications. These change. From the Middle Ages up to the eighteenth century, Europeans thought of themselves very much in religious terms and differentiated themselves from people of other faiths. In the nineteenth century, first national and then racial classification came to the fore. Now it is no longer so safe to assume that English people will be white.

It was for reasons such as these that Everett and Helen Hughes (1952: 131) observed 'a considerable part of Sociology consists of cleaning up the language in which common people talk of social and moral problems'. Sometimes 'cleaning up' means persuading the general public to make use of distinctions that have been found important in theoretical language. One relevant example is the use, since the 1960s, of the word 'gender' in places where previously 'sex' would have been used. The language is made a little more precise if 'sex' is kept for biological differences and 'gender' is used to denote the social expectations related to sexual difference. The public may have a better understanding of any moral problems if these are described in words that convey a clear idea of their nature. In parallel with the change from sex to gender, it may be possible in the future to keep 'race' for biological differences and use 'ethnicity' for the distinguishing of social groups based on common appearance or ancestry. If so, that day is still far off.

The discussion has already hinted at three steps necessary for this kind of cleaning up. First, it is even more important in sociology than in biology to appreciate *the distinction between classification and nomenclature*. Objects of study have to be classified systematically in different ways appropriate to whatever has to be analysed. The task of naming the resulting taxa, or classes, is a separate one. The names given to plants do not affect the behaviour of the plants, but humans are very concerned about the names by which they are identified. Groups claim that they themselves should be able to choose the name by which they are to be known. *People give to themselves names which show who they claim to be* rather than who they actually are. They give to others names which show how they perceive these others, and which may differ from the names these others have for themselves. Fewer people object to being identified by national origin or religion than by race, but much can vary from one context to another. Sometimes rights to names are restricted. The Turkish government does not recognize Kurds as an ethnic group within the population. A member of the legislature was sentenced in 1979 to two years' imprisonment with hard labour for declaring in public 'In Turkey there are Kurds. I, too, am a Kurd'. In France a Breton family has given its children Breton names which are not on the state's register of permissible names; as a consequence, their births cannot be registered.

Second, it is vital to recognize that *physical differences do not of themselves give rise to cultural differences*. People belong in a particular blood group whether or not they know it. A person's complexion may, to the specialist, be an indicator that the person is more likely to have a particular gene, just as being male is an indicator that the person is more likely to be colour-blind, but these are statistical associations which have no implications for the way people should behave towards each other. Only with the progress of biological science in the twentieth century has this been properly appreciated. Those responsible for health care can now benefit from studies showing the frequencies with which certain genes occur in different sections of the population, but these frequencies bear very little relation to any folk classification. In the Americas there are very many people with some African and some European ancestry. In the United States they will usually be accounted black, but (as is discussed on pp. 56–60) in many parts of the Caribbean and Latin America they will be classified differently. Individuals from a country where most people are of predominantly African ancestry may feel black when in a predominantly white country but not when in their home country. The drawing of social boundaries may be influenced by physical difference, but it is not determined by it.

Some of the differences in the behaviour expected of men and women can be attributed to their genetic inheritance, but others are culturally cultivated; they vary from one society to another and they change over time. When those who occupy a particular position (say, teacher) are expected to behave in a particular way (e.g. teach), they have a role to play; this is defined by their relationships with those who occupy other positions (pupil, employer). *In racially divided societies, roles are allocated on the basis of physical appearance* (or phenotype, to use the technical term). Appearance, like costume and names, can serve as a role sign. People think 'because she has a dark skin she may be a West African', or 'because he wears a turban he must be a Sikh'; just as they think 'because he wears a clerical collar of that kind he's presumably a Catholic priest', or 'because her name is Cohen she must be Jewish'. Behind these inferences is the assumption that people differ in important ways and should be treated accordingly, though there is much variation because the signs are not always read in the same ways and beliefs about the special characteristics of West Africans, Sikhs, Catholic priests and Jews may be wrong. When a word that describes a physical difference is also used to designate a social category this may distract attention from the process by which physical features are given social meaning.

Third, if ordinary language is to be 'cleaned up' it is essential to appreciate that the same word may be used with different meanings. Changes in the meaning of 'race' and its relation to ethnicity are discussed in Chapter 3, but one caution must be entered immediately. No one has ever seen another person's race. People perceive phenotypical differences of colour, hair form, underlying bone structure, and so on. For historical reasons, phenotypical variations came to be the basis for what, in Western European culture in particular circumstances, were called racial classifications. They could have been called something else. There are therefore three levels of abstraction which have not been distinguished in the discussion so far. On the first, *individuals perceive physical and other differences*, which lead them to infer that the others are Pakistanis or Americans or Muslims, and so on. These are proper names. On the second level they use these perceptions as *signs of expected behaviour* (Americans may be expected to be tall or rich, for example); this is what gives assignment to such categories social meaning. There may then be a third level in which they describe their ideas about who belongs where as a *racial classification*, implying that genetic differences are responsible for some of the behavioural differences. The first and second levels are common to most societies. The third is the product of a particular culture which has been exported and adopted in other cultural regions, thereby occasioning confusion and misunderstanding. 'Race' is often used as if it were an objective, scientific and culture-free designation of differences of appearance. It is not. The very use of this word to identify such a classification brings with it a host of cultural associations deriving from the historical circumstances in which the word acquired special meanings. Appearance can be misleading. For the purposes of scientific classification a better set of terms is available. In everyday speech it may be quite legitimate to use the word race, but it is best first to consider whether there is not some other word that would be more accurate.

If the speaker wishes to refer to a group of persons of similar complexion or appearance, it may be better to call them an ethnic group, while remembering that everyone has an ethnic origin, not just the members of minorities. In Britain, the English have regarded the Scots, Welsh, Gujératis, Afro-Caribbeans, Poles, etc., as groups defined by ethnic attributes. They have not regarded themselves as possessing an ethnicity, because, being the largest group and the dominant element in the population, there has been no pressure upon them to distinguish their group from the society as a whole. This mode of reasoning has been called 'minus-one ethnicity' to reflect the way that members of the dominant group, if they add up the number of ethnic groups in their country, are inclined to count all the ethnic groups except their own. In the United States it has long been customary to speak of Irish-Americans, Italian-Americans, Polish-Americans, and so on. Only recently has the expression 'Anglo-American' made an appearance as an inprovement upon 'White Anglo-Saxon Protestant' or 'WASP'. Since many whites are not Protestant, 'Euro-American' would often be more appropriate. Because it takes itself for granted, the dominant group usually identifies itself by the name of the nation. New Zealand is an exception: the main population division is that between the people of Maori and European descent. The latter are known as Pakehas, using the Maori name for stranger. So most people there can claim the national name, New Zealander, and an ethnic name, Maori or Pakeha (some do not claim the name New Zealander but maintain that the country should be known by a Maori name, Aotearoa). The position can be contrasted with that in Scandinavia where there are national names, Norwegian, Swedish and Finnish. There is also an indigenous people in the North who call themselves Saami but have in the past been known as Lapps. The majority population in each of the three countries identifies itself by a national name only and is under no pressure to coin an ethnic name to distinguish itself from the original inhabitants.

Ethnic identification in Britain and North America tends to be voluntary, because individuals have the alternative of identifying themselves by their nationality alone, but in other places, for example in parts of the former Yugoslavia, ethnic identification has often been forced upon people. A somewhat distant parallel is that of people who have changed their sex and then applied to have their birth certificate altered. The certificate records a historical fact, but one that causes them embarrassment, contrary to the respect due to their private life. They may feel that they have had a gender identity forced upon them.

Group consciousness is never easily defined because it is a distillation of personal experience. In one form it is an individual's interpretation of how his or her life is affected by membership in the group. That membership may be a mixture of voluntary identification with other members, together with an involuntary identification decided by others. In another form, group consciousness is revealed in an individual's readiness to assign others to membership of groups.

While group consciousness varies from one person to another, there are also common elements. If those who are assigned to a particular group are treated similarly, then they have experiences in common. They project their own experience when they respond to information about other groups. Men can experience a common bond with men in a different society, women with women, whites with whites, and blacks with blacks.

This discussion should have shown that the words used in everyday life to designate groups ignore differences which can be very important to anyone who wants to understand the determinants underlying the social pattern. To identify these factors, it is necessary to develop a theoretical language. The use of Latin names, as in the naming of plants, can be one way to avoid emotional associations. Mathematical symbols can be even better. It is a matter not only of making distinctions, but also of finding similarities. Theoretical languages have to help in the explanation of the observations, so they are more concerned with concepts than with names. It is unhelpful to try to define concepts in isolation, because they belong in families. The research worker needs a set of concepts to cover a range of variables, just as lines can be drawn over a map to create the kind of grid that makes map references possible.

References to group consciousness belong in the practical language of everyday life because the sentiments in question are too variable to permit precise definition. The same applies to 'nation' and 'nationalism' because they refer to units within continually changing political structures. The words 'role', 'social relations', 'relationship', and even 'social group' are different in that while they are used in practical language, they can also be employed in the theoretical language of sociology in more precise senses. Later chapters will explain how some words and concepts are components of the theoretical language that is being developed for the study of ethnic and racial consciousness.

Name-changing

When newcomers are received into certain religious communities, like monasteries and convents, they are given a new name. *The names are signs that they have* undergone a religious conversion and *become new persons*. Equally some newly independent states have chosen new names, as the Gold Coast became Ghana, and Ceylon became Sri Lanka. Name-changing may help a group redefine itself. Events in Malaysia since the early 1970s have shown how a group which is not quite half of the total population has been able to strengthen its position by the introduction of a new name. The country's constitution has been written so as to confer special rights upon Malays; this is justified on the grounds that they are *bumipu-tera* (sons of the soil). Malaysians of Chinese origin observe that it is the *Oran Asli* (aborigines) who are the true sons of the soil and that the Malays, like themselves, are immigrants. But since the Malays were established in the country well before the 'English' came to England, this objection lacks political force. The success of the Malay claim that they are the sons of the soil, and the meaning which they have given to the name *bumiputera* has given them a powerful advantage in the political realm. The association of a name with a territory can be potent.

In the United States before the First World War, there were black preachers who maintained that African-Americans were the lost sheep of the House of Israel. In 1913 a Moorish Science Temple was founded in Newark which taught that Negroes were really Moors and Muslims. The first step towards true emancipation was for blacks to appreciate who they really were, and to assume their proper name. The Black Muslims grew into an important social and political movement in the 1960s. Its leader told his followers that they were not 'Negroes'; that this was only a label that white people had placed upon them to make discrimination easier. Entry into The Nation of Islam was marked by the discarding of what was called a slave name (i.e. a surname which may have derived from some white slave owner) and by rebirth into a new identity with a new first name followed by the letter X to denote both the change ('ex') and the mystery of destiny (e.g. Malcolm X). People who suffer racial discrimination are sometimes reluctant to acknowledge that others regard their group with scorn. Unless they have the emotional support of their fellows and an explanation of why prejudice should be directed against them, individuals may find it psychologically easier to assume that they have failed to progress because of their own limitations than to face up to the full strength of the forces ranged against them. Many black people in the New World were unconsciously uncomfortable with their skin colour. Taking a new name could signify a recognition that the old identity was demeaned, a rejection of that identity, and the assumption of a new one. It could be comparable to a religious conversion.

In the United States up to the 1960s, 'coloured' was generally considered the best name for people with any degree of African ancestry, both by the people themselves and by others. Many of the people so designated had very light brown complexions and the adjective 'coloured' seemed suitable because it comprehended all the varying shades. At that time blackness was thought ugly, so that to call a person black was to say something wounding. Coloured was a kinder description. This was to change in the 1960s as African-Americans seized the leadership of the civil rights movement. If people could be brought to believe that black was as beautiful as any other colour, there would no longer be any reason to regret being black, and it could be no more hurtful to be called black than to be

Table 2.3 **Racial designations preferred by blacks in Detroit**

	1968	1971
Coloured	12	6
Negro	59	38
Black, Afro-American or black-American	23	53
Other	6	3

Source: Aberbach and Walker (1970)

called white. African-Americans outside the civil rights movement were not always inclined to change their self-definitions, so the activists retorted that those who called themselves coloured did so because they were frightened to call themselves black. Their message appealed to the younger generation and to city-dwellers. A measure of its spread is given by Table 2.3, showing the racial designations preferred by respondents of African descent in two surveys in Detroit. There had, for a long time, been groups of black people in the northern cities who thought that blacks should identify with Africa. They constituted a movement often called cultural nationalism for this reason. It might therefore have been interesting had the respondents been invited to choose between the three alternatives grouped together in the third line.

In the 1970s 'Black Americans' was the name favoured by many, but then after a while opinion settled on African-American as the preferred designation. When hyphenated, this name change brought African-Americans into line with other 'hyphenated Americans', like Irish-Americans, and so on. Discussion of preferred names also affected other groups which were moving towards a new self-consciousness. Sometimes the internal disagreements were so vehement as to give rise to a 'battle of the name'. Mexican-Americans fought this battle with a special passion. Most of those in California favoured 'Mexican-American', but the equivalent population in Texas wanted 'Spanish-speaking', while yet other groups favoured 'Americano', 'Latino' or 'Hispano'. Academics who studied the dispute said that the battle against the designation 'Mexican' – particularly in official statistics – was often explicitly a battle against the implied exclusion of Mexican-Americans from the 'white race', with all its rights and privileges. Of the various alternatives, 'Spanish' suggested a claim to an upper-class status, while 'Spanish-American' traditionally referred to the residents of the state of New Mexico who were established before the more recent immigration of lower-class Mexicans. They added that 'in recent years, *chicano* (a diminutive of *Mexicano* in Spanish) has come into increasing use as a self-referent, notably among the young and especially among the militant' (Grebler *et al.* 1970: 385–7).

The militant movement of the late 1960s and early 1970s

attempted to propagate a single ethno-national identity among all Mexican-Americans, emphasizing the Indian roots common to the entire grouping. According to Walter Connor (1985: 26) their programme included

- the popularization of the formerly pejorative self-referent *Chicano*
- appeals to a separate and unifying consciousness based upon a brown complexion
- a representation of society as polarized between 'us' and 'them', *Chicanos* and *Anglos*
- the development of nationhood by venerating *La Raza*.

But the campaign fizzled out. Its party, *La Raza Unida*, could not muster even one-third of the necessary 66,000 residents to qualify in California as a legally recognized political party. The group designation *Chicano* is still much less popular among the people than among those who write about them. In one survey only 4 per cent favoured it; in another, only 10 per cent. Results from the 1980 census suggested that more than 15 per cent of those considered to be Mexican-American had failed to identify themselves in this way when completing the form. Significant numbers denied having any Mexican ancestry. The militants fought a vigorous campaign, but they lost.

From the viewpoint of the militants it must have been a priority to try to unify as large a group as possible, in order to exercise most bargaining power. To get some of the Mexican-origin groups to join them, they may have had to make concessions, and sometimes the price demanded may have been too high. Had they won their internal battle they might then have had to fight an external battle to get others to use the name they had chosen.

The choice of a name may be influenced by its implications for the naming of other groups. When in 1948 the National Party came to power in South Africa it brought in the Population Registration Act which classified every inhabitant as White, Native or Coloured. At this time Natives were often described as Bantu. Some whites claimed to be white Africans and many maintained (with little justification) that the Bantu were also recent immigrants into southern Africa. To call black Africans 'natives' was therefore to imply that the whites were not natives. To have called them simply 'Africans' would have occasioned confusion in the Afrikaans language with the name Afrikaners used for themselves. So the Nationalists may well have been pleased when the designation 'black' became more acceptable and they could refer to blacks and whites without conceding that blacks had a better claim to be considered indigenous. Shifts in political relations were reflected in changes in nomenclature, as with the Department of Native Affairs, which became that of Bantu Affairs, then African and later Plural Affairs.

The black consciousness movement in the United States had a profound effect in Britain, giving rise to separate battles of the name which often overlapped and were confused with one another. The first was the one in which Afro-Caribbeans fought with themselves, or with the values with which they had been indoctrinated, and in favour of the self-referent 'black'. That battle was over by the mid-1970s. The second has been the longer-running struggle to get official bodies and public institutions to use the name black as a designation for all non-white persons. Waged by activists from the majority and the minorities, this campaign gained much ground during the late 1970s and early 1980s.

Afro-Caribbeans had not been subjected to so profound a subordination as African-Americans, and they could always call themselves Jamaicans, Trinidadians, Barbadians, etc. Nevertheless, many responded in much the same way as African-Americans. To change, and call themselves 'black', could be a struggle of great emotional significance. It testified to the psychological and cultural dimensions of racial subordination and liberation.

The argument for using black as a synonym for non-white was based on the proposition that whites had marked off non-whites as a separate category to whom they accorded fewer privileges. All non-whites had suffered from the racial prejudices of the whites. Sometimes it was claimed that, whether they appreciated it or not, all the peoples of Africa, South, East and South-East Asia, the Pacific, the Caribbean, and the native peoples of North and South America, had been exploited by whites and united by this experience. The proposition was one of dogma rather than demonstration. In its application to Britain, it appeared to be influenced by a desire to mobilize the largest possible constituency. It seemed to assume that the black–white boundary would not change; that blacks must attain equality with whites in the distribution of privileges (income, wealth, positions of high prestige, etc.) and in the exercise of civil rights; with the result that racial tension would then disappear.

As an argument for the inclusive use of the name, this overlooked several objections. The signal failure of the attempt in 1975–7 to create a National Black Peoples' Organization, despite a substantial grant from the Gulbenkian Foundation (Banton 1985: 64–6), might have suggested that the aspiration for so broad a coalition was unrealistic. So might the unwillingness of many Asians to identify themselves as black. Though many came from cultural areas in which a light complexion was preferred to a dark one, Asians had not been brought up to hate their colour. In the localities in which they had settled there were often important tensions between Asians and Afro-Caribbeans. In publications which adopted the inclusive use, it was often unclear whether or not Asians were included in generalizations about blacks, and this then had to be spelled out. People of intermediate appearance, or who could identify themselves with either black or white according to the circumstances, had a right to work out their own identities and to find a name or names acceptable to them; their options were not to be restricted as if they were anomalies.

In a discussion note addressed to sociologists that was first published in 1976, I drew attention to the problem of naming and went on to

pose this issue in its starkest form by asking what justification there is for our calling Asians 'black' in our research reports and discussions? ... Is it for the good of the whites, or the Asians, or both? Is there not a greater danger that the assumption that the social world is divided into blacks and whites may reinforce the very beliefs and assumptions we wish to combat?'

This article, both in its original and its reprinted form (Banton 1977), was ignored. The inclusive use of 'black', led by the white elite, some of the mass media, and political groups on the left (such as the 'black sections' group in the Labour Party and the race equality units in the Greater London Council between 1981 and 1986) became more and more common.

In 1988 Tariq Modood extended the criticism of these new usages. Some Asians accepted the designation 'black', yet there were three other groups, each one of which he thought more numerous than those who accepted it. First, the largest group were the Asians who knew that they were often called black but studiously refrained from referring to themselves in this way. Second there were those who felt politically obliged to call themselves black because of the expectations of their political champions, sponsors and sympathizers. Third, there were those Asians to whom it had not occurred that others might include them when they referred to blacks. Modood also acknowledged that the new use of 'black' was to indicate an aspiration for a wider unity, but detected in it a bias. It represented Africans as the prototypical blacks. Asians could never be as black as Africans. The price of the aspirational use, he wrote, was that British Asians had 'to define themselves in a framework historically and internationally developed by people in search of African roots'.

Several other unrelated considerations should also be borne in mind. The objection of the opposition of 'black' to 'white' as if they were mutually exclusive and exhaustive categories does not apply to the one term only. There are no circumstances in which all whites think or act alike, so that lumping them together can be misleading. Labelling them 'white' is no better than labelling other people 'black': it is inaccurate; it employs a value-laden name; and it introduces a discontinuity into what is socially as well as physically a continuous distribution. Nor should it be assumed that individuals themselves can provide a complete account of why certain names are preferred. People can give reasons for their preferences, but they may not be aware of underlying causes or of any logic which explains why the possible alternative names differ from one society to another. When a great variety of alternatives are in use, this may indicate that the social pattern is changing and fluid.

Name-changing can be observed among other groups, particularly occupational ones. In Britain, sanitary inspectors became public health inspectors. The name 'student' used to be reserved for university students, but now it is often used for those who would earlier have been called schoolchildren. For present purposes it is more relevant to note that in West European languages it has been customary for about the last two centuries to employ different titles for married and unmarried women (e.g. Mrs/Miss, Mme/Mlle, Signora/Signorina, Frau/Fräulein) while making no corresponding distinction for men. Many people in English-speaking countries now object to the differentiation of female titles in situations in which marital status is irrelevant, and prefer to use another title (Ms) for both married and unmarried women. The use of this title has been a point of principle for many women, a sign of how they saw themselves and wished others to see them. (An alternative is simply to stop using any such titles.) The use of 'gender-neutral language' is another example of sensitivity about the naming process.

Legal language

Every academic subject, and every profession, seeks greater precision in the use of words, but there is one field that should be of particular help to sociologists who study group relations. This is the branch of the law which prohibits discrimination. Law is the most refined form of practical language because courts have to be consistent in the way they define terms and how they apply them to behaviour. Members of the general public frequently accord extra respect to names and definitions that are enshrined in law. It is therefore useful to note that there is substantial agreement internationally about the definition of racial discrimination and a growing agreement about related concepts like prejudice and incitement to racial hatred.

Lawyers may be precise in their use of words but legislators have political objectives to meet. The UK Parliament in 1965, 1968 and 1976 agreed to legislation called Race Relations Acts. Parliament chose this name because members of the public were accustomed to thinking of relations between white people and people of another colour as race relations, and the government wanted to counter mistaken beliefs that physical differences in some way justified unequal treatment. In so doing it unintentionally reinforced the idea that relations between people of different appearance are in some way distinctive, that inter-racial relations differ from intra-racial relations. It would have been better had they been called Prevention of Discrimination Acts; after all, when in 1975 Parliament adopted the Sex Discrimination Act it did not consider calling it the Sex Relations Act!

The Acts prohibit less favourable treatment 'on racial grounds'; the latest (1976) Act states that 'racial grounds' 'means any of the following grounds, namely, colour, race, nationality or ethnic or national origins'. Thus in law racial grounds include ethnic grounds. If one person treats another less favourably on racial grounds, that may be unlawful even if the other person is not of the race that the discriminator believes him or her to be. For the purpose of what is called direct discrimination what matters is the intention of the discriminator. This enables a court to base its judgment upon the categories that underlie the thoughts and acts of ordinary people, without asking an expert whether those beliefs are scientifically correct.

These categories can be based on many-stranded relationships. When two people meet they can interact with one another on the basis of different relationships and they can change from one to another. Two students could interact on the basis of the same or different gender, the same or different generation, the same or different religion, as students of the same or different subjects, supporters of the same or different sporting teams, and so on. There is a social relation between them because they are interacting with one another, behaving in ways that respond to one another. The way they behave at any particular time depends upon how they negotiate the relevant relationship. For example, a female student might ask a male student for advice about something connected with her studies, in terms of the relationship between fellow-students. He might attempt to change it into a male–female relationship. She might either agree to interact on this basis or decline to do so. To describe things in this way is to draw a distinction between a relation (between individuals) and a relationship (between roles).

What the law calls race relations are therefore, in a strict sense, racial relationships. They are interactions in which the behaviour of one or both parties is influenced by a belief that it is appropriate to behave differently when the parties are not of the same race. For someone to discriminate racially it is not necessary that the person should be racially conscious in the sense that they could say, 'I know that person was of a different race and therefore I treated that person differently.' It may be that the person in question had little insight into his or her motives, or was simply confused, but others could see that this person treated people of a different race in a different way. It is also possible for someone to be mistaken in thinking that another is of the same or different race. Inferences are made from people's names and from accents heard over the telephone. There is a medical condition known as 'Nelson's disease' in which the skin of 'white' people turns brown, and they become the victims of racial discrimination; they are not of different race if this is defined in terms of their genetic inheritance, but they are if race is defined by reference to differential treatment.

If social relations are many-stranded, race may be one of the strands. A relation between a white person and a black person is not necessarily a racial relation. It becomes one only when one of them treats the other differently on racial grounds. Differential treatment may constitute discrimination in the legal sense but does not necessarily do so. The law has been drafted to protect people from being treated unfavourably in employment, education, the provision of goods, facilities and services (like housing), and the disposal or management of premises. It deals with situations in which one party can grant or withhold something of material value. There are many everyday encounters which entail no more than the granting or withholding of friendship and courtesy; these are not covered by the law, though victims of discrimination are usually offered sums of money by the courts in recognition of the injury to their feelings. A sociological approach must be broader than that of the law. Any kind of difference in behaviour associated with an assumed difference in physical appearance or ancestry can be racially motivated. Whenever such motivation can be inferred, then there are racial relationships.

Jews and Sikhs are in law ethnic as well as religious groups. This means that although in mainland Britain it is not unlawful to discriminate on grounds of religion, anyone who treats a Jew or a Sikh less favourably on the grounds of that person's group member-ship may be acting unlawfully. (How an ethnic relationship may be distinguished from a racial relationship is discussed in Chapter 3.)

Individuals who are accused of racial discrimination may be quick to protest that they have been involved in a many-stranded relation, and that it was some other strand, not a racial one, that caused them to behave in a particular way. But for the most part the general public is not bothered about such niceties. Their attention is caught more by reports of bad relations, tension, conflict, injustice, etc. What are good racial relations? Can there be good racial relations? After all, might it not be said that good relations consist in paying no attention to differences of colour? Or in paying no more attention to skin colour than to eye colour? In such circumstances there would be no racial relations at all. That is a good argument, but unhelpful as a response to present circumstances. There is implicit in the way most people approach any discussion of these matters an idea of a scale, with the 'bad' at one end and the 'good' ones at the other. Sociologists should not only study the 'bad' cases, but also be able to explain why a case appears to be at one point in such a scale rather than another. Their analyses should provide guidance about the kind of action that would make it possible for a society to move nearer to the 'good' end of the scale. This requires measurement, which is difficult for both conceptual and practical reasons. While one end of any such scale has to be based upon 'bad' things like discrimination, riots, expressions of hatred, and so on, the other end is marked by an absence of such things; it is difficult to find for it a name that suggests a positive quality. The least unsatisfactory is 'harmony'. It is unsatisfactory because highly unequal relations have often appeared harmonious. Slaves have appeared contented, and systems based upon slavery have persisted for centuries. Would 'justice' be a more positive name for the good end of the scale? Such a proposal introduces other problems. Philosophers have been trying to define justice for over two thousand years and the word's meaning is still a subject for lively debate. People appeal to justice as an ideal or standard by which to judge prevailing circumstances. It is something outside and independent of those circumstances. Sociologists need to compare different sets of social relations. They may call one set harmonious if there are no signs of friction. At the same time they may conclude that appearances are deceptive and point to other signs which lead them to expect changes; or they may reach a private judgement that the circumstances are unfair to one section of the population.

Conflict

It is scarcely any easier to define the 'bad' end of the scale. One solution would be to call the bad end 'conflict', since there is a popular concept of conflict as a fight or a struggle. The scale would then become a scale of harmony and conflict. The objection to such a proposal is that conflict is not necessarily bad. There are both constructive and destructive conflicts. Consider conflict between trade unions and employers. Worker pressure upon management (including strikes and the threat of strikes) sometimes forces firms to be more efficient and more productive. Conflict is then constructive. It is also possible that prolonged conflict can lead to the closure of an industry, the market for the product being captured by producers in another country. Such conflict is then seen as destructive. The difference between the two kinds of conflict can be represented by borrowing expressions from the language used in the theory of games.

Imagine a game between two players. If the gains and losses of the two players are added up at the end and the total is more than zero, that is a positive-sum outcome. If the total is less than zero it is a negative-sum outcome. The third possibility is a zero-sum outcome in which one party's gain has to be the other party's loss. If there is a conflict between employees and an employer, and when the net gains and losses of both sides are added up they come to a positive figure, that will have been a constructive conflict. It could be that increased wages quickly compensate the employees for any loss of earnings during the strike so that they benefit overall, or that new rates of payment result in higher output so that the employer benefits, or that both benefit. If the total benefit exceeds the losses (whether or not the benefit has been evenly divided), the conflict can then be classed as constructive. If the total losses have been greater than the gains, it is classed as destructive. Many contests are of a zero-sum character in which one party can gain only at the other's expense and the total is therefore zero. In conflicts between ethnic and racial groups only subjective assessments of gains and losses are possible, but the theory of games nevertheless offers an interesting way of thinking about kinds of conflict.

Parties to a conflict can never be sure whether they will make a net gain or a net loss, or whether the overall outcome will be positive, negative or zero. One party might initiate a conflict knowing there to be risk that in the short run it might lose, but believing that in the long run not only would it gain but also the outcome would be to the general good (after all, parties to any struggle often claim that the interests of society coincide with the interests of their own group). It is probably right to conclude that people are most likely to engage in overt conflict when they believe that they 'have nothing to lose'. The sociologist can use the word 'conflict' to identify the signs of struggle without making any assumption about the results to which it will lead. Yet if conflict can lead to harmony, that implies that conflict should not be seen as the end point of a scale but as a position in a kind of spiral. (This is discussed, with examples, in Chapter 4.)

Most human behaviour can be understood only if it is seen as behaviour governed by rules. There are rules which govern fights and struggles. Football teams struggle with one another according to rules. Players and clubs which break the rules can be suspended. Strikers and their employers are engaged in a struggle, but the state lays down rules about how it may be conducted. States go to war with one another, but there are rules of war and international conventions about such things as the protection of civilians in time of war. Only in extreme circumstances do people recognize no restraints whatever. It can therefore be helpful to distinguish the extent to which a struggle is regulated by rules. Ordinary language recognizes a distinction between competition and conflict. Football teams are engaged in competition because their struggles are limited to defined periods, in special circumstances, and closely regulated. When the final whistle is blown the struggle has to stop. The word 'conflict' is applied to struggles which endure longer, affect a bigger part of the participants' lives, and are less closely regulated. Some conflicts are between two sections of a society with both sides appealing to values shared by most members of that society. It is often said that the outcome of some industrial disputes depends upon which side gets the support of the general public. These are conflicts within societies and they have to be distinguished from conflicts which split societies and result in secession or partition. When a deep fissure is opening up and one side is demanding that it be recognized as an independent state, it may be more appropriate to speak of a cleavage than a conflict. Competition, conflict and cleavage constitute a little family of concepts useful in distinguishing different degrees of struggle. Since it is not presently possible to measure those degrees reliably it may be better to stay with the popular senses of the words and concentrate upon understanding the facts about the interaction of peoples.

Popular ideas about racial and ethnic relations reflect individual experiences and the images generated by the mass media. They do not provide a reliable basis for the understanding of what gives those relations their character any more than the experience of shoppers in the supermarket enables them to understand the workings of the economy. To understand racial and ethnic relations it is necessary to look beyond popular consciousness to the social structures which give it form. This is not a one-way relationship, for popular ideas also influence structures, and the two interact in ways that are related to the society's environment. Two racially distinctive groups whose members encounter one another in equal relationships will interpret their experiences differently from people who meet only as super-ordinates and subordinates (as, for example, used to be the case in apartheid South Africa). How they interpret that experience may also be influenced by prevailing beliefs about the results of scientific research into physical differences. Those beliefs usually over-simplify and distort scientific knowledge. Since sociologists hope to communicate with people other than fellow sociologists, they have to start from the popular assumption that certain kinds of social relations are racial relations and then go on to correct the errors that flow from popular understandings.

CHAPTER 3

Accounting for differences

'What is race?' seems a simple question, and those who ask it often think there should be a simple answer. Some make the mistake of assuming that because there is a word in the language there must be something in the natural world that corresponds with that word. This is a philosophical error. There is also a historical dimension, because the word 'race' is less than five hundred years old. There have been physical differences between humans for thousands of years, but it is only within the last two centuries that these differences have been conceptualized as racial. The use of ideas about race to organize evidence about human variation has entered popular consciousness and influenced relations between groups. To unravel its social significance it is best to proceed historically, showing how and why the word has acquired additional meanings.

One of the earliest uses of 'race' to designate a set of people is to be seen in the reference to 'the race and stocke of Abraham' in Foxe's *Book of Martyrs* of 1570. The set of persons so designated were Abraham's lineage. The word has continued to be used in this sense down to the present time. Looking back from the vantage point of a later generation it can be seen that this first sense contained an ambiguity. It designated a set of people who were (a) of common descent, and (b) similar in significant respects. They were similar because they were of common descent. Yet two humans (or two animals, or two plants) could be of common descent without being similar, or could be similar without being of common descent. If race was to be used as a name for a class of individuals, that class had to be based on either descent or similarity of appearance. The ambiguity can be demonstrated by reference to a prominent descendant of Abraham, Moses. According to the Old Testament (*Exodus* 2: 15; *Numbers* 12: 1), Moses was a Levite who married a Midianite woman, Zipporah, who bore him two sons, Gershom and Eliezer. Later he married an Ethiopian woman (who may have been black, since his brother and sister 'spoke against him' for doing so – though, of course, they could simply have disliked his marrying a Midianite). If his second wife had borne him a son, the boy would have been 'of the race and stock' of Levi, just like his father and half-brothers. To say so would be too use *race* in the sense of lineage. Yet if some contemporary anthropologist had set out to classify the individuals, taking appearance as the criterion of race, Moses, Gershom and

Eliezer would have been accounted Semites, the second wife an Ethiopian, and Moses' third son a hybrid.

Scientific understanding of the nature of variation was assisted in the eighteenth century by the much improved system of classification formulated by the Swedish natural historian Linnaeus. This scheme was based on the outward appearance of the specimens to be classified, including observations about growth and habitat. The natural world was divided into three kingdoms: animal, vegetable and mineral. Within the animal kingdom, creatures were classified in orders, humans being assigned to the order Primates. Within this then came a smaller number of classes: family, genus, species, variety. The criterion of species was fertility, and the example often cited was that of the mule. If a horse is mated with a donkey the offspring is a mule. A mule is infertile. By this criterion the horse and the donkey were declared separate species. A variety is a subdivision of a species; its members can mate with those assigned to other varieties of the same species and produce fertile offspring. So if Moses had a third son and there were other males and females resulting from crosses between Israelites and Ethiopians, they would have constituted a variety. They might indeed have been called a race. To call them such would be to use the word for a class of specimens of similar appearance irrespective of descent. Moses' third son would have been assigned to a different race if the criterion were similarity instead of descent.

The growth of scientific knowledge was influenced by the ideas that prevailed in the societies to which the natural historians and philosophers belonged. By far and away the most powerful of these influences were those which stemmed from religious faith, and particularly from the belief that the Old Testament provided a straightforward account of the creation of the world some six thousand years earlier. It declared that all humans descended from Adam and Eve. The Old Testament appeared to account for differences by rehearsing genealogies showing how, by descent, people acquired membership in groups. Eighteenth-century classifications of humans harmonized the more easily with such an outlook because of the ambiguity in the idea of race as lineage. In that century political opinions exerted scarcely any influence upon scientific discussion of race, despite the agitation over the slave trade in the 1780s and 1790s. The debate about that trade was conducted within a framework of knowledge which presumed Africans to be inferior because they lived in an unhealthy climate and lacked the kinds of political and social institutions which encouraged economic development. For the abolitionists, the central issues were the doubtful morality and necessity of the trade. Only a handful of pro-slavery writers asserted that blacks were permanently inferior; most pro-slavery writers rejected such views except in so far as they contended that only Negroes could work in extreme heat. The slave-traders had no doubt about the humanity of those whose bodies they bought. The anti-Negro opinions of one pro-slavery writer, Edward Long, are sometimes quoted as if he were representative of a large body of white opinion. Long was also a sharp critic of colonial government and of West Indian slavery, so it was the abolitionist leader William Wilberforce who in Parliament frequently cited Long as the great authority on West Indian slavery, and not the pro-slavery side. If Long's arguments are to be interpreted as an ideology advancing material interests, they were not the interests of the slave-owners.

The ambiguity in the sense of race as lineage reflected the difference between a historical view of connections over time, and a classificatory approach starting from differences in the present. The confusion increased at the beginning of the nineteenth century when the great French comparative anatomist Georges Cuvier introduced his concept of type. At this time the three lowest classes in the classificatory scheme were those of genus, species and variety. To use words like *race* and *type* for purposes of classification was confusing. Were they additional to genus, species and variety? Or substitutes? If substitutes, for which terms did they substitute? The problem arose because it was so difficult to separate the question of classification from beliefs about the history of differences.

Explanations

When, in the early nineteenth century, it was asked why the peoples of the world were of varied appearance, there were four possible kinds of answers. The first was divine intervention. It was suggested that, being descended from Adam and Eve, everyone had been of similar appearance until God placed a curse upon the descendants of Ham and made them black. God had apparently at some stage chosen to give other peoples yellow, brown and reddish complexions. The second answer was that of climate: the sun had burned some peoples black. The difficulty, though, was that while some Europeans could become sunburned (or weatherbeaten) these conditions were not passed to a father's or mother's children. There was no inheritance of acquired characters. The third answer was the one now known to be correct: that variations arising accidentally in the course of conception had been selectively preserved. Until Darwin assembled evidence in favour of the theory of natural selection this explanation seemed both improbable and contrary to Scripture. So there was support for a fourth kind of answer. This was the theory that the world was divided into a series of natural provinces. Thus it was only in Australia that kangaroos and other marsupials were found. Likewise, only in Australia were there humans with the appearance of Australian Aborigines; they corresponded to the marsupials in being the sorts of humans suited to that province. They were one out of a finite number of permanent human types which had existed without change for a very long period, perhaps since the creation of the earth; or perhaps since some great catastrophe, like Noah's flood, or a series of volcanic eruptions, had upset the pattern. This doctrine is sometimes called catastrophism. It expounded an anti-evolutionary, steady-state view of the universe; in its application to humans it is called racial typology.

Racial typology presented the main kinds of humans as distinct species rather than varieties, despite all the evidence that sexual unions between them produced fertile offspring. It taught that each type was superior in its own province and that it was futile for humans to emigrate to provinces for which nature had not intended them. Europeans would never succeed in permanently colonizing North America. Since humans did not properly understand the conditions governing their lives, they mated with people of different type, and races became mixed; but nature set limits to such deviation and hybrid lines died out. Pure types were permanent and unchanging. None of the proponents of racial typology held strictly to the logic of their doctrine. To some, it seemed obvious that the whites were taking over other regions, demonstrating a greater capacity to develop them, and were therefore a superior race. The 1850s have been identified as the decade in which theories of 'scientific racism' were first advanced.

There was nothing remarkable about belief in racial superiority in the eighteenth and early nineteenth centuries. Europeans were obviously superior to Africans in the ships they built, their navigational instruments, their development of writing, and so on, but this superiority was attributed to the methods of social and political organization they had developed in what was thought to be a congenial and stimulating environment. Africans and other 'backward' peoples would be able to catch up in a few generations. The new doctrines of the mid-nineteenth century were very different. They fostered the beliefs that whites were *permanently* superior to blacks and that the two groups were not two varieties of a common species but two species of a common genus. They encouraged anthropologists to concentrate upon measuring human heads on the supposition that differences in the capacity for civilization were the result of differences in brain size. (They also found that male brains were larger than female brains, and this seemed to explain differences in the social position of men and women until it was discovered that brain size was related to stature.) Typology was a new way of accounting for observable differences and one which could easily be understood by non-specialists. It popularized a new concept of race as type which was to acquire fateful significance in the Nazi doctrine of race. It presented blacks, whites and yellows as different species (just as lions, tigers, leopards and jaguars are different species within the genus *Panthera*) and it suggested that social relations between human types had to be different on account of these zoological distinctions. It has not yet been eliminated from the popular consciousness though it is much less influential than it once was.

Nevertheless, it is important when reading historical material not to project this idea backwards in time. When writers in the seventeenth, eighteenth and early nineteenth century used the word *race*, they did not mean by it what the typologists meant.

Two leading typologists were the Scottish anatomist Robert Knox who published *The Races of Men* in 1850, and the French Count Arthur de Gobineau whose four-volume *Essay on the Inequality of Human Races* appeared in 1853–4. Both men regarded the revolutionary movements in Europe in 1848 as the expression of racial forces. Neither provided any justification for European expansion overseas; indeed, Knox was vehemently critical of imperialism. In the United States the leading exposition of typology was *Types of Mankind* by J.C. Nott and G.R. Gliddon, published in 1854. This big and authoritative-looking volume was not welcomed by the defenders of slavery in that country; most of them relied upon the Bible as a sufficient support for their views, and rejected any suggestion that Negroes were not, like themselves, descended from Adam and Eve. With the increasing political power of the white non-slave-holding working class before and after the Civil War, that attitude changed, and doctrines of permanent black inferiority gained widespread acceptance among whites. In Britain the expression of racial prejudice seems to have become more common after about 1870, partly because of increased social mobility. One way in which individuals could advance their own claims to status was by disparaging others, and a dark skin colour was a definite social disadvantage. Imperialist policies were particularly unpopular in the 1860s; they began to gain support only after 1874, and then for reasons unconnected with racial doctrines. Beliefs in white superiority gained a strong hold upon popular consciousness in the closing years of the nineteenth century, but the nature of the change in opinion and its causes has not yet been fully analysed. At no point in that century was there any single idea of race acceptable to all scholars, and yet by the time the century ended very many people identified themselves and others in racial terms.

The typologists believed that members of each racial type inherited distinctive psychological characteristics, such as an alleged ability of Caucasians to explore other regions and to construct civilizations; humans were also believed to inherit innate attitudes towards members of other races. What later came to be called racial prejudice was, in the typologists' theory, an inherited disposition. For their generation this was not an unreasonable inference. Only in the 1920s did psychologists assemble evidence to indicate that racial prejudice was learned in the course of a child's upbringing. The processes of socialization cause humans to interpret events in the light of their own society's values; the resulting bias is known as ethnocentrism. Prejudice is something more than this: it is a rigid and hostile attitude towards members of particular groups that often has sources in the psychology of the person in question.

The word *race* was used for literary and historical as well as scientific purposes. From the sixteenth century there were French writers who saw the history of their country as that of interaction between two races, the Franks and the Gauls. Some seventeenth-century English writers maintained that the English were 'descended of German race' (and therefore democratic), as part of an argument against the ambitions of the Stuart monarchy to rule by divine right. In his novel *Ivanhoe* (1819), Sir Walter Scott told the story of Robin Hood as part of the Saxon race's resistance to rule by the Norman race. So 'race' had a popular significance in European thought before new scientific theories had any impact and before it was employed in connection with the colonization of Africa. To describe the relations of Franks and Gauls, Saxons and Normans, or English and Irish, as the relations of races, became more meaningful when in the later nineteenth century more people believed that there were distinctive racial types. The differences between peoples were *racialized* by the use of words which implied that the differences sprang from the biological determinants postulated in racial theories. This conception of racialization has been taken up by sociologists as a way out from some of the difficulties caused by the multiplicity of meanings given to the word race. To say that differences were racialized is to say that they were interpreted in the light of prevailing racial theories, without entering any debate about the validity of those theories.

Natural selection

The doctrine of racial types was pre-Darwinian. It could make no allowance for the way in which forms of life transported to another part of the world could, by changing, adapt to that new environment. The theory of natural selection was able to account for the evidence about differences between humans as part of a comprehensive explanation of diversity and change throughout the natural world. Darwin's book *On the Origin of Species by Means of Natural Selection, or the Preservation of Favoured Races in the Struggle for Life* was published in 1859. In the fourth edition, Darwin referred to 'geographical races or subspecies' as 'local forms completely fixed and isolated'. A subspecies was what had previously been called a variety. It was a division of a species consisting of individuals which differed in appearance from those in other divisions, but which, should their isolation be broken down, could still mate with individuals from those other divisions and produce fertile offspring. If the word *race* is used by biologists today, it is used in this sense.

Darwin described processes of selection, but he could not identify the unit upon which selection operated. That was the contribution made by Mendel when he experimented with the breeding of peas. Evolution comes about by the selection of genes. The 1930s saw the development of population genetics as a branch of study which took the gene rather than the species as the unit of selection and attributed to each gene a definite fitness value. By 1950 a textbook entitled *Genetics and the Races of Man* defined *race* as 'a population which differs significantly from other human populations in regard to the frequency of one or more of the genes it possesses' (Boyd 1950: 207). Since there are now thought to be over half a million different human genes, there could be a similar number of human races. In practice no one draws this conclusion because it would not help biologists in the tasks with which they are engaged.

One task which does require biologists to classify humans is in connection with blood transfusions. Nineteenth-century racial classifications are useless for this purpose, but understanding of blood groups is essential. In 1900 the ABO system was discovered. Later research showed that in this system an individual's group was determined by three genes, A and B being dominant relative to O. Someone with two A genes, or one A and one O, will have blood of group A. Someone with two B genes, or one B and one O, will have blood of group B. Someone with one A and one B gene will have AB blood. There are other systems, for example the Rhesus system, so called because it was first detected by immunizing rabbits with blood cells from Rhesus monkeys. About 16 per cent of Europeans are Rhesus-negative. When a Rhesus-negative woman has children by a Rhesus-positive man, the children are likely to inherit both a D gene and a D antigen (an antigen can combine with other bodies in the blood to make it change, for example, by clotting). Under certain conditions the mother's body will produce an antibody called anti-D which can destroy the D-positive red cells in the foetus. The resulting anaemia frequently used to cause the baby's death, but now this can be prevented by transfusions of blood from a Rhesus-negative (i.e. D-negative donor) – that is, blood without the antibody. The heredity of blood groups, like that of eye colour, is determined by only a few genes, whereas the heredity of shape, size and colour of the body is determined in a complex way by a variety of genes and is also subject to the influence of diet and other environmental factors.

The frequency of blood group B is lower among Europeans than among Africans or Asians, but the differences are not very great. Among some American-Indian populations there seem to be few if any people of this group, but for the most part the figures show continuous distributions. Moving across Europe and Asia, for example, the percentage of people of group B in Britain is 7.2; it rises to 11.2 in France, 12 in Germany, 14.2 in Bulgaria, 21.8 in Russia, and up to a peak in Central Asia, before declining. Data like these demand that research workers calculate gene frequencies, not that they divide the populations into separate categories as if there were significant discontinuities in the figures. The old, Linnaean kind of classification is of little use for solving the new problems uncovered by genetics. Nineteenth-century anthropologists could not know this.

They relied upon a method that had, apparently, been successful in arranging plants and animals into a systematic set of categories. It was an attempt to fit each individual specimen into the most appropriate place in a comprehensive scheme. It assumed that when a specimen's place had been determined, something new and important had been learned about that specimen. Unlike blood-group classification, there was no simple purpose behind the Linnaean classification or its nineteenth-century extensions in respect of humans. Therefore there was little discussion of the elementary principle – which again can be illustrated by the various blood-group systems – that the same specimens might need to be classified differently for different purposes.

Ethnicity

Charles Darwin showed that species were not fixed, but subject to continuous change. Quite how change came about remained problematic until the establishment of population genetics seventy years later. In 1935 Sir Julian Huxley and A.C. Haddon used this new knowledge to explain the errors in some prevailing racial doctrines; they went on to maintain that the groups in Europe which were commonly called races would be better designated 'ethnic groups'. They wrote that

it is very desirable that the term *race* as applied to human groups should be dropped from the vocabulary of science.... In other animals the term *subspecies* has been substituted for "race". In man ... what we observe is the relative isolation of groups, their migration and their crossing. In what follows the word *race* will be deliberately avoided and the term *(ethnic) group* or *people* employed.

(Hurley and Haddon 1935: 91–2, original italics)

The organic character of a subspecies (whether animal or human) could be explained by the methods of population genetics. It was left to social scientists to discover corresponding methods by which the cultural characteristics of ethnic groups could be explained.

About the same time it became conventional in the United States to describe Italian-Americans, Polish-Americans, Irish-Americans, and so on, as ethnic minorities. There was a potential confusion in that Huxley and Haddon were referring to large groups, often coterminous with nations or bigger than nations and usually majorities. For them, ethnic group was a synonym for race, and a preferable term for identifying groups like those in Europe. The new usage in the United States was to represent races as divided into ethnic groups.

This suggests that it can be useful to draw a distinction between primary and secondary ethnicity. The ethnicity of the Italians or the Poles in Europe is a *primary ethnicity in which ethnic alignment coincides with national alignment.* The ethnicity of the Italian-Americans or the Polish-Americans is a *secondary ethnicity in which ethnic groups compare themselves with one another within a framework of shared citizenship.*

The United States usage was a practical one for the circumstances of that country. Italian-Americans and Polish-Americans were also called hyphenated Americans and the expression 'hyphenate' had come into use to identify a kind of grouping unknown in Europe. The distinctive cultures and linguistic usages which characterized hyphenate groups were ethnic ones. One objection to this usage was that African-Americans as a group shared culturally distinctive characteristics which could be compared with those of Italian-Americans and Polish-Americans. A more important objection was that in representing ethnic groups as subdivisions of races it accepted a misleading conception of race. To distinguish African-Americans and Italian-Americans as belonging to distinctive races was to rely on a pre-Darwinian conception and ignore what had been learned about genetics. It has been defended by those who say that in ordinary speech in the United States, 'race' is a social construct and that everyone knows what is meant by it. It is taken for granted in the USA that people of, say, one-eighth African ancestry and seven-eighths European ancestry, may account themselves black and be so accounted by others. The understanding of how this concept of race in the practical language of most English-speaking countries is socially constructed, and not in conformity with genetic inheritance, has been one of the social science advances of recent times. But to acknowledge that race is a social construct is not to concede that it is a good construct. Indeed, it appears very peculiar to observers from other countries because it conflicts with the use of the word to denote a subspecies.

United States usage has spread to other regions. Xhosa, Zulu, Venda and Tswana are sometimes considered to be ethnic subdivisions of the racial category black South African. English, Irish, Scots and Welsh can similarly be represented as ethnic subdivisions of the racial category white British or white European. These are examples of the practical language of everyday use; how this will develop or change in the future is difficult to predict. As has been argued in Chapter 2, social science cannot advance without a more refined language than that of the ordinary person; at the same time it can contribute towards the cleaning up of practical language by making its vocabulary more consistent. Social scientists can follow the recommendations of Huxley and Haddon by analysing popular uses of the expression 'race' without endorsing it, and can develop the concept of ethnicity as part of their theoretical language. African-Americans and Black Britons can then be presented as ethnic groups which define themselves by their shared experience and attitudes towards their social environment. Ethnicity can be used as a concept applicable all over the world irrespective of whether the people to whom it is applied have any word which corresponds to this word in the English language.

It then becomes easier to consider the position of persons of mixed ethnic origin. They may identify themselves as members of one group, or of different groups according to context. One of the factors influencing their decisions may be the prejudices associated with beliefs about 'race' which are expressed by other persons. Many prejudgements about individuals are based upon outward differences of skin colour and costume. Differences of appearance have consequences for social relations that are more inflexible and wide-reaching than differences of culture. Most people have no option about whether others will classify them as black, brown, white or yellow. It is an involuntary assignment to a social category and it puts a lot of pressure upon individuals to identify themselves with that category. Cultural characteristics are different, in that children of immigrant parents are not obliged to identify with their parents' homeland or to speak its language. To get children to do this, there has to be a social organization which offers emotional and/or material rewards to those who maintain the cultural character-istics of the migrant homeland instead of conforming to the expectations of the ethnic majority in the new country.

Whether ethnic identification is primary or secondary is also affected by processes of interaction. Sometimes it is a matter of bitter dispute. The Kurds, who live mainly in Turkey, Iraq and Iran, consider themselves a nation and have wanted a separate state, so from this standpoint theirs can be considered a primary ethnicity. The governments of the states on which they live see them differently. Only in Iraq have they been recognized as a distinctive ethnic group, composed of citizens of the state, and therefore as a form of secondary ethnicity. A parallel can be drawn with the Tibetans. The government in Beijing claims that Tibet is part of China and considers Tibetans an ethnic minority, not a nation. In other places too, there may be members of a group who claim that their ethnicity is primary and that their country should be independent, while others, either inside their group or within the state claiming sovereignty, oppose that claim. The Quebec referendum of 1995 recorded a wafer-thin majority for the province's retention of a status which made 'French-Canadian' a secondary ethnicity. In the referendum of 1979 residents of Wales voted to by four to one against a separate assembly for their country. The nationalists in both Quebec and Wales seek to change the self-identification of their co-ethnics. Elsewhere, as their circumstances have changed, individuals have indeed altered, or been obliged to alter, the significance they accord to national and ethnic identities. In the former republic of Yugoslavia there was a significant number of people for whom being a Yugoslav was their national identity, but this identity was destroyed and they had instead to define themselves as Serbs, Croats, or the like, as these became their national identities and examples of primary ethnicity.

Going back to the earlier discussion of the different strands that can be detected in the social relations between two individuals, these definitions make it possible to maintain that whereas an ethnic strand in a social relation may, for most purposes be the same as what people consider a racial strand, the two may sometimes differ. If a racial relationship is one in which the behaviour of one or both parties is influenced by ideas about the relevance of race, so an ethnic relationship is one in which that behaviour is influenced by ideas about ethnicity. The practical difference is that ideas of race will be beliefs about the involuntary effects of genetic inheritance and ideas of ethnicity will be beliefs about the customs people choose to follow.

The popular conception of racial groups as physically defined and ethnic groups as culturally defined does not allow for the way that the same set of people can be both physically and culturally distinctive, just as they can be both a linguistic and a religious minority. Culture affects the way that people perceive physical variation and constructs the categories in which people classify their perceptions. Societies are organized in ways that make physical features relevant to behaviour in certain situations and which determine how people of intermediate appearance are classified. Popular ideas about physical classification are themselves influenced by social and cultural pressures.

Among these pressures is a tendency to highlight a group's racial or ethnic characteristics and to overlook the political dimensions. There is nothing special about differences of race or ethnic origin that they should occasion conflict. Groups may be recruited on the basis of shared attributes but what motivates their collective action is the social and political meaning they give to their common experience and their ideas for the future. In this the relation between the group and the state is often the key factor.

Racism

At the beginning of the chapter it was asserted, with reference to race, that it is wrong to assume that because there is a word there must be something which corresponds to it. That same argument also applies to the word 'racism', which has been used in a bewildering variety of senses since the 1960s. It entered the European languages in the 1930s to identify the doctrine that race determines culture, the underlying concept being that of race as type. Some types were supposed to be permanently superior in their ability to generate civilization. In the late 1960s 'racism' was given a second, extended meaning as designating the use of beliefs and attitudes to subordinate and control a category of people defined in racial terms. The word was then increasingly used to express a moral judgement. Anything which could be called racist was by definition bad, so that a concept had become an epithet. A third use of the word was as a label for a historical complex, generated within capitalism, facilitating the exploitation of categories of people defined in racial terms. Earlier this complex had been called racial prejudice, but by 1970 it was generally referred to as racism. One objection to this definition is that there are similar complexes in Japan and other regions where they cannot have been caused or developed by capitalism. 'Racism' is also used in a fourth, much more general sense, to refer to almost anything connected with racial discrimination, prejudice, inequality, and so on.

The introduction of the new word and the changes in its use reflect changes in understanding of the social world. For many centuries it had been thought natural that humans should identify with those with whom they had grown up, and that they should keep strangers at a distance. Then the evidence accumulated that these feelings were not inherited but learned, while the old assumptions were jolted by the Nazi movement's use of racial doctrines and its delusion that Jews were not strangers but subhumans who, as a threat to civilization, had to be eliminated. The lessons of that period influenced the founding of the United Nations 'to save succeeding generations from the scourge of war'. Human rights had to be respected 'without distinction as to race' because history had shown that a failure to ensure this could be a cause of war. So when it seemed about 1960 as if Nazi ideas might be reappearing, the United Nations drew up the International Convention on the Elimination of All Forms of Racial Discrimination. That the UN should favour measures for *reducing* racial discrimination should astonish no one, but it was remarkable that in 1965 the General Assembly should have *unanimously* adopted a convention which affirmed that the states parties were 'resolved to adopt all necessary measures for *speedily eliminating* racial discrimination in all its forms and manifestations' (italics added). Underlying the issue were two contrasting conceptions of the nature and causes of racial discrimination: one saw it as resembling a crime, the other as resembling a sickness. The Convention utilized a crime-like definition, but most of the delegates to the General Assembly seem to have thought of it as a kind of social sickness which afflicted certain societies and not others. Otherwise they would not have thought that it could be *speedily* eliminated. The Russians thought that it was caused by capitalism. The newly independent states of Africa thought that it was caused by colonialism, and that apartheid was its most extreme manifestation. European states could accept that it was caused or exacerbated by the propagation of doctrines of racial inequality. Those who drafted the Convention doubted if many states would ratify it, but they were proven wrong, so that twenty-five years later more than three-quarters of the world's states had agreed to be bound by its provisions.

In the years that followed 1965, UN resolutions included

references to 'racism and racial discrimination' as if the two were synonymous. That this could cause misunderstanding was demonstrated in 1975 when in the General Assembly the representative of Kuwait introduced Resolution 3379 declaring 'Zionism is a form of racism and racial discrimination'. It was a major step in a campaign by Arab states against Israel and the movement, Zionism, which had created that state. The originators of the motion did not draw any distinction between racism and racial discrimination; they saw the two as aspects of the same thing in line with the second, late 1960s, definition just quoted. They argued that under Israel's law only Jews could be proper citizens in Israel and that, since Jews were a race, the Israeli state was racist. Their arguments were criticized by Daniel Patrick Moynihan, the US ambassador to the UN, who was himself a social scientist. He operated with the first definition, of racism as a doctrine, and quoted *Webster's Third New International Dictionary* which defined it as 'the assumption that ... traits and capacities are determined by biological race and that races differ decisively from one another'. (These and the following quotations from Moynihan are in the Official Records of the UN General Assembly A/PV.2400: 152–65.) According to the *Dictionary*, racism also involved 'a belief in the inherent superiority of a particular race and its right to domination over others'. Moynihan maintained that the assumption and the belief to which the *Dictionary* referred were both alien to Zionism. He described this as a movement, established in 1897, which was to persons of the Jewish religion a Jewish form of what others called national liberation movements.

Moynihan stated that 'racial discrimination is a practice, racism is a doctrine'. The UN had defined racial discrimination, but not racism. The allegation that Zionism was a form of racism was 'incomparably the more serious charge'. One of the few occasions on which racism had been discussed at the UN was in 1968 in connection with the International Convention on the Elimination of All Forms of Racial Discrimination. Speaking very sarcastically of the intellectual precision with which the matter was being treated, Moynihan described the discussion on that occasion about the order in which 'racism' and 'Nazism' should be mentioned in a preambular paragraph.

The distinguished representative of Tunisia argued that 'racism' should go first because, he said, Nazism was a form of racism. Not so, said the no less distinguished representative of the Union of Soviet Socialist Republics, for, he explained, Nazism contained all the main elements of racism within its ambit, and should be mentioned first. That is to say that racism was merely a form of Nazism. ... If, as the distinguished representative declared, racism is a form of Nazism, and if, as this resolution declares, Zionism is a form of racism, then we have step by step taken ourselves to the point of ~roclaiming – the United States is solemnly proclaiming – that Zionism is ~m of Nazism.

This playing with words was intellectually dishonest. It was also dangerous for minorities which depended on laws to protect their rights. Moynihan's protest was eloquent.

Today we have drained the word of its meaning. Tomorrow terms like 'national self-determination' and 'national honour' will be perverted in the same way to serve the purposes of conquest and exploitation. And when these claims begin to be made, as they already have begun to be made, it is the small nations of this world whose integrity will suffer. And how will the small nations of the world defend themselves, and on what grounds will others be moved to defend and protect them, when the language of human rights, the only language by which the small can be defended, is no longer believed and no longer has a power of its own?'

In 1991 the General Assembly, by 111 votes to 25, revoked Resolution 3379.

The 1975 UN resolution was used for political ends in other places. In Britain the National Union of Students in 1974 decided that students' unions should not allow racists and Fascists to address meetings on their premises. Following the UN, student unions refused to recognize the formation of Jewish societies 'to promote greater understanding of the Jewish religion, culture and people, the state of Israel and Zionism'. They declared that such a programme was by definition racist. The National Union of Students then threatened to suspend the membership of any union which persisted in a contrary interpretation of the policy.

The idea of racism has now entered the public consciousness in many countries. A 1991 opinion poll in Britain found that 97 per cent of the white respondents were willing to answer the question 'Do you think Britain as a society is very racist, fairly racist, fairly non-racist or completely non-racist?' and that 67 per cent considered it to some extent racist. This is evidence of a major change since the early 1970s. The idea of racism has provided a foundation for an attack on some of the conditions which generate discrimination. Its power has been the greater because racism has been defined as something essentially evil, though its edge has at times been blunted by over use. As Robert Miles (1989: 52–61) has noted, there has been a process of conceptual inflation as the word has been applied to an ever greater range of things in order to stigmatize them. One French writer has even represented misogyny and discrimination against women as forms of racism (Guillaumin 1972: 84).

Racism has sometimes been represented as the racial prejudice of the powerful, implying that members of subordinated groups can never be racist. At one time there were animated debates about whether the action of Idi Amin, in expelling from Uganda Asian residents because they were Asian, was racist. Some of those who resisted such a conclusion wanted a definition that harmonized with their political philosophy. Similar issues have underlain disagreements about whether there is a 'new racism' or whether it is appropriate to differentiate between racisms in the plural.

In the English-speaking world those who sought to defend racial inequalities used to appeal to biological doctrines as providing a justification, but towards the end of the 1960s there was an important change. Those who, in Europe, opposed immigration from the non-white world often argued that the strangers' ways of life were so different that coexistence was impracticable. Instead of basing their contentions on a premiss of racial superiority/inferiority they based them on one of persisting cultural differences. This trend seems to have strengthened. In Germany the question of what name to give to such sentiments has a special dimension because *Rassismus* is associated with the extremism of the Nazi era. Most Germans prefer to speak of *Fremdenfeindlichkeit* (literally hostility towards foreigners); this can be translated as xenophobia. In France there has been more hostility towards immigrants from the Maghreb (in Algeria and Morocco) than towards blacks from Africa and the West Indies. The Maghrebins were seen as the more different because they were Muslim. One response might be to define as racist any hostility based upon beliefs about inherited biological differences, and as xenophobic any that is based upon beliefs about cultural differences. It would then be possible to describe German attitudes towards Turkish immigrants, and French attitudes towards Maghrebins, as xenophobic, and to describe a transition from racism to xenophobia in public opinion within the majority population.

Many sociologists have been unwilling to do this because they believe that a definition should grasp the essence of the thing that has to be defined. They continue in a philosophical tradition that goes back to Aristotle, and which may be contrasted with the alternative tradition called nominalism; this latter maintains that a definition should distinguish the thing being defined from other things with which it might be confused. A favourite illustration is to say that while an essentialist might define *Homo sapiens* as a rational animal, a nominalist would define *Homo* as a featherless biped! Underlying the claims that Amin's action was not racist, that there is a 'new racism', or that there are different racisms, is an essentialist philosophy. Others, who contend that for the purposes of research it is necessary to distinguish forms of hostility springing from possibly different sources, rely upon a nominalist philosophy.

Much of the argument about the definition of racism also applies to the definition of antisemitism. This word was coined in 1879 to name a movement against the race and culture of the Jews (and not their religion) because they were perceived as a threat to German culture. It has since been generalized to designate hostility towards Jews and Judaism on any ground whatsoever. It has an undoubted value, for both Jews and Gentiles, in the practical language, and is important to many Jews as an explanation for the hostility to which they are sometimes subjected. But there are at least two reasons for denying it any place in the emerging theoretical language of social science. The first is that it must be possible to condemn actions carried out by Jews if the same actions would have been culpable had they been carried out by non-Jews. This has been the more important an argument since the foundation of the state of Israel in 1948. Criticism of that state's actions might spring from antisemitic motivations, but need not necessarily do so. The second argument is that many groups besides Jews have been, and are, the objects of hostility, but their names are not given an 'ism' as if the character of the victim determined the nature of the hostility. A scientific approach to the study of inter-group tension needs to start from the influences underlying hostility in aggressor groups (such as the genocides in Nazi Germany, in the former Yugoslavia, Rwanda, Burundi and elsewhere) since they show common features independently of the groups against whom the hostility is directed. It is not the character of the victim that determines the hostility.

Looking ahead

It is possible to discuss the sociology of racial relations without using the word 'racism' provided that other words are employed to designate the things people have in mind when they speak of racism. The words used in everyday speech carry multiple meanings which have to be 'unpacked' and their component elements identified and named so that the course of events can be explained. Attitudes may be better grasped by the concepts of ethnocentrism and prejudice; systems of belief by reference to doctrines and ideologies; behaviour by analysis in terms of discrimination and incitement to discrimination or to hatred. The formation of groups has to be explained by reference both to the sharing of experiences and interests, and by the processes of mobilization mentioned in Chapter 4. These concepts are part of the new theoretical language that is being developed in order to explain social processes. They can be used to make better sense of what people have in mind when they speak of antisemitism and of nationalism.

The first requirement is always to be as precise as possible in defining the problem to be solved or the question to be answered. To explain why one category of persons continues to be disadvantaged economically, it is necessary to control for the influence of a great number of variables operating across generations. Some characters have a genetic origin but their development and transmission may be much influenced by environmental factors. Differences in the inheritance of intelligence obviously influence the advancement of individuals, but as the socio-economic position of ethnic groups improves, so may their average performance in intelligence tests. The relative success of different immigrant groups may be related to the human capital they have brought with them in the form of education and industrially relevant skills. Chance factors, like the region in which they settle and the course of international trade, can also be important.

Mention of immigration introduces a further set of variables. The inhabitants of some countries have seen themselves as a nation of immigrants (like the USA); others (like Germany) have not. Some racial minorities have been composed of persons who were citizens of the country (like New Commonwealth immigrants in the UK); others have been composed of resident aliens (like most countries in the European Union). Devising an economically appropriate and socially just immigration policy can be very difficult. To aggregate all the variables associated with physical and cultural differences, as if 'race' were a single factor, only obscures the scientific and political problems.

Some words used in practical language can be 'cleaned up'. The expression 'institutional racism', for example, is over-generalized. It is employed most frequently to criticize unequal outcomes and does not locate their source. 'Institutional*ized* racism' is not open to the same objections if it is used in a search for the assumptions which underlie bureaucratic routines that have unintended effects of a discriminatory nature. 'Race' as a folk concept differentiating present-day groups on the basis of their appearance has no theoretical value, but the adjective 'racial' used in conjunction with some other concept, like that of discrimination, may be different. In the study of genetic continuities over generations, 'race' can be used as a synonym for 'subspecies', but the latter word is surely to be preferred as less productive of misunderstanding. 'Ethnicity' is now a part of everyday English language and may one day acquire greater explanatory value than it has at present.

One possible way of continuing to use the words racial discrimination and racism with distinctive meanings, would be to keep the former for crime-like behaviour and use the latter for phenomena that resemble a sickness. If this is done, the sickness metaphor should not be employed to evade the conclusion that for every act of unlawful discrimination someone is responsible and should be brought to account.

To describe someone or something as racist inevitably implies a claim to moral superiority on the part of the speaker, but there is still an important difference between describing actions or statements as racist, and describing persons as racist. To tell individuals that their actions are racist is to suggest that they are capable of behaving in some other manner. It is to suggest that the propriety of an action can be discussed and that the parties might come to an agreement about the best way to behave in future. To tell someone that he or she is racist is to imply that there is something wrong with the actor rather than with the action. It drives the person into a corner and reduces the likelihood that he or she will behave differently in the future. This is a political tactic which is to be distinguished from the attempts of some social scientists to develop a concept of racism that might illuminate the causes of racial tension.

CHAPTER 4

Groups and individuals

Compared with other animals, human beings have some very special talents. These are cultivated during a relatively long period of socialization in which they are brought to recognize their dependence on others (notably their mothers, but also other family members). They learn that at times they must forgo immediate gratification and that they have obligations (or debts) to those who are defined as fellow group-members. They become psychologically dependent upon their identification with particular groups and upon the receipt of approval from people who represent these groups. Thus assumptions about group identity are part of the traditions transmitted from one generation to another.

Human individuals are born into groups. Some groups have a formal character; for example, almost everybody is born with a nationality. Others are the less formal groups of kin and neighbours. In the course of socialization individuals learn how other group-members expect them to behave, that group-members can reward the kinds of behaviour of which they approve and punish the kinds of which they disapprove. Individuals learn that they can derive satisfaction from conformity to the expectations of other group-members and acquire a consciousness of group belonging. Some individuals are more conforming than others, while some groups or societies demand more conformity than others.

Ends and means

In the process of socialization humans acquire goals, both material goals, like a desire for wealth, and psychic or immaterial goals, like desires for achievement and the affection of others. Some societies inculcate stronger desires for individual achievement relative to group approval than others do. Individuals seek to maximize their satisfactions (economists would say that they seek to optimize), and though they are not always efficient or rational in the way they go about this, in the long run they generally learn from the mistakes that they make and get better in using the available means to attain their ends. To do so they will at times be obliged to *join with others in collective action* or to follow strategies that assume that others will engage in such action. At other times they may be able to attain their ends by *individual action*, as when they go shopping in a super-market.

One person belongs to many groups. People identify themselves, and are identified, with others on the basis of class, gender, language, religion, and so on. The importance of any one identification varies according to the individual and his or her circumstances, but groups that combine a variety of identifications will be stronger and more long-lasting. When discussing the naming of groups, Chapter 1 observed that interpersonal relations are usually many-stranded. Even in a transitory and impersonal relationship, like that between a bus-driver and someone paying a fare, there may be an exchange of words about the coins handed over, the state of the weather or the length of time spent waiting for the bus. This idea of the strands to social relations can be a bridge between the study of behaviour and the analysis of groups.

Social groups result from and are maintained by the goal-seeking actions of individuals, but each individual has many goals with different priorities. Short-term goals may be placed in order as part of a strategy for attaining long-term goals. If the cost of attaining one goal increases, individuals may change to pursue another one and align themselves with a group that will be of more assistance for this purpose. Sometimes, too, individuals change their goals (as when someone decides to stop smoking).

Some kinds of cooperation are enforced by the nature of the goal. For example, in the contemporary world nearly everybody needs to belong in a state which will give them a passport and the rights of citizenship. The state sets out to defend them from attack, either from criminal action within the country or from aggression on the part of other states which might seize some of the national territory. It provides them with what economists call public goods. Group cooperation requires the collective action of individuals. It is more easily achieved when, perhaps because of their socialization, individuals take it for granted that they belong to the group in question.

One of the founders of modern sociology, Max Weber, maintained that collective action can be of two kinds, which can be called associational and communal. The teams formed for the purposes of some psychological experiments discussed later in this chapter were associations created for a specific purpose and dissolved soon afterwards. Associations are in theory founded upon single-stranded relationships in which the parties act together for a limited purpose. However, in the course of cooperation the parties can easily become friendly with one another and start adding other strands to their relations; their actions can then become communal, because communal action springs from a feeling of belonging together and community life is many-stranded. An association of persons sharing a common ethnic origin would appeal to a consciousness of shared experience and would therefore be communal from the outset, so it is the difference between individual goal-seeking and collective goal-seeking of a communal character that is most relevant to the study of ethnic consciousness.

In the economically less advanced societies the individual is dependent upon group support in most spheres of life. People who live by hunting or herding animals, or in a society based upon the cultivation of land, have to cooperate in order to obtain the necessities of life. Their societies are structured to promote the kind of cooperation that is needed; they often have difficulty adapting to changes of circumstance and they may not make the most of individual talent. The Protestant reformation in Europe brought in a major change when it demarcated a larger sphere in which the individual was to act as an independent unit. This opened the way for new incentives to economic action and promoted economic growth. Industrialized societies with high levels of consumption now allow much more scope for individualistic goal-seeking than previous forms of society.

People who have common interests or common attributes do not necessarily engage in collective action, but they are often brought to do so by some stimulus. This may be what is perceived as a threatening action on the part of another group or the exhortation of a political entrepreneur who evokes and directs their sentiment of community. The process by which individuals are brought to act collectively is called mobilization. In sharply divided societies (such as Northern Ireland) some groups are mobilized almost all the time and this constrains the freedom of action of their members. Group obligations take priority over individual goals.

It has already been observed that racial groups appear to be more permanent and involuntary than other groups because others assign individuals to membership of them at sight. The strength of this assignment by others (as opposed to self-assignment) means that racial groups are easily mobilized. In a racially segregated society, racial status is relevant to conduct in almost every situation. Later chapters will argue that this is one of the key factors in the increase or decrease of group consciousness.

Groups may be mobilized for different purposes. For example, those who share a religious faith may come together in an act of worship. This is collective action and it will almost certainly be communal. If the group-members believe that their faith obliges them to act for or against some practice, like, say, abortion, then theirs becomes a political group as well as a religious one. The sphere of politics is not limited to political parties and groups which share an overtly political ideology; it includes all activity concerned with the distribution of resources and competition for power or influence. This more comprehensive conception is exemplified in the use of the expression 'sexual politics' to denote ideas and actions about the relative positions of men and women. Once persons with a common attribute (like a shared racial, ethnic or national origin) engage in collective action on the basis of a group consciousness then they usually *become a political group* in this broader sense. Their actions are governed by their political strategy rather than by the attribute they have in common.

Experimental research

Very little stimulus is needed to cause humans to align themselves with others in opposition to those who are thought to be different. Having created a group boundary, they then treat those on its other side in a less favourable manner. Henri Tajfel (1970) conducted a series of experiments to discover the minimal conditions which give rise to such discriminatory behaviour. The 'subjects' of the experiments were young male apprentices who were shown slides of pictures by Klee and Kandinsky and asked to indicate which they preferred. They were then led to believe that they had been divided into teams according to their preference for the one artist or the other. Next they completed a task in which they were allocated small sums of money, and in which they could follow alternative strategies. One was that of maximizing joint profits, in which members of their own team got most money but members of the other team (identified only by a code number) did equally well. Another strategy was that of maximum difference, whereby the subjects obtained less for themselves but were able to ensure that those apparently in the other team received even less than they did. As subjects came to understand the nature of the task they increasingly preferred the strategy of maximum difference. Group discrimination could be produced by simply telling the young men that they had been allocated to different categories even though the categories themselves were of no social significance. Subsequent experiments confirmed this finding and showed that similar effects could be produced even more simply. It would seem that all that is needed to produce group alignment and competition is the belief of subjects that they share membership in some sort of group or team, even one randomly created. Similarities between people contribute to group formation by serving as cognitive cues to the formation of social categories and do not create bonds by themselves.

To start with, Tajfel interpreted these findings in normative terms. He argued that in all cultures a child is brought up to believe that certain people in given situations are allies, belonging to a 'we' group, while others belong to 'they' groups and are to be treated differently. Having internalized a 'generic' norm of behaviour towards 'they' groups, whenever a subject was faced with a situation in which people were categorized in this way, the subject could be expected to behave in a partisan manner. The weakness of this as an explanation was that, if the experimental subjects had chosen maximum joint profit or fairness strategies instead, their behaviour could equally well have been explained in terms of norms learned during socialization. So Tajfel modified his theory to claim that if individuals were to maintain their identities as members of a group they had to use opportunities to maximize group distinctiveness.

The experimental results show how easily group competitiveness can be generated among young men recruited from a population already acquainted with one another, but before generalizing from them it is necessary to allow for variables that were not included in the research. The discrimination that was measured was in the amount of money the young men would forgo. Willingness to take less money in order to beat the other team would have varied from one participant to another and upon how much money was involved. Other influences would have come into play before they would have been willing to engage in forms of discrimination that would have had more serious consequences, such as injury to members of the other group. But the study is worth recalling here to indicate how psychologists can uncover variables often neglected in sociological writing.

What Tajfel wrote about socialization also deserves some elaboration. Though there is no experimental evidence about this, it seems as if individuals invest much of their social experience with moral qualities. If they grow up in an ethnically mixed neighbourhood then they subsequently assume that it is right and proper that local communities should be mixed. If they grow up in a neighbourhood where all the other residents are of the same colour as themselves, they assume that it is proper to live with people of the same colour. What can be expected in the statistical sense of probability comes to be what is expected in the normative sense of the morally right way of doing things.

Encounters between peoples

Socialization into communal, many-stranded, relations creates groups which their members think of as natural. When these groups have an ethnic dimension, this encourages a high sense of ethnic consciousness and sometimes leads their members to attribute to others the same sort of consciousness that they have themselves. Over the centuries, Jews have displayed a high sense of their own distinctiveness; Afrikaners in South Africa, over a shorter period, displayed such a consciousness and were prepared for its development among black African ethnic groups. The belief that ethnic identities derive from causes deep in the history of groups gives rise to what has been called a primordial sense of ethnicity. It reflects the intense feelings of some group members. To it may be contrasted what has been called a circumstantialist conception of ethnicity. This reflects the conclusions of observers, who, viewing the ways that groups change as their circumstances change, maintain that the sense of ethnic belonging is influenced primarily by the group's relations with other groups. It is possible that the people themselves may believe their ethnicity to be a primordial attribute, but for the observers to be divided in their opinions. Some may believe that ethnicity is in general a quality of this kind while others believe it can be explained in circumstantialist terms.

An example of the primordialist sense of ethnicity has been offered in a study of the Parsi (or Parsee) group in India. When a change in the laws regulating adoption was being considered by the government, three Parsi leaders sought exemption for followers of their faith (Zoroastrianism). They argued that a person could become a Zoroastrian only by being born into their group (Hinnells 1994: 266). An observer might seek to explain the strength of this belief in terms of the relations between Parsis and other groups around them practising different religions. Group conflict (as in Northern Ireland) can evoke and sustain high levels of consciousness, especially when those concerned believe that they are involved in zero-sum relations (i.e. in which one group can gain only at the expense of the other group, as explained in Chapter 2).

Some of the major forms of contemporary group consciousness are the outcome of the process by which Europeans established themselves in the New World in the sixteenth century; then on the coastline of West and South Africa, and in the Indian subcontinent. The Europeans differed from the native groups in their physical appearance and in respect of their work motivations and skills, like literacy and technical knowledge, particularly in the ability to manufacture and use firearms. The Europeans were the agents of relatively large and well-ordered states with the power of those states behind them. The native peoples were often organized in states, sometimes with a single monarch ruling a substantial territory, but these states were relatively small and could not mobilize so much power. The long-term effect of this European presence, nevertheless, was to encourage native political organization on a larger scale with forms resembling those of the European state.

To start with, the differences seemed sharp. One group consisted of people who have been called white; the other of people who were black or coloured; there was a discontinuity in some ways comparable to the division of humans into males and females. The effect of contact was to reduce the discontinuities of appearance and of cultural attitudes, and to turn them into continuities. The distinction between continuous and discontinuous distributions (already mentioned in Chapter 3) is important here again; it is illustrated in Figure 4.1. Figure 4.1(a) represents the situation in many British school and university classrooms: most people in the class are of fair complexion. Figure 4.1(b) typifies that to be found in some areas of minority settlement: a bimodal distribution with two large groups of fair and dark complexion and a number of persons of intermediate appearance. Figure 4.1(c) represents the kind of development that might be expected overseas as a result of European invasion and settlement.

Figure 4.1(d) presents a unimodal distribution of a kind that might be found in some parts of Latin America. The purpose of these comparisons is to show that differences in complexion constitute a continuous distribution, whereas differences, say, of gender, do not. It would make no sense to try to prepare a graph to show degrees of gender with the most masculine individuals at one end, the most feminine at the other, and a range of intermediates. Gender is discontinuous, and if the numbers of males and females in a class are to be represented visually this has to be by a block diagram, or histogram, with one column of a height that shows the proportion of males and another column the proportion of females.

The graphs in Figure 4.1 show the distribution of persons as if their complexions had been measured scientifically. In everyday life matters are different. A continous line is divided up into sections, and names like white, coffee-coloured, and black are given to segments of it. Perceptions of people's identity are then influenced by folk concepts of racial groups. In most contact situations one group is the more powerful and its members seek to preserve and increase their privileges; the groups which result are influenced by struggles for advantage. This can best be understood from historical examples.

The New World was first colonized by people from Spain, a

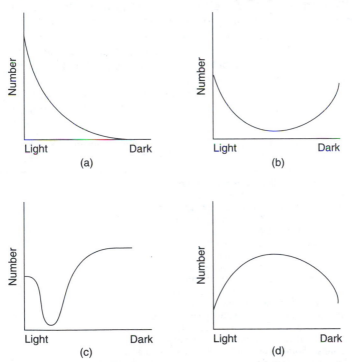

*Figure 4.1 **Distribution of persons according to complexion***

country in which lines of descent were very important for determining a person's rank in society. The Spaniards recognized that in the Aztec and Inca civilizations the American Indians maintained hierarchical social systems like their own. To start with, even aristocratic Spaniards were willing to marry Indian women of high rank. Concubinage was tolerated by both the church and the state. It was not sexual relations between persons from different groups that troubled the Spaniards so much as the fear that if such persons were allowed to marry, the children would claim Spanish ancestry and the arrangements for calculating social rank would be thrown into disorder. Descent from Africans was dishonourable not because they were black but because of the presumption that they were of slave ancestry. New names for persons of partly European, partly American Indian, and partly African origin were added to the Spanish vocabulary, as can be seen from Tables 4.1 and 4.2. The German anthropologist J.F. Blumenbach noted some of these in his 1775 book *De Generis Humani Varietate Nativa* (On the Native Varieties of the Human Genus) and added to the list in the 1795 edition from which Table 4.3 has been prepared (Blumenbach 1865). Some Spanish writers elaborated long lists of names for many sorts of possible mixture, but it is doubtful whether they were much used in everyday life. Nevertheless, their multiplicity must have made it easier for people to accept that group distinctions were matters of degree. In Spanish-speaking parts of America no sharp line is drawn between black and white. For a long time the trend has been, and still is, towards the kind of distribution shown in Figure 4.1(d), not only in appearance but also in social position.

   The case of Brazil is the more interesting because a larger proportion of slaves were brought there from Africa than were

Table 4.1 Names for persons of mixed origin in eighteenth-century New Spain (i.e. the northern Spanish territories in the New World)

1	Spaniard and Indian woman beget mestizo
2	Mestizo and Spanish woman beget castizo
3	Castizo woman and Spaniard beget Spaniard
4	Spanish woman and Negro beget mulatto
5	Spaniard and mulatto woman beget morisco
6	Morisco woman and Spaniard beget albino
7	Spaniard and albino woman beget toma atrás
8	Indian and toma atrás woman beget lobo
9	Lobo and Indian woman beget zambaigo
10	Zambaigo and Indian woman beget cambujo
11	Cambujo and mulatto woman beget albarazado
12	Albarazado and mulatto woman beget barcino
13	Barcino and mulatto woman beget coyote
14	Coyote woman and Indian beget chamiso
15	Chamiso woman and mestizo beget coyote mestizo
16	Coyote mestizo and mulatto woman beget ahí te estás

Source: Mörner (1967: 58)

Table 4.2 Names for persons of mixed origin in eighteenth-century Peru

1	Spaniard and Indian woman beget mestizo
2	Spaniard and mestizo woman beget cuarterón de mestizo
3	Spaniard and cuarterona de mestizo beget quinterón
4	Spaniard and quinterona de mestizo beget Spaniard or requinterón de mestizo
5	Spaniard and Negress beget mulatto
6	Spaniard and mulatto woman beget quarterón de mulatto
7	Spaniard and cuarterona de mulatto beget quinterón
8	Spaniard and quinterona de mulatto beget requinterón
9	Spaniard and requinterona de mulatto beget white people
10	Mestizo and Indian woman beget cholo
11	Mulatto and Indian woman beget chino
12	Spaniard and chino beget cuarterón de chino
13	Negro and Indian woman beget sambo de Indio
14	Negro and mulatto woman beget zambo

Source: Mörner (1967: 58–9)

brought to the Spanish colonies apart from Cuba. Brazil was a colony of Portugal from 1534 to 1822 when it became independent under its own emperor, the Prince Regent of Portugal. He and his successor ruled until 1889 when the country became a republic. Brazil experienced rapid economic growth over short periods with a sequence of successful export products. During these times there was a strong demand for African slaves. But the booms were punctuated by periods of depression in which the value of slaves declined and

Table 4.3 The principal names for human hybrids listed by Blumenbach in 1795

First generation	
European + Ethiopian	mulatto
European + American	mestizo
Ethiopian + American	zambo
Second generation	
European + mulatto	terceron or quarteron
European + mestizo	castiso
Mulatto + mulatto	casqua
Ethiopian + mulatto	griff
American + zambo	zambaigi
Third generation	
European + terceron	quarteron
European + castiso	postiso
Mulatto + terceron	saltatra
Mulatto + zambaigi	cambujo
Quarteron + mestizo	coyota
Griff + zambo	givero

Fourth generation
'there are those who extend even into the fourth generation this kind of pedigree, and say that those born from Europeans from Quarterons of the third generation are called Quinterons, in Spanish Puchuelas, but this name is also applied to those who are born of Europeans and American Octavons.'

Source: Blumenbach (1865: 216–18)

many of the older and less valuable were given their freedom. There was also a population of mulattos descended from unions between Portugese men and African women. They secured a special niche in the socio-economic structure as the agents of whites in supervising slaves (in agriculture and mining), pursuing those who ran off, making war upon local Indian groups and escaped slave settlements, serving as urban artisans, boatmen and cattle herdsmen. This created the 'mulatto escape hatch' whereby these men and women escaped from the bottom tier of society and secured intermediate positions. In this way there developed a continuous distribution of status in which complexion was one criterion among others. Partly in consequence, the emancipation of slaves was a gradual process. In 1871 a statute required the registration of all 1.7 million slaves and the emancipation of those in certain categories. In 1885 those aged over 60 years were brought within these provisions; by this time it was impossible to maintain a slave code that lacked any moral sanction, so that in 1888 the remainder were freed without any compensation being paid to their former owners.

In the early period of the settlement of Brazil, as of the United States, slavery assisted economic development because it provided a labour force at a time when labour was scarce. Since land was readily available, free labourers were inclined to go off and farm for themselves, so a system of unfree labour was advantageous in binding workers to the large-scale production units necessary to produce export crops. In the long run, though, slave labour was less productive than free labour because people will work hardest when they are working for themselves. It was uneconomic to use capital to purchase labour once wage-labour became available; wage-labourers did not have to be fed, housed, and looked after in times of sickness; if they died the employers had not lost their capital. Societies built upon slave labour had to undergo fundamental change once the economic balance tipped and slavery became uneconomic. In Brazil the transition was gradual; in the United States it came about only after a bitter four-year civil war.

Continuous and discontinuous ranking

A clear colour line between black and white was drawn in the United States because the whites had the power to draw it. Relations between blacks and whites were polarized and, especially in the Deep South, a discontinuous distribution of racial status was established. Whites might have done the same in Brazil (and in Latin America generally) if they had had similar opportunities, but it suited them to make allowance for variations in individual talents. What happens today in Brazil may be explained, very crudely, by reference to the idea of a continuous scale in which complexion is only one element in this computation of status. It is as if, when one person meets another, each obtains an impression of the other's wealth and education; persons are judged from their mode of address, speech and complexion, giving them imaginary points on a series of scales. A dark-complexioned lawyer might score 6 out of 10 on wealth, 9 on education, 8 on costume, and 1 on complexion, an average of 6. In Brazil this person would rank above a fair-complexioned bank cashier who scored 3, 5, 4 and 8 on these scales. (If wealth were more important than the other criteria, that scale could be weighted more heavily by calculating its points out of a larger maximum; it is the principle that matters, not the technique.) In the United States black lawyers would have been assigned to the black category. Their points would have given them a high rank in that category, but in many inter-racial situations the points would not have allowed them to out-rank white bank cashiers. There was discontinuity in the calculation of rank reflecting the existence of two hierarchies. The separation between the two was maintained by the whites chiefly in the circumstances which they defined as relating to social equality, but it was often ignored in business relations. In recent times the range of situations defined in business terms has increased so that the pattern of continuous rank has been gaining over the discontinuous one. The latter, which had its classic expression in the Deep South, has been called 'colour-caste'. It employs a two-step procedure. In the first step individuals are assigned to either the black or the white category in accordance with their appearance. This is a discontinuous ranking because black–white is a yes–no kind of differentiation, unlike placing someone on a scale. The second step is one of continuous ranking within a category, by reference to wealth, education, speech, demeanour, and so on, in which high points on one scale compensate for low points on another. Among blacks in the United States a whole range of terms have been used to distinguish shades of complexion, but they were irrelevant to the way individuals defined themselves in any situation in which the white category was opposed to the black.

It is important to appreciate that in different parts of the New World the same individuals' social positions would have been differently assessed. In Latin America a coffee-coloured person might be called a mulatto and be at a disadvantage compared with a white person, but rank ahead of a black person. In the Deep South coffee-coloured people would have been assigned to the black category and in their dealings with whites might have enjoyed no advantage on account of their lighter complexion. A set of individuals corresponding to Figure 4.1(d) would in Latin America have been described by a larger number of names referring to their individual shades of complexion. In the Deep South they would have been divided into two. The racial categories employed in everyday life both reflect and mould popular consciousness and they follow a different logic from that which directs classification in the biological sciences.

In societies in which appearance is one element in a continuous scale, a fair complexion has usually been preferred to a dark one. Thus when a survey in Puerto Rico in 1956–7 asked respondents what was the best colour to have, nearly half replied white (or *blanco*, since the interviews were conducted in Spanish); 8 per cent said mulatto (*trigueno*) and just over 1 per cent black (*negro*); nearly 40 per cent replied that there was no best colour because people were equal. When asked 'Would you say that persons of your colour have more, the same, or less opportunity to make their way in life than persons of other skin colours?' over 76 per cent declared that everyone had the same opportunities irrespective of colour (though among white respondents nearly 28 per cent thought their colour gave them an advantage). When asked, 'Would you say that persons of your colour are respected much more than, the same as, or less than persons of a different colour?', nearly 87 per cent said that persons received the same respect regardless of their colour. These replies are analysed in Table 4.4(A) according to respondents' views as to the colour categories in which they themselves belonged. The answers do not explain why so many should consider everyone equal in terms of respect when so many thought white the best colour to have.

Another part of the puzzle is contributed by Table 4.4(B), which compares the number of persons in the sample who were judged by local interviewers (themselves of all colours) to be *blanco*, *trigueno* or *negro*, with the number of respondents who assigned themselves to these categories. It will be seen that nearly 12 per cent of those considered white, and over 31 per cent of those considered black, preferred to describe themselves as mulatto. One possible explanation is that Puerto Ricans appreciated that a light complexion had

*Table 4.4 **Respect accorded to skin colour in Puerto Rico (A) and assignment to colour categories (B)***

Colour of respondent	More respect (%)	Some (%)	Less respect (%)	N*
(A)				
White	17.6	81.8	0.6	483,000
Mulatto	5.0	92.9	2.0	397,000
Black	9.4	84.9	5.7	53,000
Total	11.8	86.7	1.5	933,000
(B)		*White*	*Mulatto*	*Black*
Interviewer's assignment		608,000	307,000	80,000
Self-assignment		537,000	397,000	55,000

Note: The totals of these two tables vary because some respondents did not provide usable replies to the question about respect.
*Total size of division
Source: Tumin (1961: 227–46)

conferred an advantage, and in some circumstances still did so, but that either consciously or unconsciously they recognized this as a source of injustice and reacted against any expectation that colour should influence social position. It is as if they thought it best to do away with the categories black and white and for everyone to be mulatto. This is a speculative interpretation. What is more convincing is that, as shown in Table 4.4(A), so few of the black respondents should have thought that they were accorded less respect because of their colour. Physical differences are not always a basis for drawing social distinctions.

The contrast between Puerto Rico and the Deep South is a contrast in the importance of individual relative to group attributes. The possibility of grouping by colour was recognized in Puerto Rico at the time of the survey, but it was not a basis for social roles. In the Deep South individual attributes were completely subordinated to group membership in situations of racial conflict, but at other times people responded to the other person's individual qualities as well as to racial categorization. Groups are composed of individuals whose behaviour can bring about changes in the character of the groups themselves. Yet the individuals have been profoundly influenced by the groups with which they have been brought up and with which they identify. Group and individual influences are at work in all situations but the balance between them varies. In parts of Mexico, for example, individuals can choose to be either an Indian or a *mestizo*. They can live with Indians, speak an Indian language, dress in Indian clothes, and use an Indian name. Or they can live like *mestizos*. It is choice rather than colour which decides the issue, though choice may be subjected to the constraints of kinship and past friendship.

In Central America there has been a process of *mestizaje* (or mestizization) which seems to be exemplified in the Puerto Rican finding that 12 per cent of whites and over 31 per cent of blacks regarded themselves as mulattos. The trend probably reflects individual advantage (*mestizos* being subject to less discrimination), the feeling that this is the direction in which the society is moving, and a tendency to elevate the highest common factors of national identification. Group changes are then an aggregation of individual changes. As an index of the *mestizaje* of an Indian group it would be possible to ascertain the proportion of individuals able to speak Spanish, or speaking Spanish at home, and plot these numbers on a chart to show changes over time. This could be represented by a diagram like that in Figure 4.2 which plots linguistic change in Wales between 1891 and 1981. In 1991 18.7 per cent of the population reported that they spoke Welsh, a decline of 0.3 per cent over ten years. However, the age group with the highest percentage of Welsh-speakers (24.3 per cent) was that of persons aged between 3 and 15 years. A diagram to show the increasing use of Spanish by Indians in Mexico would contain a rising curve to show the proportion of persons able to speak Spanish and a falling curve for those able to speak only an Indian language. The first curve could be described as a measure of the assimilation of Indians to Spanish culture in respect of language, but it has to be remembered that, as the Puerto Rican study showed, *mestizaje* also affects whites. The version of Spanish spoken in Latin America now differs from Castilian Spanish. People of Spanish origin in Latin America have been influenced by Indian culture in their ways of life and national identification. When groups of different culture come together in new political units there is a two-way process by which many differences are reduced.

Sometimes encounters between peoples lead to the reduction of differences, whether cultural or (as in the case of Brazil, for example) physical; in others those differences are maintained. The effect of contact also varies between sectors of society. In sectors which do not affect the balance of power (like recreation or cuisine) or which facilitate the objectives of the superordinate group (like language or education) differences are more easily reduced. When it is a question of group control over economic resources or gainful occupations differences may be maintained.

The effects of contact between Greek and Turkish peoples at the eastern end of the Mediterranean have been very different from those in Latin America. The people known as Greeks settled in many parts of what is now Turkey and in other regions to the East. Constantinople was a Greek city until it fell to the Ottoman Turks in 1453. Under Ottoman rule Greeks and other minorities, often distinguished by religion, remained distinct over the centuries. The negotiations for a political settlement after the First World War led to fighting between Greece and Turkey and this caused the flight of a large Greek refugee population from Turkey, Bulgaria and Russia.

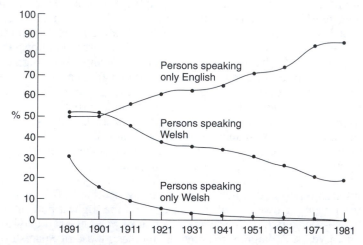

*Figure 4.2 **Linguistic change in Wales***

In 1923 there was an official exchange of population between Greece and Turkey in which Greece received some 1,300,000 refugees in return for 380,000 people considered Turkish. More than six centuries of contact had not brought the disappearance of group characteristics. This history, like that of Cyprus, shows the importance of the political framework (and the link between religion and politics) in influencing what happens as a result of group contact.

One way in which cultural differences are maintained is by distinctive costume. The reasons why Sikhs wear turbans may be religious, and so may the reasons why some male Jews wear skull caps (*yarmulkas*) and those known as Hassidim have a distinctive costume and hairstyle, but their effect is to mark them out in the eyes of others as different. Many Bangladeshis in the East End of London, Pakistanis in Bradford and others of Middle Eastern or African origin continue to dress as they would in their homelands. This sends a signal to the majority population, which may be unintentional, or, if intentional, may not be read in the way intended. It indicates that they want to maintain a difference and increases the likelihood that they will be treated differently.

Interaction

Sometimes group boundaries are dissolved and ethnic groups disappear. British history can be seen as the settlement of the country by Angles, Saxons, Normans, Huguenots, and others, and the interaction between the English, Welsh and Scots leading to a situation in which most of the differences have disappeared. This process, like that just described for parts of Latin America, can be called assimilation, in the dictionary sense of 'becoming similar'. The word sometimes occasions misunderstanding because many people now take it to denote a process by which one group absorbs another without itself being changed. The sociological concept of assimilation passed into ordinary language in the United States at a time when white Americans were anxious that immigrants from eastern and southern Europe might not make good citizens. Assimilation was equated with Americanization and with changes by minorities to conform to majority expectations. A similar distortion has been apparent in British usage since the 1950s, in that assimilation has often been equated with Anglicization. For example, in 1965 the British Home Secretary, Roy Jenkins, delivered a speech in which he said that he did not regard integration

as meaning the loss, by immigrants of their own national characteristics and culture. I do not think that we need in this country a 'melting pot' ... I define integration, therefore, not as a flattening process of assimilation but as equal opportunity, accompanied by cultural diversity, in an atmosphere of mutual tolerance. This is the goal.

(Jenkins 1966)

The speech was an example of clever political rhetoric. By disparaging the concept of assimilation as 'flattening' the speaker made 'integration' appear the more attractive. Jenkins was opposing what in the United States has been called 'straight line assimilation', an assumption that all aspects of minority life gradually conform to majority conventions at much the same speed. This is a chimera. Immigrants adopt the language of the majority if this is necessary for employment, but they may become more attached than previously to their religious practices if these give them reassurance and enable them to create a community of their own in the new land. Assimilation is not a flattening process and the word needs cleaning up if it is to be used in social science.

The concept of integration is no more straightforward. 'Integration' is a metaphor derived from mathematics to designate the making of a whole. If people are to come together in a whole they have to change, and they are unlikely to do so unless they think it will be worth their while. Immigrants learn a language to use a telephone, license and insure a motor car, pay taxes, get their children to school, and so on. They are less ready to conform to majority norms in the private sphere, particularly to norms of relationship within the family and in matters of sexual morality. It is individuals who change in these ways, but if they wish instead to maintain their previous customs, they have to combine with their fellows. If they are to continue speaking their mother-tongue, and particularly if they want their children to learn to speak it, they must get together with other speakers of the language. This is relevant to any consideration of the bargaining component in ethnic change. A simple model of change represents the receiving society as offering incentives to immigrants to conform to majority expectations. Immigrants who are willing to conform in the economic sphere may combine in the social sphere to try to keep alive the customs of their homeland, particularly if they believe that one day they will return. They offer the psychological rewards of esteem and affection to those of their number who observe the old customs and help maintain an immigrant community. The majority society often finds that it has to reward minority members in order to obtain their loyalty, or to threaten sanctions for disloyalty. The participants do not see this as part of a bargaining process, but from the outside it is apparent that individuals are exercising choices between the available alternatives. To this has then to be added the collective dimension. Some objectives can be attained only by collective action. If, for example, they want to agitate against discrimination, minority people must organize, offering to support political parties that will favour their cause, and threatening to campaign against those that will not. Here the bargaining is explicit. If young blacks in Brixton or Harringey organize to attack the police, their conduct may be interpreted as implicit bargaining. It is as if they said 'We think we are being harassed and propose to retaliate. We will do this again if the police do not leave us in peace.' It is pressure of this kind, and from many directions, which causes outwardly harmonious relations to move towards conflict, and then to find a new equilibrium.

Minority organization will be strong when the incentives for minority members to conform to majority expectations are weak. In some situations the members of a superordinate group discourage any tendencies for members of the subordinate group to adopt their ways because they assume that it to their advantage to prevent assimilation. In the Deep South the pattern of incentives reinforced the colour line. Changes in the relations between the black and white groups could be brought about only by collective action whereby the power of the federal government was used to counterbalance the policies of state and local governments. There are similarities between the Deep South and other two-category societies in which everyone is assigned to either the superordinate category (call it P) or the subordinate category (B). Since they have shared interests to pursue, the individuals organize as two competing groups. The interaction constitutes a dynamic system which is the product of a set of forces. When group P can muster sufficient strength to prevent group B from changing the relations between the two groups, and group B can prevent group P from doing the same, then inter-group relations are in equilibrium. The strength that each group can muster is the product of relations within the group.

Relations rarely stay in equilibrium for long because opinion within groups shifts. Changes in the society's environment (like the discovery or exhaustion of natural resources or alterations in world trade) may work to the relative advantage or disadvantage of either group. Figure 4.3 depicts possible consequences of change. The sequence starts on the left with a situation of harmony, in the sense that there are no overt signs of struggle between the two groups. It then changes, either because P seeks to extend its relative advantage over B by acquiring a greater share of the resources (indicated by the downward arrow representing pressure) or because B seeks to reduce its relative disadvantage by obtaining a more even share of the resources (indicated by the upward arrow). This upsets the equilibrium between P and B. Signs of struggle increase. One possible outcome is the breakdown of the system, by the secession or expulsion of one party, by partition, or by the spread of disorganization. Partition is represented by the two separate circles for P and B.

The breakup of the former Yugoslavia has provided some terrible examples of how previously amicable relations can be destroyed by the processes of political mobilization that lead to polarization. When members of one group commit atrocities against members of another, all members of the former group may be regarded as collectively responsible whether or not they were involved in the action. First of all people conclude that only in the midst of their own group can they be

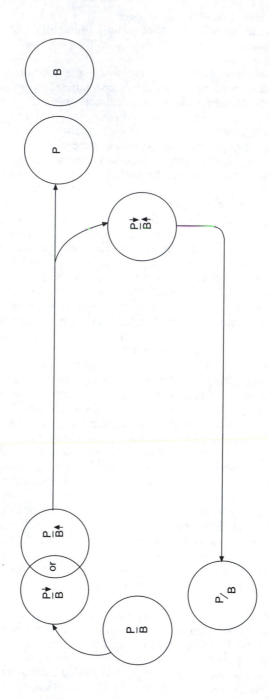

Figure 4.3 Equilibrium model of two-category racial relations

secure. Then, though they have done nothing wrong and have enjoyed good relations with their neighbours belonging to the other group, they come to fear attack from strangers who hold them responsible for atrocities committed by their co-ethnics, or strangers who simply seek 'an eye for an eye and a tooth for a tooth'. Their fears can be whipped up by politicians who exaggerate group differences in order to further their own campaigns. Anxieties can mount, just as a snowball gets bigger when rolled down a slope.

Partition is not the only possible outcome. Having mobilized their respective resources, P and B may be able to resolve the conflict by returning to a new equilibrium in which either B accedes to a deterioration in its position because of P's demands, or P accepts an improvement in B's relative position. The sources of change lie in the individuals' satisfaction or dissatisfaction with their relative positions, but the process of mobilization requires effective leadership. If one group acts in a way that outrages the expectations of people in the other group it may be easier to get members of that group to unite in collective action.

One of the skills of a political leader is the ability to seize upon an incident that can be turned to political advantage. Another important skill is the ability to bargain effectively. In any conflict between two ethnic or racial groups, just as between an employer and a trade union, there may be a good moment for one side to offer a settlement. If that opportunity is not seized, the price of harmony may increase. In inter-group relations the bargaining is rarely conscious, but the superordinate group can often avoid open conflict by making concessions before there is any trial of strength. By first sketching in Figure 4.3 an abstract model of the elements involved in two-category group relations, it becomes possible to identify similarities between inter-group conflicts in quite different parts of the world, such as those between the Tutsi and Hutu in Rwanda and Burundi, discussed in Chapter 5, and those between blacks and whites in the United States and South Africa, discussed in Chapter 6.

The argument of this chapter has been that *individual goal-seeking reduces group consciousness* and promotes assimilation, but that certain goals (like public goods) can be attained only by collective action; this is inherently political. In Western industrial societies the commonest forms of collective action are those based on the shared economic interests which give rise to class solidarities. Western political systems have been constructed for the management of the politics of class and are ill-adapted to manage the politics of religion (as in the struggles over the legalization of abortion) and those of ethnicity.

Collective action on an ethnic basis occurs most frequently when persons who share a common ethnic origin, and associated attributes or interests, organize to influence the exercise of state power or to protect a shared culture. These political aspects are discussed in Chapter 5.

CHAPTER 5

Peoples and states

Racial consciousness is greatest in societies in which appearance is used as a basis for discontinuous social classification and evokes an identification of 'us' and 'them'; this is most potent when the groups differ in their power and their access to valued resources, like well-paying occupations. The study of ethnic and racial consciousness, therefore, has to consider the political contexts within which peoples encounter one another, and this, in turn, entails a historical perspective.

Some mid-nineteenth-century authors wrote of the 'swarming' of races as if each race at some point in its history sent out swarms of its members to colonize distant parts, just as bees and some other insects swarm at some point in their annual cycle. Many human societies have indeed passed through a phase in which they sent out their members and took over new territories. The Assyrians, Phoenicians, Persians, Romans, Turks and Tartars did so in their time. From the fifteenth century many West European nations entered upon such a phase. Less is known about the extent to which the ancient African empires did likewise, but there is no reason to believe that they were very different and the Zulu provide a relatively modern parallel. In Asia the Mongols and Han Chinese expanded to take over large territories. Consideration of such cases suggests that processes of expansion include two particular forms which can be called colonization and imperialism. Colonization is the planting of outposts in new territory. They may be trading posts, in which case they are enclaves within larger societies rather than centres from which people are ruled. This sense of the word survives in the way that, say, Italian restaurateurs, hairdressers and other workers in a British city may be referred to as an Italian colony. Empire, by contrast, entails the sending out of individuals in order to rule other peoples. Imperialism cannot be defined with much precision. For most of the twentieth century the form which has been most discussed has been 'salt-water imperialism', the extension of power to rule peoples on the other side of an ocean. The extension of power by land, as in the Tsarist empire that became the USSR, was thereby excluded from the definition of imperialism. Since the Second World War the extension of power by economic means rather than by direct rule has occasioned talk of 'dollar imperialism', 'neo-colonialism' and the like, but these notions are for use in political discourse rather than social science. The distinction between colonization and imperialism has likewise been swallowed up in the tendency to speak of colonialism as if it comprehended both.

Implications of empire

The expansion of European power overseas took so many forms that generalization is hazardous. Nevertheless, for the purpose of an initial orientation it is possible to advance three propositions about the implications of empire for racial and ethnic relations. The first is that *imperialism established a framework within which people who were previously strangers to one another could interact and do business*. It was a framework of peaceable rather than warlike relations. In Africa, fighting between ethnic (or 'tribal') groups was reduced both by the black empires and by the white ones. The latter regulated both inter-African (black–black) relations and inter-racial (black–white) relations. European states extended their rule in Africa for their own ends. They wanted to raise enough money to pay for the costs they incurred. They wanted to open up markets for their own merchants. They wanted to increase their influence in the world. They could do these things best if relations were peaceable. Within this framework new alliances were created between subgroups: white administrators with African chiefs, white traders with their black customers, white missionaries with black Christians, African intellectuals and trade unionists of one group with their opposite numbers of another, and so on. In British-administered territories political structures were created that enabled Africans to form political parties and acquire political experience. The Europeans had created the new political units by drawing lines on a map, but at the end of the imperial period these lines proved remarkably durable. In some places the people of one ethnic group are divided between two or three states (e.g. the Somalis in Somalia, Ethiopia and Kenya) and it has been said that there is scarcely a boundary that does not divide some group. The newly independent governments have nevertheless been unwilling to revise these boundaries. European influence bequeathed to the late twentieth century a black Africa of some forty states instead of a much larger number of relatively small ethnic units. Imperial rule reduced a large number of small conflicts, but left a small number of large ones.

Second, *imperialism incorporated ethnic groups differentially into new political structures*. One way in which this was sometimes done was to make overseas territories constitutionally part of the metropolitan country. In the early 1960s, for example, 29 deputies were elected from African (and other) constituencies who took seats in the National Assembly in Paris. Had the constituencies been drawn so that one deputy from Africa represented as many constituents as one deputy from France, there would have been not 29 but 390. That they had seats was an indication of their political incorporation. That they had fewer seats relative to their numbers demonstrates that the incorporation was differential, or unequal.

A more common procedure was for the imperial power to create a subordinate form of government in the colonial dependency. The British pattern was for the formation of a legislative council which could make laws for a colony. These laws had to be in accordance with British ideas of natural justice and could be disallowed if they were found offensive. The legislative council represented the people of the colony; it included representatives of European commercial interests and officials of the colonial administration. Some members were appointed by the Governor, but the trend over time was for more to be elected by popular vote so that the council had come to function as a parliament by the time of independence. Some colonies, like Kenya and Southern Rhodesia (now Zimbabwe), included areas regarded as suitable for European settlement. Other colonies, like most of West Africa, did not. In the former, white settlers often became politically powerful. The contrast between Northern Rhodesia (now Zambia) and Southern Rhodesia was particularly marked. In Northern Rhodesia political power remained with the British Crown and the country was administered by British officials who formed part of a colonial civil service with a career structure that could entail their being posted to Jamaica, Sierra Leone or Hong Kong instead of staying where they were. Southern Rhodesia, by contrast, was initially under the control of the British South Africa Company, a private company operating under a royal charter. Though the British government established a legislative council in 1898, Southern Rhodesia did not formally become a Crown colony until 1923 when the whites voted against incorporation into the Union of South Africa. As a partly independent state it had its own career structure for administrators. In 1965 the governing party made a unilateral and illegal declaration of independence. Constitutionally, however, responsibility for the territory remained with the British government which in 1979 succeeded in negotiating an end to the rebellion and the transfer of power to a new government. The contrast between Northern and Southern Rhodesia could be represented as a contrast between imperialism and colonialism, since in the former there was an imperial administration but in the latter the interests of white colonists were politically dominant.

In both Northern and Southern Rhodesia Africans were differentially incorporated into the new political structures. In the former they were, after a while, represented on the legislative council, but whereas they constituted over 97 per cent of the population it was not until independence that they had a correspondingly dominant position in the country's politics. In the period prior to independence African political movements were often called nationalist because they sought independence, just as, say, national movements in nineteenth-century Europe sought independence from Habsburg rule.

It might have been more accurate to call the African movements anti-imperial or anti-colonial movements for there was relatively little sense of national belonging among the peoples of varied ethnic groups who had been brought into association by European imperialism. After independence the new states had to cultivate a sense of national belonging in order to hold the societies together and combat ethnic fragmentation. Ironically, the first authentic African nationalism was that of the Afrikaners, the white settlers of Dutch origin who, in the middle and late nineteenth century, attempted to establish their own independent republics. If, today, the Zulu were to campaign for a separate sovereign state, that too could be accounted nationalist. It would show that there was a group of people claiming a distinct identity, seeking to rule themselves, and no other peoples, in a territory which they claimed as their own. Were that to happen, many would describe it not as nationalism but as tribalism, because they would consider it politically retrograde. Third World nationalism at the end of the twentieth century is associated not with ethnic units but with states, and states are based upon the lines on the maps drawn at the end of the previous century.

Third, *when imperial rule ended, there was less friction if political power could be transferred either to non-ethnic political parties or to a dominant ethnic group.* Twentieth-century transfers of power to non-ethnic political parties include such cases as Ghana in 1956, many West Indian countries around 1960, and Tanganyika (now Tanzania) in the following year. This category should also include Burma and India, despite the religious violence associated with Indian independence. Elsewhere power was transferred to the representatives of a political system which was formally non-ethnic, but in which one ethnic group, often because of its numerical strength, had a preponderant influence upon the nature and administration of the system. Thus in Kenya successive governments have been dominated by the Kikuyu. In Zimbabwe the Shona have established their primacy over the Ndebele. In Zaire the Kongo are pre-eminent, and in Pakistan the Pathans. In Guyana the Creole or African part of the population gained greater political power than the Indian-origin group of almost equal size. In Zanzibar the dominant group had been Arab from the days before the British arrived. With economic growth, more workers from the African mainland settled there and political rivalry led to polarization. The Arab-dominated Zanzibar National Party was opposed by a party of mainland Africans. Elections became flashpoints for racial violence. After independence in 1963, the African-led party experienced the frustration of winning a majority of the votes but not a majority of the seats. Shortly afterwards a mainland African led a revolutionary movement which set off a spate of racial brutalities. Several thousand Arabs were killed; by murder, repatriation, and emigration, their numbers were reduced by over 20 per cent. So it was that there, as in some other countries, the numerically preponderant group asserted its claims.

When empires have expanded without crossing salt water the results have shown some similarities and some interesting differences. In modern times three empires have exercised sway in Eastern Europe and its borders. Under the Ottoman empire, from the fourteenth century, Greek communities settled in Anatolia and around the Black Sea. The Sultan's non-Muslim subjects were ruled by their religious leaders. This seems to have kept the communities separate, because in 1923 Greece and Turkey had to administer a compulsory exchange of Muslim and Orthodox residents (mentioned on p. 61). Despite the passage of centuries, the Greeks had not become integrated into the state in which they and their forebears had been living. Under the Russian empire (from 1721) foreigners were invited to Russia. Later it was Germans and other foreigners who staffed the imperial bureaucracy. Russians were settled on the empire's fringes in the Baltic and the Caucasus. Integration was only partial because after the dissolution of the Soviet empire persons of German and Greek origin migrated to the countries from which their ancestors had originated. Nor has there been complete integration in Transylvania, a region where, over the centuries, peoples of different ethnic origin have met and where now Hungarians and Romanians have to coexist within a single state. The Balkan region has historically been a meeting place for Turkish, Russian and Austrian influence, and for the Muslim, Orthodox and Catholic faiths. So long as one power was dominant, ethnic political movements could be held in check. The breakup of Yugoslavia (a state created after the First World War) occurred at a time when external pressures dampening ethnic nationalism were weakened.

The expansion of imperial power in East Asia merits a more detailed comparison than can be offered here. The Russians did not regard their control of the Asian portion of the Soviet Union as imperialist, but since 1989 the people who were subject to that power have been more ready to label it as such. The three propositions just advanced all apply in some degree to the Russian empire and to the post-1989 changes. Briefly, there is a large region which since the seventh century has been known as Turkestan, an Iranian name meaning 'the land of the Turkic peoples'. The western part was gradually conquered by Tsarist Russia in 1865; after the formation of the USSR in 1924 it was divided into the five republics of Uzbekistan, Kazakhstan, Kirghizia, Turkmenistan and Tadjikistan. The eastern part was invaded by the Manchu rulers of China in 1876 and on some modern maps is named Sinkiang-Uigur. While the expansion of Russian power was relatively peaceful, that of Japan was bloody. In 1931 Japan invaded Manchuria, created the new state of Manchukuo, and installed as its head the man who had been deposed as emperor of China in 1912. The Japanese army invaded the Chinese mainland, sacked several of its principal cities, and by 1938 occupied the most economically developed half of China. Seeking to encourage Japanese to settle in Manchukuo, and to rationalize its expansionist policies, the Japanese government developed doctrines of Japanese racial superiority.

Though the Chinese empire was succeeded by a republic in 1912, the state continued to claim territory in Eastern Turkestan, Mongolia and Tibet that was inhabited by ethnically distinctive peoples. In Eastern Turkestan they now complain of the steady influx of Chinese settlers and of economic and social policies which threaten their way of life and their right to self-determination. The Chinese reconquest of Tibet after 1949 was particularly brutal, though the Beijing government maintains that it was only the peaceful liberation of the people from an oppressive ruling class and that Tibet has always been part of China. Before the 'liberation' there were some three thousand monasteries. Many were bombed and machine-gunned from the air. Now thirteen remain. A national uprising was repressed. The number of lives lost cannot be accurately estimated but, including those who died from starvation during the fighting, may possibly exceed 1 million. This has given rise to accusations of genocide. At present, Tibetans complain of the massive influx of Chinese settlers and a new form of apartheid in practice, even if there is no explicit ideological rationale for it. Tibet's natural resources have been exploited with little regard for the ecology or the health of the population. Any generalizations about the sociology of imperialism should surely not neglect the recent history of East Asia.

If imperial rule established a framework for interaction, then it would seem that within the framework some group differences were reduced, others maintained, and a few increased. Political differences were reduced among groups struggling for independence while economic changes created class alliances and similarities crossing ethnic boundaries. Religious differences could help keep groups apart, especially when they were associated with political differences. Whether people sought their ends by collective or individual action may, as the previous chapter contended, have been a crucial variable, but it is difficult to test the proposition.

Rwanda and Burundi

The conflict in Zanzibar can be seen as an illustration of the changes represented by the equilibrium model of two-category relations shown in Figure 4.3. To start with, relations were tranquil. Then the superordinate group was put under pressure by an increase in the size of the subordinate group and by inter-group competition in connection with elections. Conflict increased. The previously superordinate group had to lose some of its privileges before harmony was re-established. The whole system was then changed by its incorporation into what became Tanzania. The same model is illustrated more dramatically, and more tragically, by events in the states of Rwanda and Burundi to the west of Tanzania in the African interior. In 1899 they both became part of German East Africa, passing into Belgian hands in 1916 and being administered as a single unit by that country until their independence in 1962. Rwanda had a population of 2.5 million, and Burundi of about 3.5 million. The population of both countries was composed of three strata, sometimes called races, sometimes castes, sometimes ethnic groups, namely the Twa, or forest-dwelling pygmies, who accounted for 1 per cent; the Hutu, or peasant-cultivators, who made up 85 per cent; the Tutsi pastoralists, who had conquered the region in the sixteenth century and made themselves its rulers, contributing the remaining 14 per cent. The three groups have often been described by reference to representatives. Thus the Tutsi have been described as tall, graceful and aristocratic; the Hutu as people 'whose ungainly figures betoken hard toil, and who patiently bow themselves in abject bondage to the later-arrived yet ruling race, the Tutsi'. Descriptions based upon typical representatives distract attention from the many people who do not correspond to any type. There were physical differences, the Tutsi being on average 1.75 metres tall (5 feet 10 inches) and the Hutu 1.66 metres (5 feet 6 inches), but the differences between the groups were mainly cultural and from their appearance many people could not be identified as either the one or the other.

In both Rwanda and Burundi there was an upper stratum and a lower. In the upper stratum were the king and the princes of the blood; within this elite the king was the first among equals, but, since the dynastic families were rivals, the king could play one against another. The king found among the Hutu natural allies against the dynastic families, and he relied greatly upon Hutu for the administration of his Crown lands. The Tutsi were divided by status and by region; the Hutu, being more numerous, were divided even more, but these divisions were balanced by patron–client relations linking all manner of people from the king to his lowest subject. Although the traditional social structure contained a great many sources of conflict, in practice few if any conflicts followed ethnic lines. The massacres that followed independence were traceable to the social transformations of the twentieth century and to the exploitation of ethnic differences for political ends.

The overriding political problem was that of managing social and economic change so as to bring a society at a low level of development up to the standards being demanded at the UN. The Belgian administration appreciated this, even if they could not foretell how rapid the change would have to be once international pressure was applied in the late 1950s. The Belgians reduced feudal privileges, encouraged the growth of a new class of teachers and artisans, and conducted elections. In 1956 the first popular vote took place on a basis of adult male suffrage to choose representatives to serve in electoral colleges which in turn would elect members of the Superior Council. The pace of change was faster in Rwanda, where Tutsi–Hutu tensions were sharper. Nevertheless, many Hutu voted for Tutsi candidates, with the result that the Tutsi obtained a virtual monopoly over seats in the Rwanda Superior Council. Leo Kuper (1977) interpreted the position in these words:

The reforms, however inadequate in their implementation, the appearance of an educated Hutu elite, encouragement of, and support for their aspirations by European clergy, the increasing identification of the Belgian administration with Hutu interests, the visiting missions and interventions of the United Nations, the political movements in neighbouring territories, all helped to foster an egalitarian challenge to inequality.

(Kuper 1977: 174–5)

Two political parties were formed. One which was Tutsi-dominated was primarily concerned with black–white relations and apprehensive of a coalition between Belgian and Hutu interests. The other, Hutu-dominated, was primarily concerned with Hutu–Tutsi relations; it claimed that if the country was to become truly independent it was necessary to abolish the colonization of blacks by blacks. In 1958 the king attempted to suppress this contention. He declared the problem to be one of wicked rumours circulated by a small group of enemies of the country, acting under foreign influences; those who attempted to create divisions were to be punished. So the leaders of the Hutu were attacked. The Hutu replied with incendiarism, burning and looting thousands of Tutsi huts, plundering their plantations, killing their livestock. Some Tutsi were murdered, but the attacks were primarily upon property. The Tutsi drew on the apparatus of government to assassinate suspected leaders and instigators. There were atrocities. The Hutu might have responded with civil war had not the Belgians restored order. They installed a new and more representative governing council. Agrarian reforms were introduced, but such measures could not stem the increasing polarization. The next elections were accompanied by more burnings and murder. They confirmed Hutu domination of the country by 1962 when, with UN approval, Rwanda became independent as a separate state. In retrospect it looks as if the UN should have persisted longer to keep Rwanda and Burundi together as a single political unit. The ethnic oppositions in the two states were so similar; people in each of them watched events in the other, and were influenced by what was happening on the other side of the border.

Rwanda became a one-party state with a full panoply of laws formally proscribing discrimination based on race, colour, sex, religion, political opinion, national descent or social origin. It had policies for the equitable allocation of jobs in the public and private sectors with quotas for each ethnic group. Its history for a time illustrated part of the processes described in Figure 4.3. To start with there was harmony between Tutsi and Hutu based upon the greater power of the latter. Then tension increased until there was open conflict and the possibility of a breakdown. A Hutu revolution resulted in the expulsion of the previously ruling elite of the dominant minority and the society moved round the flattened circle back to a new kind of harmony with the larger ethnic group in the politically dominant position.

This was no true equilibrium and it did not last. On 1 October 1990 the army of the Rwandan Patriotic Front invaded from Uganda with a force of 7,000 soldiers, some of whom were Tutsi exiles who had deserted from the Ugandan army. Within three years the government had lost control of the situation because of its own deficiencies. The ruling elite had used political office for its own aggrandizement. Since the invasion started, more than a thousand Tutsi had been extra-judicially executed while others had been made to 'disappear' or had been tortured in detention. As before, those responsible for the killings had been able to act with impunity.

An international commission of inquiry concluded that the massacres were not spontaneous movements but planned attacks on Tutsi and Hutu leaders who favoured power-sharing. The Rwandan state had operated so as to exacerbate ethnic tensions. Many Tutsi were hidden or otherwise saved by Hutus, some of whom paid with their lives for these acts of courage. Tutsi were killed just because they were Tutsi. Because the Rwandan soldiers could look forward to only one meal every two days, the army terrorized the local population. Rape was commonplace.

In April 1994, after the presidents of Rwanda and Burundi were both killed when returning from peace talks in Tanzania, the Hutu commenced a genocide in which the militias maintained by political parties played a major part. The UN's special rapporteur, who investigated events, came to conclusions similar to those of the international commission. Two things had been going on at much the same time. There was (a) a political conflict between the then government and the invading army; and (b) a criminal conspiracy. As part of (b), repeated appeals had been made to the Hutu proclaiming 'ten commandments' which included:

'1. Every Hutu must understand that every Tutsi, no matter who, works for the interests of his ethnic group. Therefore any Hutu is a traitor who takes a Tutsi as a wife, concubine, secretary or protégée . . .'. According to commandment 4, a Hutu was a traitor if he entered into commercial relations with Tutsi. According to commandments 5–7 strategic positions should be filled by Hutu, most teachers should be Hutu, and the armed forces exclusively Hutu. '8. The Hutu should stop having mercy on the Tutsi.' '10. The Social Revolution of 1959, the Referendum of 1961, and the Hutu ideology shall be taught to every Hutu and at every level. Every Hutu should spread widely the present ideology. Any Hutu who persecutes his Hutu brother for having read, spread and taught this ideology is a traitor.'

One radio station became notorious. The UN special rapporteur stated that

the generally illiterate Rwandese rural population listens very attentively to broadcasts in Kinyarwanda; they hold their radio sets in one hand and their machetes in the other, ready to go into action.

The criminal conspiracy seems to have been accelerated and intensified by the political conflict but might well have occurred even had there been no military invasion. An international criminal tribunal has been established to try those responsible for it.

Political change in neighbouring Burundi was much influenced by news of the violence in Rwanda. In Burundi the elections of 1961 were won by a party which stood for national unity, led by a royal prince who was popular among the Hutu. He was murdered. The Tutsi had difficulty accepting democratic reforms and relations were worsened by the actions of Tutsi refugees from Rwanda. In 1965 they murdered the Hutu prime minister. Despite their overwhelming success in the preceding elections, the Hutu were passed over in the selection of a new prime minister. An unsuccessful attempt at a coup was followed by Hutu terrorism and the murder of at least 500 Tutsi. As in Rwanda, this evoked reprisals on a larger scale. Somewhere between 2,500 and 5,000 Hutu were slain in 1965. There were repetitions in 1972 in which about 100,000 people, or 3.5 per cent of the population, were massacred in the course of a few weeks. It has been described as selective genocide. It began with Hutu attacks upon Tutsi, but led to massive Tutsi counter-attacks and the re-establishment of Tutsi rule. The Tutsi concentrated upon those Hutu who were, or might become, leaders. Soldiers and bands of Tutsi youth appeared in the classrooms of the university and at secondary schools with lists of Hutu names. Young people were loaded into trucks and taken away. Few ever returned. Hutu pupils were assaulted by their Tutsi classmates and sometimes beaten to death. Hutu priests were taken from the churches, and Hutu doctors and nurses from the hospitals. This was the selective element in the genocide. Though Hutu and Tutsi were often described, by themselves as well as others, as races, they were not so distinctive that lists were not necessary to identify individuals. Prior to the killings there had been an open and flexible system of social stratification with considerable mobility. Afterwards there was a caste-like division; access to material wealth, status and power being restricted to Tutsi.

There were further killings in 1988. Six years later, as the situation seemed more hopeful, the president was willing to call another election. It resulted in the installation of a new president of Hutu origin who included many Tutsi in his government but was assassinated after three months in office. A new massacre followed, but whereas previous massacres in Burundi had been committed by Tutsi upon Hutu, this was primarily a Hutu attack upon Tutsi and those Hutu leaders who were willing to collaborate with Tutsi politicians. The events supported Tutsi claims about the spread of an extremist ideology among Hutu in both countries. Throughout 1994–6 there were sporadic killings carried out by the Tutsi-dominated army and by political militias. The apparatus of government was collapsing.

The case of Burundi therefore exemplifies a different kind of circuit round the cycle representing harmony and conflict in Figure 4.3. Tension increased to armed conflict, but the Hutu revolutionary movement has so far been crushed and a precarious equilibrium maintained by military power. In the case of this and some similar states much has depended upon the supply of military equipment and training from outside; sometimes grants for economic development have been used for arms purchases with the connivance of the donor country.

The recent history of Rwanda and Burundi shows that ethnic consciousness did not create the conflict, but, to the contrary, the conflict has done much to increase ethnic consciousness. It also suggests that when a region is underdeveloped by international standards and has an inegalitarian social structure, change has to be gradual if it is to be peaceful. Such societies have a collectivistic character in that individuals are linked to each other by a dense mesh of ties based upon kinship, clientage and landholding. To introduce elections in which voting is by individuals is to open up a route for acquiring power and distributing resources that is in conflict with the traditional pattern. The example also suggests that no society can be isolated from the world outside. Colonial dependencies all became vulnerable to pressure mobilized through UN institutions; these bodies demanded a rate of change that made violence inevitable in regions like that of Rwanda and Burundi. Sociologists tend to emphasize the structural factors; with the advantage of hindsight, they regularly conclude that whatever happened, had to happen. It can be difficult for them to acknowledge that the course of change can also be influenced by the skill and personality of persons in positions of leadership, by unpredictable assassinations, and the ability of leaders to make use of whatever opportunities arise. No one can be sure that so many people in Rwanda and Burundi had to die.

The Rwanda–Burundi example is significant in another respect. How were, and are, the Hutu and Tutsi best described? As ethnic groups? As tribes? As races? As castes? As political groups? There is no certain answer. It is the same problem as in Chapter 1 with the reference to Jews as a group with multiple characteristics. A distinctive appearance creates a category, not a group, just as persons aged between 20 and 29 years, or persons earning between £20,000 and £30,000 per annum, are categories and not groups. They can become groups if they organize to pursue shared interests or out of a feeling that they belong together. This feeling is more easily developed when a set of individuals have a lot in common – religion, language, history, a shared alignment *vis-à-vis* competitor groups, and so on. The Hutu and Tutsi were groups with historical identities at the same time as individual members had important links with members of the other group. It is a salutary lesson that these cross-cutting ties could so easily be broken. Once the political system could no longer guarantee the personal security of individuals, there was nothing to withstand the pressure for polarization along ethnic lines. Hutu and Tutsi often looked alike. They spoke the same language and their elites often shared the same political ideals. Their experience suggests how much stronger can be the pressures for maintaining group boundaries when, because of differences of skin colour, people can be assigned to social categories from a distance. Physical differences facilitate stereotyping and discrimination. People who have not themselves experienced less favourable treatment readily identify with those who have because 'it could have been me'. It is therefore particularly difficult to reduce the potentiality for alignment on the basis of colour. The best hope is not to deny its intrusiveness but to seek to highlight alternative bases for group alignment such as those of common religious belief and political allegiance.

Genocide

Differences other than those of appearance have at times been magnified to the point at which members of another group have been regarded as subhuman, or as a kind of humanity so different that the ordinary rules were not thought to apply to them. They have made possible the crime of genocide. This is the name given to acts committed with intent to destroy, in whole or in part, a national, ethnic, racial or religious group as such (the last two words are added to indicate that the people are killed *because* they are members of such a group; it has to be a causal relationship, not simply an association). Genocide has at times been practised against quite inoffensive peoples when other groups have wanted their land. The governments of Brazil and Paraguay have been accused of failing to prevent genocides against Indian groups in their territory. In reply, they have argued that whereas people may, without authorization, have attacked Indians, the attacks were not directed against them because they were members of particular ethnic groups. The charge of genocide can more easily be brought against the Nazi government of Germany which was responsible for the slaughter of some 6 million Jews and about 250,000 Gypsies during 1941–5. The charge is also levelled against the government of Turkey for the deaths of about 800,000 Armenians in 1915. The killing of the Armenians took place as the Turks faced the threat of dissolution of their empire; the Armenians had been struggling for greater independence, so their loyalty was in question. The destruction of the German Jews, however, was remarkable because they had assimilated to the majority to a greater extent than Jews elsewhere; they posed no threat, but they proved convenient scapegoats.

Leo Kuper summarized the major steps in the process as starting with the definition of who was a Jew. The identification of Jews by conspicuous signs (such as being obliged to wear an armband bearing a yellow star of David), their expulsion from the civil service, the professions, responsible positions in business and industry, and the seizure of their property. They were vilified in political speeches, in publications, and through the mass media. To start with, the Nazi policy was to force Jews to emigrate, but about July 1941 the order was given for them to be exterminated. Death camps were organized on industrial principles. The victims were processed for slaughter as if on a conveyor belt. The camp staff, with bureaucratic efficiency, took into store the victims' possessions, their clothes, gold teeth and women's hair; they arranged for the redistribution of these things. Some killing centres were combined with slave camps where Jewish workers were treated as if they were expendable. Leading German firms established branches in the vicinity of the gas chambers and crematoria of Auschwitz.

Religious divisions can be the bases of divisions which cut as deep as racial ones. Kuper also briefly described the violence which briefly accompanied the partition of India and Pakistan when British rule ended in 1948. Tensions had been rising. The Muslim politicians have often been blamed for insisting that they had to have a separate sovereign state, but they could well have claimed that the violence only demonstated the justification for their fears. The state of Punjab was divided into two. In the village of Kahuta, where 2,000 Hindus and Sikhs and 1,500 Muslims had lived in peace, a Muslim horde set fire to the houses in the Hindu and Sikh quarters with buckets of petrol. Entire families were consumed in the flames. Those who escaped were caught, tied together, doused with petrol, and burned alive. In Lahore, a previously tolerant city of some 500,000 Hindus, 100,000 Sikhs and 600,000 Muslims, a Sikh leader precipitated the violence with his cry of 'death to Pakistan!' In the resulting riots 3,000 people were killed, mostly Sikhs. In the Sikh holy city of Amritsar, Hindus walked up to unsuspecting Muslims and threw vitriol or sulphuric acid into their faces. While the authorities performed the Independence Day rituals a horde of Sikhs only a short distance away was ravaging a Muslim neighbourhood. The men were slaughtered without mercy or exception. The women were repeatedly raped, then paraded through the streets to the Golden Temple where most of them had their throats cut. Muslims in the part of the Punjab that was to be Indian tried to move westwards across the boundary to Pakistan. Hindus and Sikhs on the other side of the line tried to move eastwards, but it was as dangerous to move as it was to stay still. Refugee columns on the roads became targets for looting and massacre. On the railways, trains were stopped by assassins. There were periods of between four and five days at a stretch when not a single train reached Lahore or Amritsar without very many dead and wounded passengers.

Since that time a religious movement among the Sikhs has generated a special brand of Sikh nationalism. There was a wave of assassinations of Hindus. The Golden Temple was stocked with arms, so the Indian army attacked and occupied it. Sikh zealots struck back.

Mrs Indira Gandhi, the Indian prime minister, was assassinated. Killings continued. Nor is Sikh–Hindu hostility the only religious conflict in India. In the state of Gujerat, on India's west coast, tensions between Hindus and Muslims in the 1980s has caused riot and massacre. In 1992 Hindu militants demolished a mosque in Ayodha and exacerbated Hindu–Muslim conflicts in Britain as well as in India. Mrs Gandhi's son Rajiv, while prime minister, was also assassinated, though the Tamils responsible for his death were seeking revenge as part of a political rather than a religious dispute.

Religious divisions may be the basis of conflict in that they define who are the contending parties. The motives behind the conflict may be more complicated. Not everyone takes part in rioting or approves of it. Those who instigate violence may be highly strung personalities or even psychopaths, but many ordinary people take part. In situations of collective excitement, humans are capable of acting as members of a crowd in ways that they could not act were they on their own. It should also be remembered that political or economic interests may lie behind the formation of groups identifed by religion. In Northern Ireland, as already mentioned, the contending parties are often identified as Protestant and Catholic, but the more fundamental opposition is that between the Unionists who want to keep the province part of the United Kingdom, and the Republicans who seek a united Ireland. Religious differences can also give a special character to conflicts defined in political terms, like the long war between Iran and Iraq. The Iranians and Iraqis follow different traditions within Islam and many of the states which at that time supported Iraq were influenced by the fear of the Iranian tradition.

The UN Convention on Genocide was not drafted so as to bring the mass murder of political groups within its scope. The social processes which lead up to such murders are, however, basically similar to those underlying genocide. A strong sense of 'us' and 'them' is so manipulated as to make it possible for people to treat others in ways they would not use were they dealing with men and women whom they identified as members of the same 'we' group as themselves. In Stalinist Russia whole national groups were deported. Khrushchev, in his denunciation of Stalin in 1956, referred to such actions as 'not dictated by any military consideration'.

Not only a Marxist-Leninist, [he declared], but also no man of common sense can grasp how it is possible to make whole nations responsible for inimical activity, including women, children, old people, Communists and Komsomols, to use mass repression against them, and to expose them to misery and suffering for the hostile acts of individual persons or groups of persons.

In 1965, in Indonesia, there was a massacre of communists, mostly Chinese, on a massive scale. Estimates of the numbers slaughtered range from 200,000 to over 1 million. In Cambodia the Khmer Rouge forces between 1974 and 1979 turned the country into an agricultural work-site, with the loss of possibly 2 million lives. The Pol Pot regime was then overthrown by an invading Vietnamese army. The government of Idi Amin in Uganda from 1971 to 1979 practised political massacre on an almost comparable scale.

Linguistic differences rarely become a basis for such violent opposition as physical differences and religious or political cleavages, but they can evoke powerful reactions when they serve to differentiate groups with opposed interests. In Quebec, French-speaking Canadians have referred to themselves as the country's 'white niggers'. The opposition between French-speakers and Flemish-speakers has brought down several governments in Belgium. Language differences have posed major political problems in Switzerland and in Wales. India has been forced by the strength of linguistic feeling to alter the boundaries of some of its states and in three instances to create new ones by dividing old states along linguistic boundaries.

All these kinds of opposition can have the effect (discussed in Chapter 4) of reducing harmony, increasing tension and, at times, pushing the state either to breakdown, or, after a paroxysm of violence, of re-establishing harmonious relations based upon a new balance of power. Racial differences can occasion a particularly sharp divide, but they differ from the other sorts in degree rather than kind. What is fundamental is the process of polarization when people are forced to identify themselves with one side or the other and no intermediate positions are tolerated. Tensions grow until each group wishes to have a life of its own in which the others will have no part. If they stand in the way of this objective, they must be expelled or eliminated.

Opposition can evoke solidarity among members of a socio-political category and transform them into a group. African-Americans in the New World came from a variety of peoples in Africa. They had little in common except their experience of abuse at the hands of others, but this shared experience brought them together. A comparable example of this process, which may be called ethnogenesis, is that which has been at work among the Palestinians. Their experience of the Israelis has given them a consciousness of belonging to a distinctive people that they did not have before 1948. In Africa new ethnic groups have formed in quite recent times, while in India the formation of new *jatis* (subcastes) has long characterized mobility within the Hindu system. Old groups can always dissolve and new ones form as circumstances change and individuals align themselves in new ways.

One of the principles on which United Nations action has been founded is that of self-determination. The accession to independence of a large number of previously dependent territories has fashioned the majority view about the circumstances in which this principle is applicable. Since many of the new states experienced salt-water imperialism they contend that it is colonies such as they were which are entitled to self-determination. They deny its application to groups like the Gibraltarians and Falkland Islanders. They assume that self-determination is fully realized when a colony becomes independent, and that it is ·a right which can be exercised only once. The government of Burundi has hitherto been dominated by the Tutsi. Any Hutu claims to self-determination would get little support from the Organization of African Unity or the UN. Both of these bodies are organizations of states rather than of nations. The rulers of one state are reluctant to interfere in the affairs of another, even when there are gross violations of human rights, lest by doing so they give other states a justification for interfering in what they see as their own affairs.

From a sociological standpoint, however, the kinds of conflict which arise within independent states, as groups struggle for power over others or for self-determination, may be little different from the struggles that hastened independence. In Nigeria large numbers of energetic and talented people from the Eastern Region moved to work in the North, making a significant contribution to the economic and social development of the places to which they moved. Their relative success aroused resentment, and in 1966 getting on for 30,000 of them were massacred. Those who could, returned to the Eastern Region which shortly after declared its independence under the name Biafra. There was a long war which led to the death of between 600,000 and 1 million Easterners, yet there was no independence for Biafra.

Compare this with Bangladesh. From its foundation in 1948 Pakistan was divided into two parts, separated from each other by over 1,500 kilometres (1,000 miles). They had been made a single state because in each section most of the people were Muslims. West Pakistan was composed of Baluchi, Pathan, Punjabi and Sindhi peoples with Urdu as their common language. East Pakistan, composed predominantly of Bengali-speaking people, had a very different culture, geography and economy. In 1948 the income per head was 10 per cent higher in the West than in the East. This disparity increased steadily until by 1969 there was a 60 per cent gap. The bulk of Pakistan's foreign exchange was earned in the East, but most of the foreign aid went to the West. The senior military personnel, the senior civil servants, the central government apparatus as a whole, all were overwhelmingly West Pakistani. Many East-erners maintained that they were subject to a colonial domination by Westerners. In 1970, the then military ruler, a Westerner, promised elections and constitutional changes which would have given the East a fairer deal. The Awami League campaigned in the East for the maximum autonomy short of separation. It won 167 out of the 169 seats in the National Assembly allocated to the East. The first meeting of that body was postponed while, apparently, negotiations were undertaken. In reality, the government used the delay to mobilize its military might. In March 1971 it struck. The International Commission of Jurists described the outcome as the indiscriminate killing of civilians, including women and children and the poorest and weakest members of the community; the attempt to drive out of the country a large part of the Hindu population; the arrest, torture and killing of Awami League activists, students, professional and business men and other potential leaders among the Bengalis; the raping of women; the destruction of villages and towns; and the looting of property. All this was done on a scale which it is difficult to comprehend.

(Quoted in Kuper 1982: 78–9)

In December, after the intervention of the Indian army, the war ended. Estimates of the numbers of Bengalis killed in what then became Bangladesh vary, but the total may have approached 3 million. Account should also be taken of the 10 million Hindus forced to take refuge in India; the attacks upon them probably came within the legal definition of genocide. At the UN (on which see Kuper 1985: 44–61) Pakistan accused elements within the Awami League of plotting secession with encouragement from India. The government had to act in order to prevent the state from being broken up. Pakistan expressed regret that the international community had done so little to restrain India from a course which violated 'the two most fundamental principles of the Charter of the United Nations – non-interference in internal matters, and refraining from the threat or use of force against the territorial integrity or political independence of any state'. The right of self-determination could not be extended to an area that was an integral part of a state's territory for 'Pakistan is only one among the many multiracial, multi-linguistic or multi-religious states that would then be exposed to the dangers of fission and disintegration'. So the UN concentrated upon what it does so well: talking.

Thanks to India the people of Bangladesh were not denied self-determination, but the general pattern has been for states to channel ethnic sentiments so that they support the state structure. In the days of decolonization African leaders promised that once they were independent they would be able to revise state boundaries and make them harmonize with ethnic boundaries. With the exception of the Cameroons–Nigeria boundary, no such revision has occurred. The pressures on the new leaders have been those of trying to hold together political entities dependent upon only flickering sentiments of national unity.

Constitutional engineering

The governments of the newly independent states of the 1960s took office after winning elections, but many of them were reluctant to hold any more elections unless they could be sure that they would be able to retain power. In some cases the leaders of the parties, the political elites, yielded to the temptations of ethnic politics. Such a criticism is to be directed not only against some of the politicians of Rwanda and Burundi. It is a criticism that has been levelled at politicians in Belgium and those responsible for the division of the former Czechoslovakia into two separate states. Above all, it can be applied in the former Yugoslavia.

Political theorists have asked whether it is possible to design a system such that there will be no rewards for those who play ethnic politics but instead there will be positive incentives for politicians to cultivate support across ethnic boundaries. One way of reducing conflict is to encourage the *cross-cutting ties* that can be noted when sets of people who are opposed to another on one issue find themselves allies over another issue. Two such theorists are Arend Lijphart and Donald Horowitz whose proposals for constitutional engineering in South Africa are compared in Chapter 6.

Political leaders are frequently in a position to change a country's constitution so as to promote national integration, to secure a privileged position for their own group, or provide a system of representation that recognizes ethnic differences. Claire Palley (1974) describes these three as assimilationist approaches, domination devices and pluralistic techniques. In the first are counted measures to eliminate discrimination, such as special laws, bills of rights, supervisory commissions, and bodies charged to enforce legislation, conciliate parties in dispute, monitor appointments, and so on. In the second come various manipulations of the electoral process, by making it more difficult for certain kinds of people to vote, varying the size of constituencies, and drawing the boundaries so as to favour one group ('gerrymandering'). In Malaysia, civil service posts have been awarded disproportionately to Malay applicants. In the award of business licences and government contracts, preference has been shown to Malays or to partnerships between Malay and Chinese entrepreneurs. The law has been used to enforce the grossly unequal ownership of land by a dominant minority, as in South Africa and the former Rhodesia, but it has also, on occasion, been used to protect indigenous groups (e.g. Melanesians in Fiji, Indian reservations in the USA) and even to make restitution (to Maoris under the Waitangi Tribunal in New Zealand). Regulations concerning the use of an official language may be seen as a form of domination. National holidays, the national flag and national dress may reflect only the culture of the majority group.

Pluralist policies are varied. They include federal constitutions, territorial devolution and arrangements to see that the number of elected representatives is in a fixed ratio. There may be separate electoral rolls for the different groups or a fixed distribution of important offices. The danger of organizing political life on the basis of distinct ethnic communities is that it reinforces the lines of ethnic differentiation and reduces the occasions for people to ally themselves with members of other groups. Separate electoral rolls with separate blocs of seats have been tried in Fiji, Rhodesia, South

Africa, British East Africa, Cyprus, New Zealand and India (for the benefit of the tribal peoples and the Adivasis – the so-called untouchable castes). Sometimes separate rolls have been maintained with voters allowed to vote for candidates on other lists so as to build up support across ethnic lines. In Mauritius the population is divided into four categories: Hindu, Muslim, Sino-Mauritian and General (i.e. Afro-Creole, Coloured, *mestizo* and white) each of which returns two Members of Parliament, and then a further eight are chosen as 'best losers' in proportion to the state of the parties but on the basis of representing any under-represented community. The system produces a House of Representatives which reflects the population mix. In Bermuda, with a population divided almost equally between black and white, each constituency elects two members, and this enables a party to nominate one black and one white candidate. Where communal representation exists, it may be be supported by the stipulation that this representation can be amended only with the support of each set of representatives, or with a majority of two-thirds, or even three-quarters, of the legislature. There may be special provisions to ensure power-sharing. For example, the Cyprus constitution of 1960 required a 7: 3 ratio of Greek to Turkish ministers. In Northern Ireland a scheme was introduced, unsuccessfully, for elections using a single transferable vote followed by the Secretary of State's appointing an executive to include Protestant and Catholic members from several political parties. The Lebanese National Pact of 1943-75 required that the president be a Maronite Christian, the prime minister a Sunni Muslim, and the chairman of the Parliament a Shi'ite Muslim. These can be accounted examples of deliberate constitutional engineering. Only in Switzerland has power-sharing developed organically over more than a century. There a federal assembly elects a federal council of seven, such that there are usually four or five German-speakers, one or two French-speakers, and one Italian-speaker. This has promoted relatively good inter-communal relations.

A further consideration is that though electoral rights may be given, they are not always used. In the United States in recent times less than half the eligible population has voted in presidential elections. A recent proposal to combine electoral registration with the procedure for obtaining a driving licence, which might have increased the numbers of ethnic minority and poor people who use their votes, was not adopted. In Australia, by contrast, voting is compulsory.

Federal systems may provide for different political units within a federation to have different official languages and an important measure of independence. Where peoples of different ethnic origin are intermingled, but political tensions persist, federation has much to offer provided those involved are willing to accept the constraints that derive from the region's history. One such example has been that of Yugoslavia. The conclusion of the First World War saw the recognition in 1918 of the Kingdom of Serbs, Croats and Slovenes as an extension of what had earlier been the Kingdom of Serbia. In 1929 it adopted the name Kingdom of Yugoslavia. Attacked by German, Italian and allied forces in 1941, the government collapsed; bitter fighting between those who supported and those who opposed Germany led to the disintegration of the state. In 1945 it was reconstituted as the Federal Republic of Yugoslavia. There were six national republics, Bosnia-Herzegovina, Montenegro, Macedonia, Croatia, Slovenia and Serbia; within Serbia after 1974 there were two autonomous provinces, Voivodina and Kosovo (the former had a substantial Hungarian population and the latter a majority Albanian population). Under President Tito the federation was held together by sometimes brutal measures. Following his death in 1980, the strains increased, largely because the mode of government was failing to deliver the standard of living the people expected. Communist ideology became discredited. For a while there was a collective presidency of eight members, each representing a republic or province, and having equal rights. The official view as stated to the UN in 1985 was that to elevate the provinces to the status of republics would be a concession to those who wanted 'the dissolution of Yugoslavia and the establishment of ethnically pure states on the basis of what were clearly nationalist and racist ideas'. Nevertheless, political tensions between Serbs and Albanians in Kosovo led to abrogation of the separate status of the provinces and their absorption into Serbia. The power of the federation over the republics, particularly over the largest of them, Serbia, weakened. The Serbian government was willing to allow Slovenia to leave the federation. It would accept the secession of those parts of Croatia which had a majority Croat population, but was concerned for the rights of the Serbs who had lived for centuries in territory that was part of the Croat republic. The Croat nationalists were no more ready to respect the rights of minorities within their republic than were the Serb nationalists. Croatia declared its independence without the consent of its Serb minority. The states of Western Europe could have acted to calm the situation, but they were insufficiently cautious. Serbia intervened with military force to support the Serbs in Croatia and then to support the Serbs in Bosnia-Herzegovina who had not agreed to the composition of the government which declared the independence of that state. Thousands of people who had been ready to live in peace with their neighbours without worrying about their ethnic origin found themselves forced to identify themselves ethnically, and many thousands were killed. The whole experience showed that while constitutional provisions are important to ethnic peace, they can be undone by political ambitions.

A different example is offered by experience in Nigeria. That country's politicians recognized the dangers in the British model of single-member constituencies with first-past-the-post elections when they introduced a constitution which required a candidate for the presidency to win votes in all of the then eighteen states.

Many attempts to promote harmonious group relations by constitutional measures have not brought the results hoped for. Much may depend upon economic circumstances. When there is no economic growth one group can gain only at another's expense, so there is a zero-sum conflict in which the losing group becomes resentful. This can develop into a cleavage, as for example in the expulsion of Asians from East Africa. When there is economic growth, one group can advance without the other group's losing thereby. It is probable, for example, that there has been no further ethnic rioting in Malaysia since 1969 because that country's continuing economic growth has supported the preferential policies in the Malay interest without thereby reducing the economic level of the Chinese group. The positive-sum result has come about not because the internal conflict has been constructive, but because the terms of trade have moved in Malaysia's favour and new sources of mineral wealth have been discovered.

Conclusion

The conclusion of this chapter must surely be that it is impossible to construct any meaningful scale of group harmony and group conflict because so much depends upon the particular characteristics and circumstances of the groups in contact. Nor is it easy to derive sociological generalizations when so much depends upon political relations that may change with great rapidity. The international order recognizes the legitimacy of state power rather than the rights of nations because it is difficult to take account of nations and national consciousness except in their expression through state institutions. Where there are national, ethnic or racial divisions within states relative harmony and conflict depends upon competition to control state institutions and the use that is made of that control. Some generalizations about such use are advanced in Chapter 6.

The twentieth century has seen a great increase in the services that a state can provide to its citizens; this is partly because technological advance (e.g. road, rail and air transport, mass communications, increased trade) has necessitated new forms of regulation, new opportunities for the distribution of benefits, and new modes of collective action. Political institutions suited to relatively homogeneous Western societies have been copied in new and ethnically heterogeneous states which were unable to regulate the resulting competition or to prevent it turning into conflict. Imperial rule often increased ethnic heterogeneity, but state power was exercised from a distance and the competing interests of different groups were balanced against one another. This led to accusations that they divided in order to rule, but in so doing they kept the peace and made possible the growth of new interests and new alliances. When imperial rule ended, indigenous groups contested the succession to state power and those which succeeded often used their advantage to further their sectional interests.

In previous centuries a disaffected group might have rebelled; a neighbouring state might have moved in to control this part of the territory. The growth of international political organization, reflected in such bodies as the United Nations and the Organization of African Unity, has made it more difficult for frontiers to be changed; governments now often support one another (though there have been open and armed interventions by India and Tanzania, and many covert interventions). Ethnic movements may gain support when (as in Sri Lanka) a minority believes that state power is being used against its interests, or (as in Malaysia and Fiji) when a majority believes that it must organize to defend its interests against an ethnic threat. When (as in Burundi) a particular regional and ethnic group holds the military power and uses it for political ends this can bring ethnic loyalties into situations in which previously ethnic group membership was not very important.

Collective action on an ethnic basis also occurs in support of a shared culture, most particularly a shared language since language is so central to any distinctive way of life, and of a shared religion. Almost by definition, *the support of shared interests, in the exercise of state power or the protection of shared culture, requires collective action*. These goals cannot be attained by individual action. This is one of the core problems of social science. Any attempt to explain the nature of the action that results is necessarily sociological.

CHAPTER 6

Increasing group consciousness

The powers of the state can be used to advance the interests of whichever group is politically dominant. Thus white people in the United States and in South Africa at times reinforced their position of privilege in relation to black people in a more systematic way than that employed by the Tutsi in Burundi. To this end they cultivated white racial consciousness by supporting doctrines of permanent differences in the capacities of races, for if people believed in the existence of such differences they would think there was less scope for modifying black–white relations by political action. Their measures at the same time, and inadvertently, led to the growth of racial consciousness among the subordinated group or groups. The subordinated peoples came to believe themselves oppressed and created a wider political unity in opposition to their oppressors. A good way of uncovering the dynamism of such relations is to consider five steps that might appeal to any government which wanted to construct a caste-like society in which racial inequality was unchallenged.

Racial classification

The first step would be to establish a *comprehensive system of racial classification*. If some people are to enjoy special privileges and others to have lesser rights, there must be a systematic classification which makes clear who is entitled to what. Societies in which privilege is based upon race need no such system in order to classify people of wholly European descent as white and wholly African descent as black. They do need a system, however, for determining the status of people of mixed descent and people from regions in other parts of the world that do not fit into a European–African division.

When they first settled in the United States, people from England described themselves as English, as Christians, and as free; not until the end of that century did they start calling themselves white. From the Spanish language they borrowed the names Indian and Negro. In the eighteenth century they referred to Negroes as blacks and as Africans, but scarcely ever called them heathens or pagans. The child of a black–white union was called a mulatto. By 1705 a mulatto was defined in law as 'the child, grandchild or great-grandchild of a negro'. This meant that people of one-quarter or one-eighth African origin were assigned to the same category as people of entirely African origin. However, it is likely that, whatever the legal position, in everyday life some distinctions were drawn by whites on the basis of colour. There were parts of the United States where distinct communities of persons of mixed origin formed (most notably in New Orleans after the purchase of Louisiana from the French in 1803).

In South Carolina also there was a significant mulatto class and the courts were inclined to regard its members as occupying a status diferent from that of the blacks. Especially in Louisiana the terms quadroon, octoroon and mustee were used to denote persons of mixed origin. Then, from the late eighteenth century, there was a boom in cotton production; when the importation of slaves was stopped, those already in the country became more valuable. As the number of coffee-coloured persons, whether free or unfree, grew, and with the existence of a class of 'free persons of colour', who in their cultural attributes were superior to many poor whites, there were forces operating to blur the colour line. But the free mulattos and blacks could not seize the intermediate positions in the economic structure because of the hostility of the well-to-do whites, and the continuing influx of workers from Europe who wanted the artisan-style jobs for themselves. The slave-owners feared that the free mulattos and blacks threatened the slave order. The white workers saw them as competitors for jobs and benefits. As the white workers secured the vote, they used their power to restrain black competition, and so there was never any room for a mulatto escape hatch. The names for persons of mixed origin dropped out of use as the system polarized.

At the time of the American Revolution in 1776, the gradual emancipation of slaves seemed possible, but the growing demand for cotton and North–South tensions made the Southern states commit themselves to the slave order. Slavery was effectively ended by the defeat of the Southern army, and legally ended by the Thirteenth Amendment to the federal constitution. The period from 1865 to 1876 is called that of Reconstruction, as the federal government then attempted to reconstruct the Southern political order on a more equal basis. Its success was limited, for the white Southerners reasserted racial inequality, basing it upon custom and informal understanding instead of upon law. Sociologists often called this new order 'colour-caste' because it denied any possibility of mobility from the one stratum to the other, unlike systems of social class.

Colour-caste continued the form of racial classification which had been created under slavery. Anyone with any ascertainable degree of African descent was considered Negro (or black). This practice spread to the rest of the United States. Persons influenced by the culture of that country (as most Westerners now are) believe this classification to be natural when it is nothing of the sort. The contrast with other parts of the continent was highlighted by James Bryce (1912) when he wrote that 'In the United States everyone who is not white is classed as coloured, however slight the trace. In Spanish America everyone who is not wholly Indian is classed as white, however marked the Indian type.' It was repeated in more recent times in a story about a US journalist who interviewed the President of Haiti. He asked what proportion of the island's population was white. The president replied, 'Oh, about 95 per cent.' The journalist was puzzled and enquired 'How do you define white?' The president responded by asking, 'How do you define coloured?' The journalist said, 'Well, anyone with Negro blood is coloured.' Said the president, 'Yes, that's our definition too, anyone with white blood is white.' This must be an imaginary tale, but it helps drive home the lesson that when there are only two categories and people of intermediate appearance have to be assigned to one or the other of them, they do have to be assigned to the lower one. When they are, it is because people in the upper category want to limit the number of persons entitled to share their privileges.

There were others besides blacks and whites who had to be found places. There were significant numbers of Native Americans (formerly called Indians) living in the South. How were they to be categorized? If they travelled on the railways, for example, were they to use the white or the black carriages and waiting rooms? The white or black drinking fountains? What about the Chinese who settled in Mississippi in the latter part of the nineteenth century? Such questions were settled not by doctrinal argument but by practical, everyday solutions. In Mississippi, Native Americans were counted as black in those parts of the state where they were numerous, but not in areas where few of them were to be seen. Thus a Choctaw Indian could change racial status by travelling forty miles. The Chinese had been brought to the state around 1870 as contract labourers. Some stayed after the expiry of their contracts and a small Chinese community was established. To start with, its members were counted socially as black, but in areas where their numbers were sufficient, separate schools were built. By the late 1930s more white schools were willing to admit Chinese pupils. They were the more welcome in those towns where whites were a minority relative to blacks and where, perhaps, the schools had difficulty recruiting sufficient pupils. As they prospered economically, the Chinese came to count as white.

Racial classification has been used to defend privilege. In Nazi Germany it was used to despoil and isolate a scapegoat group. A law was issued that

A Jew is anyone who is descended from at least three grandparents who are racially full Jews. A Jew is also someone who is descended from two full Jewish parents if (a) he belonged to the Jewish community at the time this law was issued . . .; or (b) was married to a Jewish person; or (c) was the offspring of a union between Jews.

The law stated: 'A Jew cannot be a citizen of the Reich. He has no right to vote in political affairs and he cannot occupy public office'. After the Nazis took power in Austria these laws were applied there. Persons who wished to demonstrate that they were Aryans had to produce the baptismal certificates of all four of their grandparents. A friend of mine has described how he shared a school desk in Austria with a boy whose grandparents had all converted from Judaism to Christianity. Therefore he counted as an Aryan, although his parents, despite being Christians, were legally 'full Jews'. His parents both perished in the extermination camp at Auschwitz, while the son was conscripted at the age of 16 and died on the Russian front in a uniform several sizes too large for him, defending the values of his *Vaterland*.

Consciousness of racial differences in South Africa has undergone important changes over the centuries, particularly in the interior. A study of the parentage and marriage of the Afrikaans-speaking whites showed that in 1807 at least one-quarter (and if unions outside marriage be included, up to one-third) of that population had a black or brown grandparent. By the middle of the twentieth century, on average 7 per cent of the Afrikaners' genetic inheritance was from black Africans (Afrikaners are the descendants of Dutch settlers; they have often been referred to as Boers, *boer* being the Dutch word for farmer). In the first half of the nineteenth century Afrikaner settlers living in the interior, and herding sheep and goats, dressed themselves in skins from their own animals. They had adapted to their environment. On the frontier the whites needed to cooperate with the native people. Whites were not all masters; non-whites were not all servants. The big change came in the last quarter of the century as a result of the discoveries first of gold and then of diamonds. The rapid development of mining brought new capital investment and attracted fortune-hunters; it transformed the basis of social and political life. South Africa was at this time a British colony. The Afrikaners attempted to establish independent republics, free of British rule. This resulted in what the British saw as a rebellion, and they crushed it with great loss of life by the South African War of 1899–1902. Afterwards the British promoted cooperation between the English-speaking and Afrikaans-speaking whites, and made concessions to the latter with this in view. In 1910 the country acquired a degree of independence as a dominion within the Commonwealth under the name Union of South Africa. Three territories remained under British protection; although in 1966 they became the independent states of Botswana, Lesotho and Swaziland, they remained economically dependent upon South Africa

In the period following the war, any reference to race relations in South Africa was likely to relate to what were thought of as two white races distinguished by language, by two forms of the Protestant religion, by history and culture, but not by appearance. The Afrikaners saw themselves as a *volk* (a people) or a *nasie* (nation);

they saw the various African groups – Zulu, Khosa, Swazi, etc. – likewise as peoples or nations. The Afrikaners had a high consciousness of membership in their own group, and of white solidarity (as incorporating the English-speaking whites). They did not readily think of themselves as a race, or refer to themselves as one, unless they had been influenced by the way people in Europe and North America used this word. Nor did the other whites, the Indians, the Cape Coloured, or the African group necessarily think of themselves as races. The Cape Coloured people (who are partly European and partly of African descent) mostly speak Afrikaans. It is interesting to note that by 1977 more than half the Afrikaners questioned in surveys should have said that they would count an Afrikaans-speaking Coloured as an Afrikaner. Chapter 2 maintained that ethnic and racial groups are composed of groups of persons who can be distinguished on several dimensions, by shared history, appearance, religion, language, and so on. The relative importance of the different criteria may change over the years, and the groups that in different countries are called racial are not differentiated in quite the same ways. So it is important not to assume that 'race' in South African usage has denoted the same kind of difference and the same kinds of feeling as it has in some other countries.

South Africa provides another example of an imperial power transferring power to a dominant ethnic group. The political dynamic behind the policies of the white parties during the first half-century of independence was the white workers' fear of competition from black labour. Most of the poor whites were Afrikaners forced off the land to seek a living in the towns and at the mines. They demanded a privileged position in the labour market and found their champions in the National Party, which was voted into office in 1948 and immediately set about implementing its dream of apartheid or separateness. The period from 1948 to the assassination of Prime Minister Verwoerd in 1966 can be seen as one in which the politicians tried to create a social order resembling that of colour-caste in the United States. It envisaged parallel white and black societies with the whites in control of the region. With classification went the control of education. From the beginning of the century Africans had owed their educational opportunities primarily to the foreign churches and missions that created and sponsored schools. Under apartheid, according to Hendrik Verwoerd, 'There is no place for the Bantu in the European community above the level of certain forms of labour' so educational opportunities had to be restricted. Apartheid could not be reconciled either with the pressures generated by a capitalist economic system or with the expectations of international opinion, so from about 1970 leaders of the National Party started to look for compromises.

One of the first actions of the new Nationalist government in 1948 was the enactment of the Population Registration Act 1950, which empowered the Director of Census to assign all persons to racial categories. Prior to that time people had been able to pass as members of a more privileged group if their physical features allowed it. Sometimes this brought a significant improvement in their social position, such as higher rates of pensions, greater freedom of movement, rights to reside in more attractive localities, send their children to better schools, and so on. The 1950 Act provided for a register, based in part on the census of 1910, which would classify all residents as White, Native or Coloured according to their appearance and how they were socially regarded. Nine years later the Coloured category was divided into seven subgroups so as to differentiate Cape Coloured, Cape Malay, Chinese, Indian, etc. Some whites who associated with non-whites found themselves classified as Coloured. Under the Registration Act persons were sometimes assigned to a category different from that to which they were allocated under the Group Areas Act, or the one for voting, or the one to which they had been assigned by the courts. An inter-departmental commission was appointed to formulate a uniform set of definitions for the purposes of all legislation, but in 1957 it reported that the task was beyond its powers. There were no objective criteria by which all persons of mixed ancestry could be classified. Therefore such classifications had to be arbitrary. Yet once they had been officially recorded it was extremely difficult for individuals to have their classification changed. Much depended upon these official records. For example, a white person was unable to contract a lawful marriage with someone who was not classified as white. The legal strengthening of the system of racial classification therefore did much to increase racial consciousness and racial tension (Kuper 1960).

Segregation

The second step to be taken by a government seeking to prevent change would be to ensure that *racial classification was the basis for determining a person's entitlements in as wide a range of situations as possible*. If some people enjoy special privileges and others have lesser rights, the rationale of the differentiation will be more difficult to enforce if a distinction is held relevant in one set of circumstances but not another. If blacks and whites are segregated on trains and buses they have to be segregated on aeroplanes too. By the end of the 1950s the following situations were in South Africa regulated by laws based upon racial criteria: marriage; 'illicit carnal intercourse'; proximity between neighbours and traders; inclusion on a common electoral roll; school education for Africans; reservations of occupations; control of contact in trade; black–white contact in churches, schools, hospitals, clubs, places of entertainment, public assemblies; university education. In the Deep South of the United States there was at the end of the nineteenth and in the early decades of the twentieth century a similar trend, which, in 1930, led Birmingham,

Alabama, to legislate against blacks and whites playing at dominoes or checkers together; while in 1935 Oklahoma separated the races while fishing or boating. Being socialized into a expectations of such a kind will have led most whites and many blacks to regard segregation as part of society's moral order.

The trend towards comprehensive segregation has to contend with opposing pressures because it may be in the economic interest of individuals to base their relations on economic rather than racial criteria. In the Deep South this stretched into the white household. Many white children were brought up by black mammies and domestic servants. It was said that in Southern society the black person could be very close to the whites but must not be allowed to get any higher. In Northern society the racial communities were physically and socially separate; the black person could climb high in the economic scale but never come any closer to the whites. The Southern system operated by exempting from many of the requirements of segregation any situation in which the white person established a personal relation with the black person. This was a kind of safety-valve which could enable people to get round the rigid application of the principle of segregation. That principle depended upon each party knowing the racial classification of the other party. In an agricultural society like that of the South in the early decades of the twentieth century, this posed few problems, but the position changed with urbanization and technological developments like the motor car and the telephone. The rules of the road could not be based upon the racial status of the drivers. It could be difficult to tell whether the person at the other end of the telephone was black or white. The legislation of the federal government became increasingly important. Though the implementation of federal law was sometimes distorted by the belief that blacks were not entitled to equal treatment, these were the deformations of a formally egalitarian structure.

Sociologists started to describe the situation in the Deep South as one of 'caste and class'. In the sphere of 'social relations', the caste norms of black subordination were enforced, often brutally. But in the sphere of 'business relations', the white person who ran the country store and sold gasoline to car drivers would treat black customers as customers rather than as blacks. White responses depended upon whether a situation was defined as questioning the norm of social inequality, and therefore a group interest, or simply as individual goal-seeking in the sphere of 'business'.

In South Africa there was a greater degree of physical segregation of blacks and whites. Racial classification was reinforced by an apparatus of control encompassing residence, occupation, education and movement. People had to know the racial status of other persons before entering into relations with them because status determined the kind of behaviour that was appropriate. To give just one example, cases were reported of black people who died after accidents because no ambulances for black people were available to take them to hospital. White ambulances were available but could not be used for black patients. As Nelson Mandela wrote:

Africans were desperate for help in government buildings: it was a crime to walk though a Whites Only door, a crime to ride a Whites Only bus, a crime to use a Whites Only drinking fountain, a crime to walk on a Whites Only beach, a crime to be on the streets after 11 p.m., a crime not to have a pass book and a crime to have a wrong signature in that book, a crime to be unemployed and a crime to be employed in the wrong place, a crime to live in certain places and a crime to have no place to live.

(Mandela 1994: 139)

Sanctions

A third step to hinder change would be needed to deal with those in either the superordinate or the subordinate group who broke the rules. In a racially divided society, people on either side of the divide will exploit the rules about classification when it suits them and try to get round them when the rules run counter to their interests. For example, if a colour-bar confines black workers to unskilled occupations, this is likely to increase the supply of unskilled labour. A colour-bar will then be in the interests of those employers (like mine-owners and farmers) whose businesses require much unskilled labour; it may be against the interest of employers of skilled labour who may as a result have to negotiate with white trade unions exercising monopoly powers over the supply of scarce skilled labour. Employers of skilled labour who find black workers able to perform the work they want carried out, may create new job categories which are not classed as skilled even if the distinction is artificial. Since the employers will not need to pay workers in these new job categories the same wages as are paid to skilled workers, it is very much to their advantage to get round the rules in this way. The government may have difficulty stopping them.

If inequality is to be enforced there must be *sanctions to reward the obedient and punish the disobedient.* The informal pressures of life in small communities may generate sanctions that are more effective than a government's rules. More than three and a half centuries ago, Francis Bacon wrote that 'he that hath wife and children hath given hostages to fortune'. The force of this observation was exemplified in the Deep South, for a white man who failed to observe local norms of racial propriety in his dealings with blacks would find that his wife and children suffered on his account. With social and economic life based upon relatively small communities and a slowly changing technology, there were real risks for the person who attracted social disapproval. When, in the 1960s, the 'freedom-riders' rode into Southern towns on inter-state coach services to enforce the desegregation of those services, they were met by white vigilantes who assaulted both blacks and whites. When civil rights activists campaigned in the Deep South to get more blacks onto the electoral rolls, white workers as well as blacks were murdered. But the considerable force mustered by white supremacists could not prevail against the power of the federal government supported by public opinion across the continent. By enforcing new civil rights laws, the president, the Congress and the judiciary carried through what has been called a 'second Reconstruction', enabling black Americans to acquire a political influence more nearly proportionate to their numbers. For them this was the fulfilment of the transfer of power nearly two centuries before.

In South Africa the Nationalist government acted quickly against the threat to its policies posed by dissident whites. In 1950 it introduced the Suppression of Communism Act based upon a loose but comprehensive definition of communism. The Nationalist government always chose nice-sounding names for repressive legislation, just as one of the more unpleasant Nazi laws was entitled the Law for the Protection of German Blood and German Honour. The South African definition of communism included 'the encouragement of feelings of hostility between the European and non-European races' if the consequence of such hostility was to 'bring any political, industrial, social or economic change'. So if the government passed a law that, because it was discriminatory, caused racial hostility, that was not 'communism'; but it was 'communism' if anyone protested against it in a manner which caused disorder. By this Act the minister was empowered to name as a communist anyone who had ever 'advocated, advised, defended or encouraged the achievement of any of the objects of communism' either actively or by any 'omission which is calculated to further the achievement of any such object'. If someone was named as a communist it became impossible for that person to engage in normal political activity. This was a powerful weapon against dissent within the white population, but by identifying communism with opposition to government policies it may have made communism seem the more attractive to some. Nor was it completely successful, for whites who believed in democracy continued to cooperate with blacks in resisting apartheid.

Later the government gave itself far-reaching powers to censor the reporting of unrest in the mass media, further illustrating the principle that the preservation of racial inequality means less freedom for the privileged as well as the subordinated group. Political control of the mass media can be used to increase group consciousness. Many observers have stated that the mass media in the former Yugoslavia hastened the escalation of ethnic tensions. In the 1970s the frequencies available to Yugoslavia for television transmissions were shared between eight agencies serving the republics and the two autonomous regions, leaving one federal frequency which the Yugoslav People's Army could activate in an emergency. When Ante Markovic took office as federal prime minister in 1989 he found that mass communications were dominated by the republican governments which presented highly partisan accounts of events. They described the leaders of other republics in terms which revived old conflicts (like *cetnik* and *ustase*) and called the armed forces of the legal government of Bosnia *mujahedin*. Markovic created a federal television station, *Yutel*, to ensure that the federal viewpoint was presented. Because of republican control of the frequencies it was unable to reach more than one-quarter of the population. By this time, in any case, there was so much suspicion of the federal government that it could not get its message through.

The government of the German Democratic Republic could build a wall through Berlin and fortify its frontier with the German Federal Republic to prevent people crossing, but they could not prevent their citizens in the East watching the television programmes transmitted in the West. This is said to have played a major part in the disaffection of the public in the East and in the pressure for change. Authoritarian governments everywhere seek to control the diffusion of information by the mass media, but with the development of satellite communication it is becoming more difficult for them to do so.

Group competition

A fourth kind of step to hinder change has to be taken in the economic sphere. The individual's search for his or her own advantage is one of the major sources of social change, and if this is not regulated it will undermine relations based upon racial rather than economic status. Consider the position of a white person with a house to sell in a middle-class white neighbourhood. Assume that blacks have hitherto lived mostly in working-class neighbourhoods because their incomes have been low, but that some blacks now have higher incomes and wish to live in the sorts of localities favoured by white people with similar incomes. If blacks have previously had difficulty moving into such areas, a property will be more valuable to them than to a white purchaser whose chances are less constrained. The vendors of the house might therefore be offered, say, £100,000, by prospective white purchasers, and £110,000 by prospective black purchasers. The vendors might prefer to sell to a white, but, unless some other factor intervenes, there must be some price at which they will sell to a black purchaser who offers more. If the vendors are unwilling to sell to a black until the price reaches, say, £115,000, the extra £15,000 represents the price that the vendors set upon their racial preference (or prejudice). If vendors are free to act in this way there will gradually be a reduction in racial segregation in residence. There will be similar effects in the employment market and in other fields of economic activity. So a government which wants to prevent such change will pass laws to prevent people acting in accordance with their individual interest if this disregards the racial status of the parties. It will seek to channel the search for economic advantage in directions which strengthen the racial order rather than weakening it.

The general proposition is that when people compete as individuals this tends to dissolve the boundaries that define racial groups; *when they compete as groups this reinforces those boundaries*. In an open housing market, properties will be sold to the highest bidder because, over a sufficient period of time, preferences for sale to purchasers of similar race will diminish. But if the market is divided up, with some houses being for whites only and some for blacks only, some people will suffer because of the restrictions upon the alternatives open to them. Others will be anxious to defend their privileges. These forces will make them more conscious of racial differences and more inclined to organize as groups either to defend the prevailing order or to overturn it.

Group competition can be seen with greatest clarity where racial groups lay claim to particular occupations and prevent members of other groups obtaining employment in them. The study *Deep South*, conducted in a Mississippi town in the early 1930s (Davis *et al.* 1941: 424–8), reported that blacks could not secure employment as clerks, bookkeepers or secretaries in white businesses, but only as porters, messengers, janitors and maids. In automobile repair shops they were not given the status of mechanics. In one instance where a Negro worked as a mechanic he was paid a lower wage and given additional duties of a menial kind. Skilled and mechanical work was reserved for whites, but there were circumstances (e.g. in businesses not in local ownership) in which Negroes did skilled work but were paid less than whites. White workers were not supposed to accept unskilled employment in what were considered 'Negro jobs'. During the depression years of 1930–5, this changed because there were white workers who preferred the 'Negro jobs' to being unemployed. The employers would have preferred to keep their black workers who worked harder and were more obedient, but the white workers had the political influence which enabled them to force blacks out of municipal employment as street-cleaners and garbage collectors. They took over the labouring work on construction sites. On the railways, ten black firemen were shot, six fatally, by whites who wanted them to resign their posts. The firemen were members of a union, and, since other black members of it were willing to take the places of the men who had been shot, the black workers were able to repulse the attempted take-over. The incident shows how fierce the inter-racial struggle in the job market can be.

In South Africa the white workers' claims to the skilled positions were enforced by law. In 1904 when the mine-owners were desperate for labour, the government arranged the importation of over 50,000 Chinese labourers on contract. To mitigate protest from white workers, a schedule was compiled of jobs from which the Chinese would be barred, and this list subsequently became the basis for excluding black workers from the same posts. The principle was then extended, by legislation, from mining to agriculture, manufacturing, transport, public administration and professional work; in this last-named, exceptions were made only to allow for non-Europeans to serve as teachers and ministers of religion for their own group. In the years following the National Party's victory in 1948, these laws were extended. For example, the Nursing Act 1957 laid down that the Nursing Council, which dealt with the registration, training and discipline of nurses and midwives, was to consist of white persons only. It was to keep separate registers of nurses and midwives of the separate races, and was empowered to prescribe different qualifications for registration and different uniforms and badges. No white nurse might be employed under the control or supervision of any non-white nurse. One of the impulses behind government policy from the 1920s was the desire to help poor white Afrikaner workers forced out of agriculture into urban employment. The Nationalists objected to the idea that white workers should have to compete for jobs with black workers. Job reservations enabled the poor whites to acquire a middle-class life-style. By the end of the 1950s this objective had been achieved and the Afrikaans-speaking whites were starting to catch up with the English-speaking whites. After 1970 the ideological impulse behind government policy weakened. Employers were allowed to upgrade black labour if they could do this without evoking protest from white workers. Non-Europeans were allowed to form trades unions. The rules regarding racial segregation at work were eased or abolished.

When social relations are regulated by law in such detail as was employed in South Africa, a large bureaucracy is needed to administer the laws. In apartheid South Africa that bureaucracy was staffed primarily by Afrikaans-speaking whites, though many of the police have been black. People employed to administer a structure of this kind have an interest in preserving a structure than gives them a livelihood, and in South Africa they were strong enough to delay some projected reforms. Government policy regarding employment, as in other fields, created distinct racial categories; people have been obliged to compete as group-members opposed to men and women who are members of other groups; this reinforced the racial boundaries. Yet there remained major tensions and differences of opinion within the racial categories. The whites were divided about the political policies appropriate to their minority status. The non-whites were divided in their assessments of their prospects, in their ethnic allegiances, and in the concern of the various socio-economic groups to preserve their gains relative to other groups. The government had some success in channelling the search for individual advantage so as to make non-whites concentrate upon possible short-term gains relative to other non-whites, and in this way deflecting their attention from bigger inequalities.

Individual competition for jobs and other goods does not generate hostility between groups to the same extent as group competition, but a society cannot organize everything on an individual to individual basis. Collective action is needed for the production of what economists call public goods, like certain government services, most notably defence. Group identifications built up in previous generations are not easily overcome even when there are no physical differences between people (as the experience of the former Yugoslavia surely demonstrates). When physical differences are present then group reactions are almost certain. Shown pictures on television, viewers seem readily to identify with one or other party on the basis of colour.

Transmitted inequality

The fifth step to be taken by a government seeking to preserve a political order based upon racial inequality is of a negative kind. It is to *permit and encourage the tendencies for socio-economic inequalities to be transmitted from one generation to the next.* These tendencies exist in all societies except the very simplest, so no government has to create them. It can increase them or it can reduce their effect by taxing the inheritance of property and wealth, by promoting equality of opportunity in education, and so on. It cannot prevent some parents giving their children a better start in life than other children get. One of the reasons why people respond to the incentives of higher pay for more difficult work, or for working longer hours, is that they want to give their children additional benefits. It is not in the interest of any economic system to try to combat so important a motivation to work, but many societies do seek to limit the extent to which this motivation restricts equality of opportunity in the next generation.

In any racially divided society racial inequalities will be transmitted from one generation to the next. Where there are distinct racial groups with differential privileges, like the Deep South and South Africa, group membership will be transmitted. In many other societies, including Britain, the associations between group membership and socio-economic status will be of a statistical character. There may be proportionately fewer blacks in the upper classes and more in the lower. As a result there may well be an image of blacks as lower-class people, and this image may work to the detriment of all blacks. It will be strengthened by the psychological process of stereotyping. In most societies unequal achievement in one generation has consequences for the next generation. If whites do better than blacks in the first generation, white children in the next generation will have an advantage, but the extent of the advantage will vary. The children of high-achieving black parents may have a greater advantage than the children of low-achieving white parents. Circumstances could arise in which no individuals are handicapped because of their colour, and there is no point at which discrimination occurs, but a statistical association between a white skin colour and a higher income is maintained by the inter-generational transmission of relative advantage. A government which does nothing to reduce that association will be able to maintain a racially unequal social order. It will be able to defend its inactivity by arguing that inequality between groups results from differences in the natural ability of individuals, just as inequalities within groups result from individual differences.

Five steps have been outlined:

- classify racially
- segregate
- introduce sanctions
- channel group competition
- permit the transmission of inequality.

A government which succeeded in implementing them could follow a policy of 'divide and rule' and persuade its subjects that the resulting inequalities were natural rather than social. For many centuries people all over the globe have accepted positions of inequality as no more than their due. In Rwanda and Burundi the structure of inequality was facilitated by the belief of the Tutsi in their superiority, and the acquiescence of the Hutu. It has often taken generations for a genuinely political consciousness to emerge among subordinated peoples, but the pace of change has been speeded up in the late twentieth century. Contact with other peoples prompts the revision of inherited expectations. The media of mass communication flash new images and new assumptions around the world. As already noted, elections were a catalyst stimulating the Hutu to believe that their votes were worth as much as the votes of their traditional masters. The extension of the suffrage, and the basis on which it has been granted, has everywhere been full of significance for racial relations.

Political groups usually seek to divide their opponents, but tensions within their own ranks often limit the extent to which they are able to do so. In the United States plantation system a distinction was drawn between house slaves and field slaves. There was a small population of free blacks, mainly in the towns. A superordinate group which set out systematically to preserve its privileges would have cultivated such divisions. When the suffrage was extended it would have used a property qualification to create an alliance with the richer blacks and check the aspirations of the poorer whites. Over-confident, unable to take a longer view, and solicitous of poor white support, leaders of the whites saw no need for such policies.

The same comment applies with at least equal force to South

Africa. At the beginning of the twentieth century, qualified male members of the Coloured population of the Cape province could vote in parliamentary elections. From 1910 they were allowed to vote only for whites who were to represent them. Proposals by Afrikaner political leaders to allow additional privileges to the Coloured and Indian groups, building them up as buffers between the whites and the blacks, never received much support from white voters. The strength of the Afrikaner rural vote and the nature of the political forces within the white group dictated the drawing of a boundary around white privilege.

In South Africa policies of divide and rule were intertwined with the Afrikaners' conception of nationality. They had survived as a *volk* although the might of the British Empire was deployed against them. They recognized the possibility that African ethnic groups might demonstrate a comparable ethnic spirit. After 1959 it was government policy to preserve the main ethnic divisions within the African population and count the blacks as citizens of ten national states. Between 1976 and 1983 four of these (Transkei, Bophuthatswana, Venda, Ciskei) were declared independent sovereign states able to send out their own diplomatic, sporting and other representatives, just like other sovereign states. The governments of every other country in the world refused to recognize these 'Bantustans' as independent, regarding them as puppets created to serve the political and economic convenience of the whites. The other six 'national states' within the republic declined to follow them into a bogus 'independence'.

The Pretoria government could call on substantial financial resources. In the early 1980s the head of the security service told a US journalist that the African National Congress (ANC) was crippled by the knowledge that any effort it might make to recruit large numbers of blacks to its membership would increase the number of informers in its ranks. The president of the ANC confirmed that this was the case: well-trained infiltrators were often not detected by their screening processs. The powers of the state apparatus were so great that many of the chief advances in black political consciousness resulted from miscalculations by those who exercised these powers. On 21 March 1960 a crowd of some 10,000 Africans gathered at Sharpeville to protest at the pass laws. The local detachment of white police panicked and fired into the crowd, killing 67 people and injuring 186. R.W. Johnson (1977: 17) suggested that the event was in many ways comparable to the Russian Revolution of 1905. It took everyone by surprise, the government, the liberals, and the revolutionaries, just as when the police fired on the workers' rally in St Petersburg. It transformed the political scene. The ANC (no revolutionary organization) and the Pan-African Congress (which had split from it on the grounds that the ANC was dominated by white communists) were both banned. International pressure mounted so that in 1963 South Africa left the

Commonwealth and the Dutch Reformed Church withdrew from the World Council of Churches. Overseas financiers took fright and investment faltered. As the government tightened its control, the main anti-apartheid movements within the country either dissolved or went into exile, in which case they risked losing touch with events in the black townships and lessened their ability to influence political movements there.

On 17 May 1976 the pupils of a secondary school in Soweto (an African dormitory town for Johannesburg) walked out. They said they would not return until a new rule that they should be taught in Afrikaans was withdrawn. Implementation of this rule was being pressed by a right-wing Afrikaner minister more concerned to win the favour of Afrikaner voters than to ascertain whether there was a realistic chance of making the schools toe this ideological line. Pupils in other Soweto schools left their classrooms and marched to the school where the strike had begun. Confronted by police armed with machine guns and tear gas, they attacked buildings and property associated with white authority. Rioting spread. The police refused to give any figures for the number of deaths resulting from the disturbances, but unofficial estimates put the total well above a thousand.

When governments have introduced and enforced laws which preserve racial inequalities they may not have been working consciously from a blueprint designed to create a new kind of caste system, or one intended to promote racial consciousness or social tension. The actions of governments are usually impelled by a mixture of motives among their members and those whose votes they want to attract. In South Africa, National Party leaders had such a blueprint, but usually policies have reflected what seemed expedient at the time. If, however, a government did wish to preserve a racially unequal political order and sought sociological advice about how to do it, that advice would have to recommend the five steps just described. If a government wanted to implement policies of the opposite effect, that advice would be diametrically opposite.

The history of black–white relations in the United States and South Africa can be interpreted in terms of the equilibrium model represented in Figure 4.3. To do so it is necessary to see the superordinate group (P) as internally divided (along class or ethnic lines, for example). The subordinate group (B) may also be divided. The effect of the P group's divisions will be considered first. In the United States the whites established themselves as the superordinate group in the cotton-growing South. Under the slave regime the white upper class began building a paternalistic social order which (with exceptions) encouraged the establishment of settled slave communities with their own social hierarchies. Upper-class whites could be contemptuous of 'poor white trash'. The policies of their class were challenged in the course of the nineteenth century by non-slaveholding whites and immigrant white workers who demanded preferential treatment by comparison with blacks. Their demands for equality among whites added to the pressure for a sharp white–black split and for racial status to regulate all social contacts. It was, metaphorically speaking, their descendants who attacked the 'freedom riders' in the 1960s. The system of colour-caste as it developed towards the end of the nineteenth century represented a new equilibrium in which the privileges of the poorer whites were protected by new methods. It was the outcome, not of planning, but of political struggles among whites. In the South African P group the main division was between a commercially oriented English-speaking group and the rural Afrikaners. As events leading to the 1922 miners' strike suggested, the business class was prepared to relax the job colour-bar. This kind of change was blocked by white workers, both Afrikaans- and English-speaking, who used their political power to increase their privileges relative to the voteless black workers. Their alliance with Afrikaner ideologists became the foundation of apartheid as a scheme for buttressing a political equilibrium. Whereas the United States stumbled upon steps corresponding to the first four of the five steps mentioned, the National Party in South Africa had them planned.

The sphere of the state

Policies of racial subordination had some distinctive features associated with beliefs about the differential inheritance of talent, but they also had features in common with other forms of inequality. While in some societies individuals can pursue a career by individual action, elsewhere individuals' career possibilities may be limited because they are assigned to a racial or gender category, or start off with disadvantages associated with a structure of social class. People who feel disadvantaged by some attribute, such as gender, social origin or disability as well as by race, may conclude that if they and those like them are to advance, they must engage in collective action. If they do, then they are likely to develop a group consciousness. Max Weber recognized this when he wrote that classes are not necessarily communities but bases for possible communal action. The same principle applies with greater force to racial categories because it is more difficult for a person to escape from racial assignment than from class assignment.

The main arena for collective action is the struggle over what shall be the powers of the state and who shall exercise them. In eighteenth-century Europe the privileges of the aristocracy could be defended on the grounds that only powerful subjects could hold in check the despotic tendencies of monarchs. The nineteenth century saw both aristocrats and monarchs pushed aside by parliaments which then sought to balance the competing claims of classes. In most European colonies, at any rate in Africa, the traditional rulers and the new middle classes were never strong enough to balance the colonial administrations. So that at their independence the peoples of the new states became subject to rulers who had succeeded to huge powers without the checks and balances to which the colonial administrators had been subject. One result was the increase in that form of group consciousness which has often been called 'tribalism', but which some say might be better called 'clientelism'.

Members of any ethnic group share features of a common culture, but they are unaware of their distinctiveness until they encounter others of a different culture. 'Tribalism' is a product of urban neighbourhoods, workplaces and labour camps where people meet others who have previously been strangers. After independence, any office-holders in government or commercial life who were able to influence the distribution of resources were expected to act in favour of members of their own ethnic group. All leaders had to reward a clientele who voted for them or provided some other kind of support in a relation of mutual dependence that was open to accusations of corruption. Sectional interests were put before national interests. Tribalism, or clientelism, was a response to the inability of the state to protect the citizen's right to equal treatment. Often it coexisted with the booty state, in which the power-holders simply enriched themselves.

The opposition of interest groups in such a structure leads more often to rebellion (in which one group ousts another) than to revolution (in which the political system is changed). There are political structures which seem to encourage change of a cyclical character: a would-be reformist group seizes power, then uses it to serve its own interests and is consequently ousted by the next reformist group. Rebellion can be institutionalized, especially when the military is involved. Bolivia, a state created in 1825, experienced its 192nd coup in 1981, an average of one every ten months. A régime which wished to escape from such an inheritance and promote long-term stability would be well advised not to attempt to suppress group conflicts, but, by constitutional engineering, to balance one conflict with another, so that individuals who were opposed to one another on one issue became allies in opposition to a different group on some other issue. The institutions of civil society are strongest when they serve the interests of all sections.

The less power that is concentrated in the state, the less there is for ethnic groups and classes to struggle over, but without some arrangement to regulate competition, the greater may be the incentive for individuals to form groups which struggle for control of resources. The United States is famous for having a pluralistic structure, for the dispersal of power, and for political philosophies critical of state regulation. Yet consciousness of group membership there does not appear to be any the less. State power has to be exerted if markets are to be kept competitive. The struggle over who shall exercise power, and in what ways, is an escapable feature of all human social life.

Conclusion

In comparing the processes by which group consciousness was increased in the Deep South of the United States and in South Africa, this chapter has compared societies organized round a division into two racial categories. In each instance groups that are intermediate between white and black could have been built up so as to weaken the discontinuity between black and white, but the contrary pressures were too strong. There seems to be something distinctive about two-category systems that impels them towards either ever-greater repression or partition, unless the system itself gets absorbed into a larger social system. Both societies developed for a time in ways resembling the sequence depicted in Figure 4.3. Change in the Deep South then took a different course as this region was forced to conform more closely to the norms of the wider society of the USA. Change in South Africa came about when leaders of the P group recognized that they were facing what could only be a negative-sum conflict. In both the question then arose whether a new order would be built upon the continuation of separate black and white groups, or whether these would be submerged in a shared citizenship. In neither is the answer yet certain.

CHAPTER 7

Decreasing group consciousness

If ethnic and racial consciousness is increased by a series of steps, then reversing those steps should be the simplest way to reduce it. Yet, for at least four reasons, so simple a prescription has to be questioned. In the first place, it should be remembered that Chapter 6 described the increase in group consciousness by the dominant group's use of state power. Action designed to counter the effects of such use could indeed consist of reversing *the use made of state power* to favour the oppressed group; alternatively, it could equally well seek to *reduce the concentration of power in the state apparatus*. There is also a second possible course, since the popular tendency to line up politically on the basis of racial or ethnic characteristics can be weakened by encouraging *countervailing alignments, such as those of class and religion*. When one form of group consciousness gains importance, others must lose it. In the third place, a society that has previously encouraged racial or ethnic consciousness can turn round and move in the opposite direction only with *responsible leadership in a high degree, and discipline on the part of the public*. Many political systems are geared to the short-term perspectives of the next election and any rewards for long-term changes come only later. Favoured groups fight to retain their privileges. When a previously subordinated group gains power, its members may be impatient for immediate benefits; discipline may depend on the level of their political education. This is another way of expressing the fourth consideration, that policies to reduce group consciousness may be difficult to implement because *previous oppression has evoked solidarity on the part of the oppressed*.

The second Reconstruction in the USA

The response of African-Americans to racial subordination has been the more complicated because they came to think of themselves as a people in what was, to start with, an alien land. Without having had any opportunity to offer much collective resistance to enslavement, they suffered dispersal and exploitation. The men, women and children, who were for the most part sold by their fellow-Africans, loaded onto the slave ships, and transported to the Americas, came from a great variety of ethnic groups. Under the slave regime they resisted white prejudice as individuals and in small communities. Only rarely could they plan wider revolts and all those in the United States failed. After the Civil War of 1861–5 Afro-Americans remained economically and politically weak. The experience of white discrimination gave them a sense of being a people, though unlike other peoples they could not base their grouping upon ownership of a territory (a partial parallel to their case has been that of the Palestinians, who, after losing territory to Israel in 1948, came to a new consciousness of their distinctiveness). Afro-Americans had to contend with the problems that beset conquered peoples, but experienced them in more acute form than, say, the Germans after 1918 or 1945. The Germans could look back with pride upon a long sequence of historical and cultural achievements. Defeat was seen only as a setback. Yet it still had momentous political consequences, contributing to the rise of Nazism in the interwar period and to an extremist strand of nationalism that is still a political threat.

The African-Americans' predicament was the more acute because they could not look back to such a history. Were they to see themselves as a people in captivity? Or were they immigrants, like the whites, and with as much right to be settled in the new land, and to be participants in building a new society, even if that society was as yet unable to live up to its professed ideals? Were they primarily blacks or primarily Americans? They spoke the same language as the whites and, for the most part, embraced the same versions of Christianity as the white population. In resisting oppression they had drawn heavily upon the Christian message of human equality in the sight of God, so it was not surprising that a minority thought that in religion there were clues as to their special identity. Even when it apparently took a religious form, the movement was always political, as has already been discussed in Chapter 1 in connection with name-changing.

In the first half of the twentieth century the movement for racial equality organized round the attack on mistaken racial beliefs and their use to justify racial inequalities. The idea that people could meaningfully be divided into racial categories and that they should be treated according to their category membership rather than their individual merits, was vigorously denied. The campaigners, white and black, believed that the categories should be dissolved. This movement reached a high point in the 1954 decision of the Supreme Court that racial segregation in schooling was unconstitutional. A crucial step in the court's reasoning was based upon social science research indicating that the subordination of the black population could have deleterious effects upon the personal psychology of black children.

Action to desegregate schools was only a beginning. One day in 1960 four black students sat at the lunch counter in a store in North Carolina and waited to be served. Within a month, thousands of black and white students 'sat in' at lunch counters throughout the South, and began a wave of sit-ins, drive-ins, wade-ins, play-ins, dive-ins, kneel-ins, teach-ins, and so on, wherever services were segregated. Blacks seized the leadership of the civil rights movement. They demanded that all people of African or partly African descent in the United States call themselves black and that others call them black. They adopted or adapted African hairstyles, items of African costume and African names. They demanded black studies and the opportunity to learn African languages. Their slogans were the call for black power and the insistence that 'black is beautiful'. Their brothers and sisters should display 'black pride'. If there was no more reason to be ashamed of a black colour than any other kind of colour, then it could no longer be hurtful to be called black. This movement inspired a series of similar attempts to raise group consciousness on the part of other minorities in the United States. It influenced the strategy of the women's movement in that country. It was imitated overseas, and in South Africa was referred to as the Black Consciousness Movement. Seen internationally, that is perhaps the best name for it.

In the next decade the administration of President L.B. Johnson, by committing itself to stronger legislation, inaugurated what has been called a second Reconstruction. Each step in its progress depended upon a special impetus. The Civil Rights Act 1964, passed after the assassination of John F. Kennedy, banned discrimination in public accommodation and employment, and made it possible to deny federal funds to those who engaged in discrimination. The Voting Rights Act 1965, passed after the beating to death of the Revd James Reeb in Selma, Alabama, restored the franchise to blacks in the South. For years there had been unsuccessful attempts to persuade Congress to act against discrimination in housing, then in 1968, only one week after the assassination of Martin Luther King, the Fair Housing Act was passed. The old equilibrium, based on the power of Southern whites within the federal system, had been upset by increased pressure from blacks and from whites outside the South. Yet the changes would not have happened as they did without the president's leadership.

The 1954 Supreme Court decision made possible a series of applications to federal courts throughout the USA to order school desegregation by changing the catchment areas for neighbourhood schools and the bussing of pupils so as to achieve a more equal distribution. Under the 1964 Act federal courts at times ordered companies to change their hiring policies in order to employ a stated percentage of minority employees. Companies which tendered for federal contracts had to be able to demonstrate that their employment policies met similar criteria. In this way the courts and the federal government introduced an era of racial quotas and this, unsurprisingly, heightened consciousness of racial difference. The system of racial classification was maintained, but used for new purposes.

Just as governments can promote competition in the economic sphere by action to restrict monopolies, so they can promote it in other spheres by legislation against discrimination. As part of the second Reconstruction new institutions were created to counter racial discrimination and the sanctions which had supported it. Yet the investigation of complaints is a labour-intensive and expensive process. Governmental agencies have never had sufficient resources to investigate more than a fraction of the complaints made to them or to take offenders to court. The transmission of inequality from one generation to the next has also been a potent factor. To cite just one statistic, in the early 1990s the official rate of unemployment in the USA was 5.6 per cent. Among 'Latinos' it was 17 per cent and among Native Americans 46 per cent. Allowing for the number of persons who have given up looking for work, the real rate of unemployment for African-Americans was put at 26 per cent and for African-American youth at 58 per cent. This is an indication of the relative disadvantage of blacks, not of discrimination, but there is other evidence to show that racial discrimination is one of its causes.

The biggest failure of the United States to reverse its heritage of racial discrimination has been its neglect of residential segregation. At the beginning of the twentieth century the pattern of black residence in northern cities followed lines of class more than of race. Members of the black elite could be optimistic about the prospects of an eventual integration of blacks and whites into a single society. Continuing black migration from the South put these trends into reverse. Between 1900 and 1920 blacks who lived in, or moved into, white neighbourhoods were forced out by all manner of threats, including the bombing of their houses. Which sorts of whites participated in these actions, and how they were organized and motivated, is not altogether clear, but there is no doubt that residential segregation soon came under systematic management. Realtors, or estate agents, controlled the expansion of black ghettos and profited from changes in property values as black demand for housing pressed against the restrictions upon its availability. Local governments used their powers to confine the areas of black occupation. As a result, residential segregation increased dramatically.

While it was under consideration in Congress, the draft Federal Housing Act 1968 was stripped of its provisions for effective enforcement. This was to some degree rectified in an amending Act in 1988, but by then great damage had been done. Massey and Denton (1993) have given good grounds for concluding that residential segregation has been both the prime obstacle to the social and economic progress of the African-American middle class and the principal force behind the creation of a black underclass. Dollar for dollar, blacks are able to buy fewer neighbourhood amenities than other groups. Calculations show that as the income of a white middle-class family increases, it can move to a locality where house values are higher, there are fewer births to single mothers, and academic standards in the neighbourhood school are higher. For the same increase in income, black families can obtain only smaller improvements on these measures. Disadvantages of these kinds have cumulative effects.

As blacks were forced into ghettos, so they developed a sense of collective identity based upon opposition to that of white Americans. If they could not get a fair reward for their efforts and accomplishments, why should they hold the same values as the whites? Anthropological studies suggest that if whites speak Standard American English, succeed in school, work hard at routine jobs, marry, and support their children, then being 'black' requires the opposite. Bright, motivated and intellectually curious, ghetto schoolchildren are put under tremendous pressure from their peers to avoid 'acting white'. They risk being stigmatized as 'pervert brainiacs' or as 'Oreos' (in reference to a chocolate biscuit that is white inside; the commonest equivalent expression in Britain is 'coconut'). Those who grow up in the ghettos rarely travel outside, even to the city centre. They have little chance of employment in clerical work if they cannot communicate effectively in Standard English. Community studies point to an intensification of these trends since the 1970s. The growth of the drug culture has led to an escalation in the rate of violent death among black men, the spread of prostitution among black women, and a great increase in the number of babies who are already drug-addicted at birth. With the decline in marriage as a social institution, hostility between black males and females has sharpened and found expression in the lyrics of popular music. No one can be trusted.

Ghetto-dwellers are little inclined to participate in the political process, but black politicians see the maintenance of residential segregation as a way of maximizing black political influence. The revision of boundaries for the 1992 congressional elections aimed to do just this at the very time when apartheid was being dismantled in South Africa. One observer (Bonney 1996: 194) noted that many of the black middle class were employed in public sector control programmes as police, social workers and teachers serving black neighbourhoods. They had been unable to distance themselves from poor black Americans and from the negative images of their crime and drug-ridden neighbourhoods. These images then served to justify the prejudices of other groups. This writer went on to say that

> When a group is excluded and withdraws from the wider society and claims the desire to control its own affairs exclusively, it also, by default, withdraws at least some of its moral claims on that wider society and lays itself open to the charge that its fortunes or lack of them are its own responsibility.
>
> (Bonney 1996: 194)

The economically successful, both white and black, are having to spend ever more on protecting their personal security, on the construction of prisons, and on the control of the dangerous social elements. Black–white distinctions are being built into the structure of post-industrial society.

Blacks and whites in the United States remain highly conscious of racial differences in many but not in all situations. People may be busy getting on with their everyday lives when something happens to evoke group oppositions, for example some action by the police can bring the young men onto the streets in a riot which derives from and reinforces racial sentiment. Circumstances in a big city can still resemble those of the caste and class model intended to represent relations in a small community. This model relies upon what has been called 'the W.I. Thomas theorem', after the sociologist who maintained that *when people define situations as real, they are real in their consequences.* An illustration was provided by public reaction to the trial in 1995 of the black football star O.J. Simpson. He was charged with having murdered his wife and a man who was with her, so in the eyes of many persons, and particularly whites, the issue was one of responsibility for horrible crimes. For other persons, and particularly blacks, the issue was that of an accusation brought by a racist police force relying on some questionable evidence. Racial motivations may have played no part in a decision to charge an individual with an offence, but if others see such an accusation in racial terms it is their perception which will decide how they respond. Some situations are seen as evoking the caste-like loyalties shared with others of a person's racial group, while in other situations people are free to follow their individual interests.

Something happened to black–white relations in the USA round about 1960 that calls for sociological interpretation. The policies and practices described in Chapter 5 can be interpreted as the outcome of the way the more powerful groups, by collective action, sought to attain their shared goals. While black resistance to segregation (the Montgomery bus boycott of 1955, the sit-ins of 1960) can equally be seen as motivated by shared interests, some more fundamental change was occurring among African-Americans. The initial goal of the civil rights movement was racial equality, the creation of a colour-blind society in which the colour of the skin would be no more a basis for differentiation than the colour of the eyes. This was an ideal formulated in terms of interpersonal relations; it ignored the possibility that the parties might see themselves as belonging to groups and want equality as group members rather than as individuals. Chapter 3 noted that sometimes individuals change their goals; it seems as if in the 1960s African-Americans changed their shared goals to set a higher value upon blackness and membership in a black community. Malcolm X asked his fellow blacks 'Why should we integrate into a burning house?' If they were to integrate, then they wanted to discuss the terms on which they would do so. Their withdrawal from what they saw as unequal relationships led to forms of self-segregation. Colour-blindness was to be replaced by racial consciousness.

The change in direction revived an earlier controversy. Jean-Paul Sartre (1948: xli) had expressed it in dialectical terms: white superiority was the thesis; *la Négritude* the antithesis; the clash between them would prepare the way to a synthesis in the form of a raceless society. Eminent scholars in the United States restated the argument; they concluded that what had happened in their country would have to be repeated in all societies where skin colour was associated with inequality, and that this was indeed for the best (Banton 1983: 68–71). Their sociology was questionable. Were a society to be polarized into racial categories, children would be socialized into believing that such was the natural order, and many people would acquire material interests in the maintenance of that order. No one explained how polarization would be transformed into racelessness.

The ideal of a colour-blind society should be given up only reluctantly, yet, paradoxically, it may be impossible to combat racial discrimination without introducing forms of monitoring to check upon whether the rules are being followed. This entails the introduction of racial classifications in the belief that they will help eventually to overcome racial classification. It prompts the question: *in what circumstances may it be beneficial to increase racial consciousness in order ultimately to decrease it?* Any answer has to depend upon political judgements about the tensions in particular societies.

Many people envisage the United States of the future as a country in which there will still be distinctive black and white groups but with a more equitable sharing of privileges. Some of the differences are being reduced, particularly those associated with the rise of the black middle class. In a modern industrial society there is less scope for group competition than there was in the agricultural economy of the South before the Second World War. Everyone in the United States, whatever their group membership, is now increasingly influenced by the media of mass communication, by consumption patterns and economic trends which show little regard for group differences, and by the technology of communication, transport, etc., which shows none at all. Blacks who visit African countries discover how American they are. So while there is still much segregation, there are more situations in which racial classification is of little relevance. If so the United States may be seen as passing round the circuit towards an equilibrium in which black and white are roughly equal or the distinction has ceased to matter. This is contested by those who conclude that residential segregation, combined with changes in the industrial structure and the inter-generational transmission of poverty, has created two societies within the state. The influence of the mass media and the emphasis upon consumption serve to increase the alienation in the ghettos. In other circumstances the pressures could lead to partition, but in the USA they are simply bottled up.

The prospects for South Africa

Many commentators expected bloodshed in South Africa. The relative success up to 1996 in managing the transition to democratic rule owes much to the political responsibility and the willingness to compromise shown by the National Party and the ANC. Either side could have played a negative-sum game and reduced the country to a desert, but both sides knew this and made concessions on a scale that could scarcely have been predicted. The ANC could respond to the challenge of events because its political philosophy had matured over a long period and had been supported by programmes for the political education of its members.

The ANC was founded in 1912 and developed from the 1940s as an urban-based mass movement relying primarily upon passive resistance. It was one of the sponsoring bodies for the Freedom Charter of 1955, which declared that 'South Africa belongs to all who live in it, black and white' and that 'all national groups shall have equal rights'. Later on, divisions developed between the 'Charterists' who favoured non-racialism and two more radical groups, the Pan-African Congress (PAC), which broke away in 1959, and the Azanian Peoples' Organization (AZAPO), founded in 1978, which were both committed to black leadership and socialism. The PAC spoke on behalf of the less privileged and less educated Africans whereas AZAPO was more representative of the black intellectuals. Both the ANC and the PAC were banned organizations between 1960 and 1990.

The retreat from apartheid was at first scarcely perceptible. It seems to have started round about 1970 and to have been accelerated by demographic projections indicating that the black population could be expected to increase from 19 million to 46 million by the year 2023. From 1980, while P.W. Botha was state president, apartheid went gradually into reverse. Restrictions on black trade unions were abolished, sports integrated, uniform tax laws introduced, and the laws against mixed marriages, laws requiring African to carry passes, laws for the segregation of hotels and public transport were all repealed. The all-white legislative assembly was briefly replaced by three assemblies, for whites, Coloureds and Indians. A 'whites-only' referendum in 1983 endorsed the direction of change, but the rate of change was not fast enough to avoid urban rioting by young blacks and guerrilla warfare conducted by the ANC's military wing operating from exile.

The banning of the ANC, PAC and the Communist Party created a gap that was filled first by the Black Consciousness Movement and then after by 1984 the United Democratic Front which resurrected the ANC doctrine of non-racialism. This spoke for a civic nation, based upon equal individual rights, regardless of origin, and equal recognition of all cultural traditions in the public sphere. The civic nation is to be based on consent rather than descent, in contrast to the philosophy of ethnic nationalism based on blood and ancestry. The Black Consciousness advocates dismissed non-racialism as a liberal illusion and a strategic error (Adam 1995: 459).

From 1976 onwards the government tried to negotiate with the imprisoned Nelson Mandela. When in 1985 the government offered to release him, Mandela reckoned that it was the sixth such conditional offer in ten years. He did not accept it. More serious negotiations started the following year and speeded up when F.W. de Klerk became president in 1989. The following year Mandela left prison on his own terms, and to a hero's welcome. It was the outcome of a lengthy process which contrasted with the precipitate grant of independence to so many formerly colonial territories. After Mandela's release South Africa's politicians engaged in intensive discussions that led to the adoption of a provisional constitution.

They sought to learn the lessons of constitutional engineering as discussed in Chapter 4. One of these was to avoid an election in which all the blacks voted for the first party, all the whites for the second party and all the Indians for the third party, and so on. This would be what Horowitz (1991) has called a racial census; everyone votes for his or her racial or ethnic party; in such circumstances there is really no need for an election at all because the census would serve the purpose. To avoid such an outcome it is necessary to encourage the formation of alliances across ethnic boundaries. The question then is whether that is a task best undertaken by the political parties or by the voters themselves.

Arend Lijphart (1994), the advocate of 'consociational democracy', maintained that for South Africa in the 1990s the task was best left to the parties. He favoured the kind of scheme in which a voter chooses a party. The party puts forward a list of candidates who become members of the legislature in proportion to the number of votes obtained by the party. This creates an incentive for the formation of a relatively large number of parties, reducing the likelihood than any one of them will obtain an overall majority. It increases the likelihood of coalition government by the pooling of seats to secure a majority in Parliament; the more seats a party has, the bigger will be its share in the coalition. Such a scheme can work where the politicians govern in the interest of the country as a whole. Pointing to the many instances in which they have instead governed in their personal interests, Horowitz (1991) is disinclined to trust the politicians in multiracial societies; he believes that they have to be given incentives that will make it in their interest to cooperate. These can be created by a system of proportional representation in which voters have to list a number of parties in an order of preference. Candidates then have an inducement to seek voters' second and third preferences as well as first preferences. It will be in their interest to avoid exciting the kind of antagonism that will cause some voters to put their party at the bottom of the list or to leave it off altogether. This amounts to a scheme in which it is votes rather than seats which are pooled, because a candidate's chances of election will depend upon much more than first preferences. A voter will have to choose 'next best' candidates from other ethnic groups. Constitutional engineering along these lines will make it easier to decrease ethnic consciousness.

Those who negotiated the provisional constitution opted for a bicameral Parliament with a four-hundred-member national assembly elected by proportional representation from national and regional party lists, and a senate elected indirectly by regional legislatures. The president was to be both head of state and head of government. He or she was to be elected by the National Assembly and that body was given the power to require the president to resign if it thought that necessary.

The election held in April 1994 was historic as the first in which blacks could vote and the first in which all electors had an unrestricted range of political alternatives. It was especially important as a decision about who should draw up a definitive constitution. Voters were asked to choose a party, not a particular candidate, so the arrangement was closer to the proposals of Lijphart than those of Horowitz. In the new assembly just over half of the new members were black, over one hundred were white, and forty were Indians. Ministerial posts were then shared between the main parties in a grand coalition.The election went very well for the ANC which achieved 252 seats, 62.65 per cent, and therefore just short of the two-thirds majority which would have empowered it to push through its own plans for a new constitution. This result was considered good for the country as a whole because it necessitated further negotiation on the crucial issues. The election also went well for the National Party which succeeded in dissassociating itself from its previous policies. It obtained eighty-two seats in the National Assembly and won control of the Western Cape Provincial Assembly because most of the Coloured voters there preferred it to the ANC. The Inkatha Freedom Party (a mainly Zulu party) obtained forty-three seats, the Freedom Front (a far right white party) obtained nine, the Democratic Party and the PAC seven and five respectively. These results were not far from a racial census and brought little cheer for supporters of multiracialism, black or white. Yet both the ANC and Afrikaners saw it as a success, the ANC for having achieved power through the ballot box, the National Party for having locked the ANC into a Western democracy and secured the survival of the capitalist order.

The ideal of a 'non-racial South Africa' will be even more difficult to attain. Black consciousness in South Africa was reinforced at every turn by the political opposition between black and white. Differences between black ethnic groups (Zulu, Xhosa, Tswana, Venda, etc.) and between socio-economic strata, were the less important. With the political changes, ethnic differences may become more salient, as in some other African states. Other worries remain. Heribert Adam (1995: 472–3) observes that 'The emerging xenophobia towards an estimated two million illegal immigrants from other African countries hardly differs from the bigotry in California against Mexican migrant workers or the *Ausländer 'raus!* demands of skinheads in Germany'. Violent crime is now more frequent and more serious than in the United States, and is one of the fears prompting the emigration of the persons whose talents are needed if the economy is to generate the wealth needed to reduce the social inequalities. Nevertheless, a transition to democratic government has been achieved with much less bloodshed and hatred than commentators expected. Much of the credit for this has been due to the remarkable personal qualities of Nelson Mandela.

Ethnic consciousness in Western Europe

No European government since 1945 has followed policies of the kind that increased racial consciousness in the United States and South Africa, but experience in Western Europe is relevant from a different angle. It was observed in Chapter 1 that when people are conscious of belonging together they may identify their group by a proper name: 'We Jews', 'We Scots', 'We blacks', and so on. It is usually an outsider who defines that consciousness as being ethnic, national, racial, or whatever. The peoples of France, Germany and the UK all had a group consciousness before they experienced the post-1945 waves of immigration from outside Europe. Even where outsiders might agree that these were all forms of national consciousness, they still differed in ways that influenced the terms on which they were prepared to admit newcomers to their group.

In 1789 the French created a secular republic based on a constitution articulating distinctive values. Over the next one hundred years and more they built a nation, a *political* community, founded upon commitment to these values. In 1991 the Constitutional Council decided that the legislature could not refer to *le peuple corse*, even as part of the French nation, because this would admit a distinction based upon ethnic origin contrary to Article 2 of the constitution. If Corsicans, Bretons and Basques cannot be recognized as minorities, nor can those from North Africa. The French have worried about maintaining the size of their population and have been ready to extend citizenship to everyone born or schooled in France on the assumption that they accept republican principles. They have not minded if new citizens retained citizenship in some other country, at least until recent times when doubt began to be cast on the loyalties of Muslims from the Mahgreb. Girls who come to school wearing an Islamic scarf challenge the school's mission to train pupils in republicanism.

Germans felt themselves to be a people, a *Volk*, before they were able to come together in 1871 as members of a state. They were an *ethnic* community, and continue to see themselves in this way. They start from a conception of *Volkszugehörigkeit* (ethnic belonging). They have accepted as fellow-Germans all those descended from people who lived on what counted as German soil in 1913, plus persons of German origin whose ancestors settled in Russia but no longer spoke German. To become German by naturalization an applicant must renounce any other citizenship because no one can be allowed to identify with a second ethnic community. Representatives of the state maintain that Germany is not a country of immigration, though there are problems when *Gastarbeiter* (guest workers) decide to remain. Most children of Turkish immigrants are and will remain Turkish nationals.

Most European governments maintain that citizens must be treated equally, and therefore the state must be blind to anything, like colour, which would introduce an improper distinction. They collect very little information on any inequalities associated with the distinctions which are observed in practice. Colour is certainly not the main divide in France, where there is much more hostility towards Mahgrebins than blacks. In France during the 1970s people on the left challenged the claim of the state to dictate the terms of assimilation and argued for a 'right to be different'. This was reflected in the UNESCO Declaration on Race and Racial Prejudice, of November 1978, which in Article 1(2) stated 'All individuals and groups have the right to be different, to consider themselves as different and to be regarded as such'. The sentiment was well expressed in a 1984 SOS Racisme demonstration by someone who held up a placard that declared 'La France est comme une mobylette. Pour avancer, il lui faut du mélange.' ('France is like a motor-scooter; to move forward it needs a mixture of fuel.') (Taguieff 1988: 38). This was the French counterpart to the Anglophone conception of multiculturalism; both would have been anathema in Germany.

The British, deeply divided on class lines as they are, have seen themselves as a *historical* community. People enjoy the rights of British subjects which Edmund Burke, reacting against the French idea of universal human rights, represented as a patrimony from their forefathers. Their citizenship has derived from their shared rights as subjects of the monarch and because the British constitution is not written, Britons have tended to work from implicit assumptions about the nature of their society rather than from explicit proposi-tions. Because immigrants from the New Commonwealth were already British citizens, the difference in ethnic origin was not confounded with a difference in citizenship. This may have made it easier to concentrate on the lack of justification for less favourable treatment on grounds of race.

Immigration from regions outside Europe had an impact first upon the UK, then Switzerland, France, the Netherlands, Germany, and the Nordic countries until by the 1990s practically all the countries of Western Europe were affected. This discussion will be centred upon the UK, France and Germany.

Although there had been a black presence in Britain for four centuries, it had always been small. A completely new phase started in 1948 with the arrival of people from Jamaica, many of whom had been in Britain in the services during the war years. In those years overseas students from British colonies were a visible minority in most university cities. Whites then perceived all university students as a privileged elite, while the colonial students were the more special because they would be returning to occupy positions of importance in their homelands; it was therefore in the national interest that they should acquire a favourable impression of the 'mother country'. Later, and in other towns, a dark complexion came more and more to signify instead a low social status. West Indian immigrants moved into jobs that were both unskilled and visible to others (like bus-conductors and hospital staff). They, and other non-white people, were still for a time seen as temporary visitors who would be returning in due course to other countries within the Commonwealth. The whites regarded a dark complexion as a sign that a person belonged elsewhere, probably in India or one of the colonies. Surveys in 1951 and 1956 recorded respectively 38 per cent and 18 per cent of the population of England and Wales as being opposed to free entry to Britain for immigrant workers from the colonies. In 1956 72 per cent of respondents favoured free entry, nearly half adding the proviso 'provided there is work'.

At this time there was no conception of New Commonwealth settlers buying their own homes, or qualifying for council housing. Only rarely were they seen as competing with white people for houses, jobs and other services. Among whites, the sense of 'us' and 'them' was very much stronger than in the 1960s and 1970s. To start with, very many English people were unaware that the mother-tongue of black West Indians was English. Many knew nothing about the differences between the various immigrant groups. I remember a Nigerian telling me in 1951 how his employer had called him to explain to two Bengali-speakers the nature of the work for which they had been engaged, as if, because they both had dark complexions, a Nigerian and a Bangladeshi would understand one another's speech.

As immigration from the West Indies and the Indian subcontinent increased in the late 1950s, a dark complexion came to be associated with a low position in a structure of social class based upon the inter-generational transmission of social inequality. White consciousness of competition grew, and with it opposition to free entry for New Commonwealth immigrants. The white public thought that there was an immigration problem and that the stopping, or reversing, of immigration was the best way to deal with any problem of racial relations. This put pressure on the first-generation settlers to legitimize their presence in the UK. They responded by referring to their war service, to the way workers were recruited from the West Indies because of the labour shortage in Britain, and by remarking on the number of Britons who had settled in British territories overseas.

Since the law governing the immigration of aliens did not apply to British citizens, new legislation, such as the Commonwealth Immigration Act 1962, was required if immigration from the New Commonwealth was to be restricted. In all countries, such laws have to recognize several different categories of entrant. Tourists and students have to be distinguished from refugees or asylum-seekers who want to stay for a longer period but nevertheless hope eventually to return to their native countries. All these persons may be barred from taking up employment unless they obtain specific permission. Others may be admitted if they have a definite job offer, though sometimes the government requires the prospective employer to establish that the vacancy could not be filled from within the UK. Those admitted to take up employment constitute primary immigration, because after they have settled down they may want their dependants to follow them. Since most states recognize a right of family reunification, the entry of dependants and the prospective spouses of residents constitutes a secondary immigration. The original immigrants often intend to return to their countries of origin after saving sufficient to set themselves up in business or to enjoy a comfortable retirement. But after the families have been reunified, children who have been brought up or born in the country of immigration often wish to remain in the country they know best. If their parents 'go back' this will undo the family reunification. So the decision often gets postponed and a man who thought of himself as a migrant worker may find that he has become an immigrant.

Immigration into Britain from New Commonwealth countries in South Asia (primarily India, Pakistan and Bangladesh) built up more slowly than that from the West Indies, but was eventually greater in volume. According to the 1991 census, about 3.4 per cent of the total British population was then of Asian origin and 1.6 per cent of African or Caribbean origin. In Britain New Commonwealth immigrants developed new forms of group consciousness. Those from the Caribbean, first thought of themselves as Jamaicans, Trinidadians, Barbadians, and so on; they were sometimes surprised to be classified as 'West Indians'. Then, as Chapter 2 has explained, they nearly all came to call themselves black, which would usually be accounted a form of racial consciousness. Some wished the category 'black' to include South Asians and any other group victimized by white prejudice. Most of the South Asians, however, thought of themselves as members of homeland communities, usually defined by their caste status, engaged in competition for status with similar groups. Most brought up their children to speak the language of their community of origin. The larger groups built up in their new country small communities which in many ways resembled those they had left behind, so that their members were conscious of belonging in a series of groups. At the lowest level membership of family groups with a particular caste status could be vital, but in their relations with the native British they wished to be classed as Hindus, Muslims or Sikhs. So in this sense they displayed a religious rather than an ethnic or racial consciousness. Members of the next generation have lacked their parents' intense ties with the homelands and they may continue to define themselves by their religion even if they do not practise it any more assiduously than most British people practise Christianity.

The immigration into France of non-European workers during the 1950s was the easier because Algeria was accounted part of metropolitan France, so that Algerian workers and their families could move freely between the two countries. The period of decolonization from 1958 to 1962 was the beginning of a massive and largely uncontrolled immigration, driven by the desire of private employers to recruit additional workers. The trade unions denounced the employment of foreigners as a way of exploiting the native working class but they were unable to stop it. By the end of the 1980s, foreigners constituted 5 per cent of the population. When a Eurobarometer survey of attitudes was undertaken in 1988, and respondents were asked 'When you think about people of another race, whom do you think of?', respondents in all the twelve countries except France and the UK cited blacks in the first place. The French respondents cited 'Arabs' first and the British, 'Indians'. When asked a similar question about people of another nationality, the French indicated a preoccupation with North Africans, the Germans with Turks, and the British with Asians. The findings concerning France fit with other evidence (see p. 44) that more prejudice is displayed towards North Africans than towards blacks from West Africa or the Caribbean; together with the figures from the UK they offer support for the view that in Western Europe since the 1950s the tendency of whites to see non-whites as racially inferior has been replaced by a growing tendency to see people from other cultures, and especially Muslims, as so different that they should be allowed no permanent place in the receiving society. It could be called a transition from racism to xenophobia. In France the second genera- tion of persons of North African origin (*beurs* as they are often called) seem sometimes to hesitate between defining themselves as French or as Muslims, as if neither identity corresponded fully to their self-consciousness.

The economic growth of the Federal Republic of Germany ('West' Germany) in the 1950s was fed by the immigration of ethnic Germans from the East, but with the construction of the Berlin wall in 1961 and the sealing of the frontier, the influx was halted. Thereafter immigration was characterized by a much higher degree of state control than had been the case in either Britain or France. In 1961 the federal government concluded the first of several agreements with the government of Turkey. The Turkish Employ-ment Service recruited workers and the Bundesanstalt für Arbeit (which also had recruitment offices in Italy, Greece and Yugoslavia) placed them with German employers. On occasion people were transported to barrack-like company quarters which were patrolled by security guards. Then many of the migrant workers found employment on their own account and there followed a period of family reunification. They were called 'guest-workers', indicating that they were expected to leave when they were no longer welcome. This fitted with the economic doctrine sometimes known as *konjunk-turpuffer*, whereby foreign workers would be recruited on contract to ease labour shortages in boom times but their contracts would not be renewed when the boomtime came to an end. Indeed, the first sudden rise in oil prices in 1973 led to restrictions in the employment of foreign workers throughout Western Europe. Nevertheless, by the end of the 1980s, foreign workers represented 7.3 per cent of the population of the Federal Republic and 7.7 per cent of its workforce; the latter figure was the highest of all EU countries except Luxembourg.

Because of the war in the former Yugoslavia, hundreds of thousands of refugees fled westwards. At much the same time, political changes in Eastern Europe inspired many economic migrants to seek their fortune in the same direction. Technological change was reducing the demand for unskilled labour, so whereas migration to Western Europe had earlier been a response to employer-demand, it switched to one driven by excess labour supply. These trends had unwelcome consequences for settled migrants, because their appearance identified them as suspects in the eyes of those responsible for checking on illegal immigration.

All the West European societies could well learn from experience in the United States of the enormous influence of cyclical effects. When individuals fail to complete school, or to get a job, or a decent home, that failure increases the possibility that they will fail again at the next stage, and the cumulated disadvantage will be passed on to their children. The growth of urban ghettos in which the sources of disadvantage reinforce one another is one of the prime explanations for the failure of the second Reconstruction to ameliorate the position of the black underclass (that category of persons who are excluded from the main opportunities and institutions of working-class life).

Negotiating change

Everyone is accustomed to the idea of negotiation in commercial dealings. It can usefully be applied metaphorically to the politics of integration, as the discussion in connection with Figure 4.3 may have already suggested. Yet it has to be remembered that while the parties may be ready to negotiate in some fields of activity, they may take up a different stance over matters of political or religious faith.

Political faith may be exemplified by the continuing commitment of the French to the first Article of the 1789 Declaration of Human and Civil Rights: *Les hommes naissent et demeurent libres et égaux en droits. Les distinctions sociales ne peuvent être fondées que sur l'utilité commune.* (People are born and remain free and equal in their rights. Social distinctions may be founded only on the common good.) This is a non-negotiable presumption of French society, from which the legislature has deduced that the state must be colour-blind. It is exemplified in the French data protection law of 1978 which specifies that data on racial origins may not be stored electronically without the express agreement of the person concerned. Any offender is to be imprisoned for a period between six months and five years or fined up to 2 million francs.

In France, racism is conceived as an ideological problem that threatens the state, and therefore as something to be punished under the criminal law. When it touches upon such issues, the exercise of freedom of speech may be restricted more severely than in some other democracies. For example, in 1993 the mayor of a small town in central France permitted the publication in the community bulletin of an article which contained a passage reading

L'immigration submerge maintenant notre commune. Autre fait aggravant, elle est de nationalité unique, ce qui favorise le sentiment de dualité anti-français ... pourquoi cette prolifération, cette occupation, où est l'intégra-tion? L'insecurité découle déjà en partie de cette immigration: problème au lycéee, racket, agressions.... De Charles Martel à Charles de Gaulle, les Français ont su balayer quand cela était nécessaire, je crois qu'ils sauraient le faire encore si on le leur démendait.

(Immigration is now submerging our community. It is the worse in that the immigrants are of one nationality, which encourages an anti-French sense of dualism ... why this proliferation, this occupation, what has happened to integration? Insecurity is already growing as a result of this immigration, a problem at the grammar school, racketeering, fights ... From Charlemagne to Charles de Gaulle, the French have known how to sweep up when it was necessary and I believe that they will know how to do it again if they are asked.)

The mayor was convicted at the appeal court for incitement to racial hatred, made subject to a suspended fine of 10,000 francs and required to publish the judgment of the court. This stated that while it was not illegal for the mayor to give his views on immigration and crime, he should not have implied that the town's Turkish colony was the source of all the trouble or done so in pejorative terms.

The Haut Conseil à l'Intégration in France defines integration as a process that evokes the active participation in the national society of varied and different elements, while at the same time accepting the continuance of distinctive cultural, social and moral features and believing that the whole is enriched by this variety and complexity.

The Council asserts that the French conception of integration must follow a logic of equality and not a logic of minorities. It claims that in Europe the French conception is shared with Germany and Belgium, whereas the Netherlands and the UK follow a *politique des minorités* (Hant Conseil à l'Intégration 1993: 34–6).

Another non-negotiable presupposition of West European societies is the equality of the sexes. The UK government regards polygamy as unacceptable within the country, though it accepts the legality of polygamous marriage contracted according to the laws of other countries. Under the Immigration Act 1988, a polygamous UK citizen may introduce only one wife into the country in exercise of the right of abode derived from the marriage. The practice of female genital mutilation (clitoridectomy), though customary in some parts of Africa, is unlawful in Britain. Nevertheless, legislation governing private behaviour is not easy to enforce if it does not have the support of the people in question. It has been estimated that in the Paris area more than 2,000 persons, mostly from Senegal, Mali and Mauretania, live in polygamous marriages. A man may go back to his native village, marry again, and then bring a second or third wife to share a tiny dwelling in France. Household income may be more than doubled by the state benefits paid to children and pregnant women, regardless of their status. A Malian construction worker who was planning to introduce a third wife, when asked why he wanted more than one wife, replied 'My father did, my grandfather did, so why shouldn't I?' He apparently had no intention of altering his ways to suit the country in which he lived, but the French government now says that it will recognize one spouse only, and will consider other marriages to be annulled. (*Guardian*, 27 January 1996). Recognition of the 'right to be different' cannot be unconditional.

The German government does not recognize that Turkish settlers in Germany constitute an ethnic minority. In German law a minority has to be a group of citizens, living in a distinctive area and following some distinctive customs. Most of the Turkish settlers are not citizens and they are scattered over many cities. In France they could quite easily have become naturalized French people, but, as has been explained, the German conception of citizenship is different. Thousands of people of German origin but no longer speaking German have been able in recent years to 'return' from countries to the East to live as citizens in the Federal Republic. Unlike the position in France, the German outlook is hostile to the idea of dual citizenship. A person can belong to only one people. Most Turkish settlers in Germany have not wished to give up their Turkish citizenship. German law provides extensive protections against any racial discrimination on the part of state institutions, but is much weaker when it comes to the actions of employers and others in the private sector.

French and British policies may differ more in the realm of

abstract conception than in practice. The French believe that where they follow a logic of equality, the British follow one of minorities; but it would be equally valid to maintain that the French start from a belief about how people should behave and the British from evidence about how they actually behave. The British and the French should treat the immigrants and their descendants as equals but they do not – especially if they have a dark skin. To reduce the difference between actual and expected behaviour the British believe it necessary to monitor conduct and keep records of people's ethnic origin. The French find this a contradiction.

State policies reflect principles of political faith. In most of Western Europe the religious faith of the majority may influence attitudes towards the new minorities but it has not set strict limits to negotiation. Many religious leaders have advised fellow-believers to look with tolerance upon religious pluralism rather than campaign to spread their own faith. In England and Wales, the Education Act 1944 required that schools conduct a daily act of collective worship and provide religious education. Religious schools can qualify for financial support from the government. The Committee of Inquiry into the Education of Children from Ethnic Minority Groups chaired by Lord Swann recommended in 1985 that this be reviewed 'given the multiplicity of beliefs now present in society' and 'in favour of a non-denominational and undogmatic approach to religious educa- tion'. The government rejected this recommendation. In 1986 a local authority in London recommended public support for an Islamic primary school which some criticized as inspired by 'fundamen- talist' beliefs. Leading figures associated with the National Secular Society protested. Soon, they said, there would be proposals for Sikh, Hindu and other schools. Children attending them would be isolated from the wider society. Self-segregation would build up an animosity greater even than that seen in Northern Ireland. People have a right to combine and establish private schools, but they should not be able to claim support from the public purse. Therefore Parliament should phase out all subsidies to denominational schools. In reply it was stated that most denominational schools do not indoctrinate their children with sectarian beliefs, and that they should not lose their status on account of the extremism of a small minority. Since secular ideas had not improved the moral standards of the society, taking religion out of the schools would not be a progressive step.

The Education Reform Act 1988 required that all new locally agreed syllabuses for religious education be based on an under- standing that the religious traditions of the UK are mainly Christian, and at the same time take account of other principal faiths. There was to be scope for variation in the light of local circumstances and for schools sponsored by churches, but collective worship was to be wholly or mainly of a broadly Christian character. Parents might withdraw their children from religious education and worship, and

such pupils might receive alternative religious education or participate in alternative worship.

The Islamic faith is not tolerant of religious pluralism. Muslims
believe themselves to be under a duty to spread the true faith. In
Britain some of their leaders are uncomfortable about multifaith
religious education classes in school because they convey an
impression that all faiths are equal. So in some localities Muslim
parents have withdrawn their children from such classes. For many
of them, as for some Christians, the truth of their faith is a non-
negotiable dogma. From the standpoint of the schools system,
religious education is one classroom subject. Some believers consider that its purpose should be to inculcate faith in their religion.
When they are then told that the propagation of their faith is for
private institutions outside the classroom, and that this is incompatible with an educational syllabus, they are understandably dissat-
isfied. A second difficulty arises because in neither faith are the
believers agreed on what is essential to it. For example, Christian
missionaries have contended that polygamy is un-Christian, whereas
other believers (like the poet John Milton) have insisted that there is
ample biblical authority for its practice. Muslims are divided about
their faith's requirements concerning the status of women. In all
faiths believers are apt to assume that their religion requires them to
follow practices which are no more than the customs of their
localities. The schools can become battlegrounds in which sectional
groups propagate their own versions of their faith.

Some parallel issues were raised by the dispute over the allegedly
blasphemous character of Salman Rushdie's novel *The Satanic
Verses*. Certain kinds of offensive statements about Christianity can,
under English law, entail punishment for blasphemy, but no other
faith can claim similar protection. Some of those who favour
religious pluralism would argue for abolishing the offence of
blasphemy and indeed for breaking the link between church and
state by disestablishing the Churches of England and Scotland. Tariq
Modood (1994: 72–3) has described the present position as an
'uneven three-cornered contest' between

(i) a secular hegemony; (ii) a Christianity which albeit in a dilute way still
gives to most people their understanding of divinity and moral conduct, yet
is fading as an organised religion; and (iii) an emergent multi-faith society.

He warns that if reformers who favour the first position squeeze
religion out of the British state, they should prepare contingency
plans to deal with aggrieved and militant minorities demanding a
share of the public space (above all, tax-funded education) in the
areas of their settlement.

Chapter 5 showed that while racial consciousness varies with
social and political circumstances, there are discernible factors
which underlie increases and decreases in its intensity. Any superordinate group will have its internal divisions. Each segment of that

group or class within it will play a double game, seeking to use the P–B division to strengthen its bargaining position within the P group and using its position within that group to reinforce its privileges with respect to the members of the B group. The game is complicated by a whole series of factors outside the parties' control. Among them is the obvious consideration that, irrespective of race, some individuals are more talented or hard-working than others. Racial discrimination works to prevent the rise of competent members of the B group and the fall of incompetent members of the P group. Those who enjoy privilege may wish to keep members of the B group divided, but by drawing a racial boundary they stimulate them to develop a consciousness of oppression which helps them to mobilize a new strength and upset the prevailing equilibrium. The subordinate group is also internally divided. The members of some divisions will be chiefly concerned to pursue their individual goals; only those who passionately resent their subordination may be willing to run the risks of open opposition to the prevailing order. The structure of caste-like subordination in the Deep South of the USA and in South Africa has been superseded by one that is class-like, the inequalities between the racial groups being maintained by the processes which are responsible for the inequalities within the groups.

Chapter 6 has fleshed out the description earlier in the book of the interaction between the 'macro' and 'micro' levels of social behaviour. Social structures set the limits of individual liberty and influence the alternatives between which individuals may choose, but individuals are not robots. Pursuing their ideals as well as their interests, they steadily modify the structures of their societies.

Governments have greater powers than they sometimes realize to regulate the integration of immigrants, but their policies also have unintended effects. Important, and sometimes unexpected variables can be uncovered when there are opportunities to compare the experiences in different receiving societies of immigrants who are of similar ethnic origin. One such opportunity was seized in 1985 by Jan Hjarnø in his brief but suggestive comparison of Turkish migrant workers in Copenhagen and Stockholm. The government of Sweden followed an explicit policy of integration (formalized in 1975) which favoured the reunification of migrants' families.

In Sweden many of the Turkish workers, both men and women, had found employment as cleaners, and accommodation in publicly owned flats in a suburb where they lived side-by-side in just three streets. Stockholm was a new and strange place for them; they said they preferred to live near other families from their village. The whole neighbourhood became stigmatized as one harbouring a mixture of the most socially disadvantaged Swedes, together with migrant workers and refugees. In the local shopping centre many shops stood vacant, the neighbourhood had a neglected appearance and the crime rate was high. This seemed not to worry the Turks, whose community was encapsulated, isolated from its social environment, and living as a sort of extension of the village community back in Anatolia. There had been little time for the men to meet Swedish girls before their own womenfolk had joined them. There were few broken marriages, and no complaints of problems controlling their children. Very few had ever visited a Swedish home, and their ideas about Swedish family life were far from accurate. Altogether, they have not as yet been any model of how the official policy of integration was supposed to work.

The group in Copenhagen had developed differently. The initial phase, when it consisted of adult males only, had lasted for about ten years. The receiving society called them foreign workers rather than immigrants, expecting them to return to Turkey when Denmark no longer wanted their labour. To start with, many lived in poor accommodation near their workplaces. Many found Danish girlfriends; some moved in with Danish single mothers, and in this way became acquainted with Danish family life and ideas about child-rearing. Many came to know Danish people privately; some started their own businesses with the help of their Danish girlfriends or Danish wives. After a few years some became members of the local Special Housing Associations and in due course were offered apartments. The rents were high, but not out of reach if more than one person brought an income into the household. The males had built up an ethnic community dispersed over several local council areas by the time, about ten years after their arrival, that family reunification started. Partly because of their dispersal, the parental generation had more difficulty than the Stockholm Turks in bringing up their children. Some wanted their children to marry someone of Turkish origin (preferably Kurdish, for the groups studied were both of Kurdish origin) and complained that their sons showed too much interest in Danish girls. The Turks in Copenhagen were more at home on the receiving society than their counterparts in Stockholm. Some were active in Danish politics. Some ran their own businesses. Yet they found it difficult to balance Turkish and Danish expectations and the cultural conflicts created tensions within families.

Some of the differences between the two Turkish communities stemmed from differences between Denmark and Sweden that had nothing to do with immigration. In Denmark more generous tax deductions were allowed for payments to dependants outside the country than appeared to be the case in Sweden. Because they had remitted money home, this had reduced the incentive for the Turks in Copenhagen to have their relatives join them. Someone who was not a Danish citizen was not on this ground at any disadvantage in obtaining a bank loan or standing as a guarantor for one, which had made it easier for Turks in Copenhagen to purchase used vehicles and ship them to Turkey where they were more valuable. In Sweden only Swedish citizens were ordinarily eligible for loans or able to stand as guarantors. In Denmark, a person could draw unemployment benefit for two-and-a-half years; thereafter there would be a special attempt to place the person in work, but if it was unsuccessful certain benefits would still be paid. Many of the older Turkish men were content to live on unemployment benefit without seeking work, perhaps in part because, in the agricultural society from which they had come, older men were not expected to work so hard. In Sweden unemployment benefit was paid for 300 days; thereafter applicants might have to accept retraining, but after ten years they were eligible for a full pension. In Denmark, people qualified for a full pension only after forty years. Elderly Turks in Stockholm were therefore unconcerned about their old age. They could continue drawing their pension after returning to their homeland, and it would be quite sufficient. The Turks in Copenhagen felt much less secure in the receiving society.

The experience of the Turkish groups can be compared with that of the Pakistanis who had come to Copenhagen at much the same time but moved into Special Housing Association apartments earlier. Finding them expensive, they obtained mortgages to purchase private housing; this gave them good tax exemptions, and, in a market in which the value of houses was rising, this proved a highly advantageous decision, taken at what subsequently proved to have been a good point in time. The Pakistanis became established among the Danish middle class.

Another interesting comparison is that between the migrants from Jamaica who appear to have prospered more in New York than their counterparts in London. Nancy Foner (1979) has observed that, in order to compare like with like, it is necessary to allow for the migration to New York's having begun fifty years earlier, so it is not surprising if they are further ahead. Those who went to New York seem to have been, on average, better qualified, while the presence of African-Americans meant that from the outset there was a large market to which tradespeople and shopkeepers could cater without experiencing strong competition from white businesses. Why they should have been successful in comparison with black Americans is an interesting and contentious issue, but it should be noted that those who migrate to seek work in another country usually have high motivation.

Just as it can be important for a group to be in the right place at the right time, so also it is possible for governments to capitalize on events that bear only indirectly on group relations. The success of the South African team in the 1995 World Rugby Football Cup appeared, at a crucial time, to encourage the conception of the transracial national identity in that country. Rugby had been mainly a white sport, and the South African team consisted mostly of white players, but President Mandela's appearance in a 'Springbok' jersey seems to have caught the imagination of both blacks and whites. (At the same time, sporting events can also reflect divisions, as at the 1968 Olympics when some United States athletes gave 'black power' salutes.)

Conclusion

The possible use of state power to decrease group consciousness can pose policy dilemmas because, as Chapter 6 concluded, the state is rarely neutral. Its actions are apt to reflect the interests of the groups which, perhaps through the electoral process, dominate the legislature and the administration. A policy of 'benign neglect' may be preferable to some forms of intervention (even if experience in Brazil is no good advertisement for it).

Benign neglect may mean leaving matters to be regulated by a market. Much then depends upon whether groups form of persons wishing to pursue a shared interest. Consider how parents' select schools for their children. Reports from many West European countries indicate that parents belonging to the majority ethnic group prefer schools with few immigrant pupils; they will exercise their options or move to private schooling to achieve this aim and social segregation will result. The enforcement of anti-segregation measures, like the bussing of children from one locality to another, arouses much resentment. Better policies might be founded on the assumption that for most parents there will be a 'trade-off' between their ethnic preferences and other considerations, like the academic standard of alternative schools, and the length and nature of the journey that the child will have to undertake to get to school and come home afterwards. Similar considerations will be in the minds of the parents of children with minority ethnic origins; they too will have their preferences. Those responsible for schools can often take steps to increase the attractiveness of some schools so as to mitigate the tendencies towards segregation. Equally, it may be possible to prevent the creation of ethnic ghettos by modifying the incentives attaching to residence in particular neighbourhoods.

International action to combat racial discrimination, the subject of Chapter 8, is premised upon the responsibility of states to use their powers for the greater good, and is opposed to any belief that state intervention is bound to make matters worse.

International oversight

As the Second World War came to an end, governments concluded that strong measures were needed to prevent any repetition of so terrible an event. So in 1945 they created the United Nations. Since then governments have slowly but steadily come to accept that they have an obligation to protect human rights, that the rights should be enshrined in law, and that what they do, or fail to do, to protect these rights should be subject to international oversight. As was emphasized at the beginning of this book, ethnic, national and racial tensions within or between states can become threats to world peace. Concern about them has been the greater because of the magnitude of the problems associated with refugees. Ethnic conflicts in the former Yugoslavia, in Rwanda-Burundi, in the Horn of Africa, and elsewhere, have led millions of people to seek refuge in neighbouring countries.

Any system of oversight must be based upon states and upon their agreement to be subject to some form of monitoring. The biggest obstacle was that many states would not accept criticism of their internal affairs from states which, in their view, themselves failed to protect the human rights of their citizens. When they talked of human rights, states in the West thought first of civil rights, whereas states in the East believed that economic rights should take priority. Debates about human rights revealed contrasting political philosophies as well as the suspicions of the Cold War. States were reluctant to yield any of their sovereignty to a supervisory body, even to the International Court of Justice, despite its highly restricted jurisdiction. At the same time their diplomatic representatives at the UN, charged with furthering their states' national interests, manoeuvred to win the support of other states and therefore had to take account of their priorities.

Regional organizations

International oversight may be achieved either by institutions able to cover the whole world, or by those limited to a particular continent or region. Though the tensions may be less acute within regional organizations, only in Europe are they as yet well developed.

The main regional organizations are the Organization for Security and Cooperation in Europe (OSCE), the Council of Europe, the European Union (EU), the Organization of American States (OAS), the Organization of African Unity (OAU) and Asia–Pacific Cooperation (a more loosely organized body). The regional organizations have on occasion acted to counter human rights abuses within member states of their organizations, and have sometimes called upon the UN Security Council for assistance. Whenever the Security Council has authorized intervention it has sought to involve the regional organization in that action. For example, the OAS attempted to negotiate a return to democratic rule in Haiti after the military coup of 1991, but then passed the problem to the Security Council. In 1994 that Council authorized military intervention by a nominally multi-national but basically US military force. The OAU has been involved in the interventions into African states but it was the Economic Community of West African States which supplied troops to restore peace in Liberia.

The regional organizations vary in the extent to which they exercise oversight over member states' policies concerning ethnic and racial minorities. Historically, the Council of Europe led the way by drawing up the European Convention for the Protection of Human Rights and Fundamental Freedoms (ECHR). The American and African organizations have adopted conventions with what, on paper, are stronger provisions for the prevention of discrimination and the protection of minority interests.

The OSCE includes among its fifty-three member states the USA, Canada, the Russian Federation, and states of the former USSR stretching to Uzbekistan and Tadjikistan, so it is larger than the Council of Europe (when Russia was admitted to membership of that body in January 1996 it became the thirty-ninth member state), and the Council in turn is larger than the EU (with fifteen states). Some of the states of Eastern Europe have been attracted to membership of the EU for economic reasons. Their path to entry lay via membership of the OSCE and admission to the Council of Europe, but the Council would admit them only if they conformed to its human rights standards and became parties to the ECHR.

In 1992 the OSCE established the office of High Commissioner for National Minorities. The Commissioner was to identify and try to resolve national minority tensions that could affect peace, stability or relations between states participating in the Organization. His first concerns were with the Baltic states of Lithuania, Latvia and Estonia. Under the USSR ethnic Russians and others from the USSR had settled in these states so that they represented over one-third and nearly one-half respectively of the populations of Estonia and Latvia. The new governments were preparing laws concerning the rights of citizenship, language use, the franchise and education which the minorities saw as discriminatory. The High Commissioner was able to mediate. He then took up concerns relating to the Hungarian minority in Slovakia, Roma (or Gypsies) in Romania, and Albanians in the Former Yugoslav Republic of Macedonia. The government of this new state wished to join the OSCE and the question of the rights of its Albanian-speaking minority was one of the issues determining whether or not it would be admitted.

The ECHR provides both for actions between governments (as when other states objected to breaches of the Convention by the 'regime of the colonels' in Greece and forced its withdrawal from the Council between 1969 and 1974) and for individual petition. Under Article 25, any person complaining to be the victim of a violation of his or her rights may appeal to the Court in Strasbourg. International oversight is therefore of two chief kinds. One state may complain that another state has not kept its promises, or an individual may petition for redress. In either event the Court may issue an opinion about how the facts stand in relation to the law set out in the Convention, and the state concerned will regard itself as bound by that opinion.

In 1993 the Council determined to prepare a convention which will specify principles to be observed by states for the protection of national minorities; it adopted a declaration and plan of action on combating racism, xenophobia, antisemitism and intolerance; and it established the European Commission against Racism and Intolerance. Action can be expected to improve the effectiveness of the ECHR in combating ethnic and racial discrimination.

The EU is founded upon the Treaty of Rome, and the provisions of that treaty have empowered the European Commission to issue directives on such matters as sex discrimination in employment which have been enforced by rulings of the European Court of Justice. The Treaty of Rome does not provide any comparable basis for regulating action against racial discrimination, so in 1993 a Consultative Commission on Racism and Xenophobia was appointed to explore ways in which the Union could respond to what was seen as a problem of increasing importance.

UN treaty bodies

Within the UN, oversight is exercised in two main ways. There is preventive action, of a legal character, undertaken by treaty-monitoring bodies acting under the authority of the treaty to which the states in question have acceded. The treaties require the state parties to submit periodic reports on the legislative, judicial, administrative, or other measures which they have adopted in order to give effect to their obligations. Some of the treaties include a provision allowing states to recognize the competence of the treaty body to receive individual complaints and issue opinions on them.

There can also be preventive action of a political character. This may be undertaken under the authority of the UN Charter, as when the Commission on Human Rights appoints a special rapporteur to investigate and report upon the situation in a member state. If preventive action is unsuccessful, the Security Council may embark upon remedial action. Individual states may be requested to supply troops who will then don the blue berets or blue helmets which indicate that they are acting as part of an international force. Remedial action has included the expulsion of Iraqi forces from Kuwait in 1991 and the dispatch of peace-keeping forces to a variety of countries, including Cyprus, Lebanon and Somalia. Observer missions have been sent to a greater number of trouble-spots.

The theory of a human rights treaty is that states embody a set of standards in a legal instrument. Each state undertakes to observe specified obligations, to report on its actions, and joins in establishing a body to monitor events on behalf of the states' parties. This treaty body will notify them how well the others are keeping to their bargain. The states and the treaty body are supposed to have a common commitment to furthering the object and purpose of the treaty. The reality is rather different. The actions of states are usually determined much more by internal politics than by external obligations. A government may, for its own reasons, legislate or take other action within the field to which the treaty relates. It then sends one of its officials to present a report so as to give the best possible impression of what it has done to fulfil its obligations. When members of a treaty body are critical, some states will object that they are acting as if they were a court, but the reality is that states are disinclined to take action on reports that other states are not meeting their obligations. States see such things as matters for their foreign policy and pursue them through diplomatic channels rather than through international institutions over which they have less control.

The chief international instrument for the prevention of ethnic and racial conflict is the International Convention on the Elimination of All Forms of Racial Discrimination (ICERD). Like other human rights conventions, it takes the legal form of a treaty which requires (in Article 4) that states make any incitement to racial hatred a punishable offence, and (in Article 5) that they protect the enjoyment of human rights from racial discrimination. The states' biennial reports are considered by a committee of eighteen persons serving in their individual capacities whom the states themselves elect. This is the Committee on the Elimination of Racial Discrimination (CERD) which reports annually to the UN General Assembly. Over 148 states are parties to the Convention but so far only 23 have made the declaration permitting individuals within their jurisdiction to petition the Committee if they consider themselves victims of a failure on the state's part to fulfil its obligations. Though it has few powers, many states take a lot of trouble to create a favourable impression before the Committee.

It must be unusual for a state to accede to such a treaty from altruistic motives and some try to secure the diplomatic advantages of being a state party without accepting all the legal obligations that flow from ratification. For example, when the United States eventually ratified ICERD in 1994, it entered extensive reservations which in effect declared that it was unwilling to modify any of its domestic practices. No document exposes the gap between the theory and the reality of human-rights treaty-making more clearly than this reservation.

The UK has been more conscientious than most parties to ICERD in the regularity, informativeness and frankness of the reports it has submitted every two years, but it would appear that most of its actions have been in response to domestic pressures rather than international obligations.

The development of policy in the UK

The key period for the formulation of policy in the UK was what has been called 'the liberal hour', from December 1965 to February 1968. It had two main components: legislation against racial discrimination and assistance to local authorities in dealing with the problems of the inner cities where ethnic differences were caught up in the cycle of disadvantage. The then Labour government enacted the first law against racial discrimination with the support of the Conservative opposition. The proposal had a relatively easy passage through Parliament because it was part of a package deal. As Mr Roy Hattersley said, 'Integration without control is impossible, but control without integration is indefensible.' There was a widespread demand for immigration control. Legislation against racial discrimination was part of the political price for it. The complementary part of the policy was implemented by giving the Home Secretary powers under section 11 of the Local Government Act 1966 to make grants to local authorities 'in consequence of the presence within their areas of substantial numbers of immigrants from the Commonwealth whose language or customs differ from those of the community'. Two years later the government brought in the Urban Programme which extended this approach.

The 1965 Act not only made it an offence for anyone to stir up hatred against a section of the public distinguished by race, but also provided remedies in civil law for racial discrimination in places of public resort. What has distinguished British action from that taken by many European states is the relative priority given to the second provision. All European states prohibit the incitement of racial hatred (to meet the requirements of Article 4(a) of the International Convention), but they have been slower than the UK to take effective action against racial discrimination, particularly in the private sector.

To evaluate the effectiveness of the 1965 Act, research was undertaken which found a significant incidence of racial discrimination in employment, housing and other public services (Daniel 1968). Three testers were employed, an Englishman, a Hungarian and a West Indian. They were of similar age and good appearance.

Claiming identical qualifications, they applied for jobs, for housing, for car insurance, and for certain other services. When they sought jobs, the Englishman got fifteen offers out of forty firms; the Hungarian applying to the same firms for the same jobs got ten offers, and the West Indian one. Out of sixty applications to rent accommodation, in fifteen cases all three were treated alike. On thirty-eight occasions the Englishman and the Hungarian were told that the accommodation was available and the West Indian turned away. On four occasions the West Indian was asked for a higher rent; on one occasion both the West Indian and the Hungarian were asked for a higher rent. On two occasions the Englishman was the only person to be told that the accommodation was available to him. Asking for a higher rent is an example of a *colour tax*: this is the price differential paid by persons of a different colour to obtain services of a quality similar to those obtained by persons not subject to discrimination. Such a tax was also evident in the case of car insurance. All three testers claimed identical driving records. In six out of twenty applications the West Indian was refused insurance cover altogether; on eleven occasions he was quoted a higher premium. The average premiums quoted by the fourteen firms who offered cover to all three testers were: West Indian £58, Hungarian £49, Englishman £45. In this, as in other parts of the study, the experience of the testers proved that the incidence of discrimination was higher than minority people had themselves estimated in interviews. The findings of the studies attracted much shocked comment in the press and helped create a climate of opinion in which Parliament could be persuaded to extend the scope of the law to provide protections against discrimination in employment, housing, education, provision of services and trade unions; it also banned advertisements of a discriminatory character.

Like its predecessor, the 1968 Act relied on arrangements to effect a conciliation of the parties. Only in 1976 were significant sanctions upon discriminators introduced in a new Act modelled on the Sex Discrimination Act passed the previous year. This enabled the victims of job discrimination to take their cases to the industrial tribunals which had been established to offer redress to persons who had been unfairly dismissed. The way in which the Act works may be illustrated at its simplest by a case in which a young man saw in his local Jobcentre a notice of a vacancy. It was for a paint-sprayer in a small privately owned car repair workshop. The centre's assistant telephoned on his behalf. The employer asked if Smith was coloured. She said he was. The employer then refused to see him and persisted in this refusal. So an application was filed with the local Industrial Tribunal alleging racial discrimination. A hearing was scheduled. The employer did not attend. The tribunal was satisfied that there had been discrimination and ordered the employer to pay £500 for the injury to Smith's feelings and a further £858 for loss of earnings to cover the period between the discrimination and his finding other employment.

The employer's action was an example of intentional discrimination, of less favourable treatment on racial grounds. This is usually called direct, as opposed to indirect, discrimination. In the latter case the discrimination is sometimes unintentional. It occurs when someone, without justification, imposes a condition which is disadvantageous to persons belonging to a particular racial group (the same provision also applies to discrimination on grounds of sex).

The leading case in this field is that of *Mandla v Dowell Lee*. It arose from the action of a headmaster of a private school in Birmingham. It was a multiracial but Christian school which included among its pupils five Sikhs who did not wear turbans. Mr Mandla wanted his son to attend, and to wear his turban. The headmaster's policy was to emphasize what the pupils had in common and to minimize differences, so he was willing to admit the boy provided he observed the school's dress code, which meant that he would not be able to wear a turban. (Ironically, the father would not have wished his son to attend this school had he understood that all pupils had to attend classes in the Christian faith.) When he learned of the headmaster's decision, the father persuaded the Commission for Racial Equality to bring a case against the school in the County Court. The judge there ruled that Sikhs were not a racial group in the meaning of the 1976 Act. The evidence suggested that they were a religious group, and discrimination on grounds of religion is not prohibited by law. This decision was upheld in the Court of Appeal, but overturned in the House of Lords. The judges there declared that a group was an ethnic group in law if it regarded itself, and was regarded by others, as distinct by virtue of shared history and cultural tradition. Characteristics of geography, language, literature, religion and minority status might be relevant but were not essential.

This means that if English people treat Sikhs (coming from the East Punjab) less favourably because they are Sikhs, the English people break the law, because Sikhs are recognized as an ethnic as well as a religious group. If English people treat persons coming from the West Punjab (over the border in Pakistan) in a similar fashion, they break the law if their action is associated with the persons' ethnic or national origin, but not if it is associated with these persons' religion. It is the more difficult to prove a breach of the law because most of these West Punjabis identify themselves as Muslims. As was mentioned in Chapter 1, a group which is identified by religion can be an ethnic group as well if it includes persons who do not practise the religion but still regard themselves, and are regarded by others, as members of it. In future the name 'Muslim' in Britain, as in Bosnia, could be accepted as a designation for a group larger than one of persons sharing a religion.

Applicants before industrial tribunals need to prove their cases according to the civil law rather than the criminal law standard (i.e. on the balance of probabilities rather than 'beyond reasonable doubt'). Civil law procedures are more flexible; they enable the parties to come to a private settlement at any stage, without requiring any admission that discrimination has occurred. Cases are first referred to the Advisory, Conciliation and Arbitration Service (ACAS) which may be able to assist the parties in coming to a settlement, or one may be reached privately or before the Tribunal itself. For example, one case concerned a Sikh engaged to work in a chocolate factory who was required, on grounds of hygiene, to wear a company hat, although he maintained that this would be contrary to his faith. The dispute was settled on the basis of a declaration that 'The Tribunal recommends that the respondents should obtain and maintain a supply of white turbans for the use of their Sikh employees in the production department who object on religious grounds to wearing the respondent's cap'. During 1994 2,324 cases within the scope of ACAS were commenced under the Race Relations Act. In France, where racial discrimination in employment is a criminal offence, the years 1990–3 saw an annual average of three convictions for such matters.

The 1965 Act's criminalization of racial incitement was of only limited effect because, to secure a conviction, the prosecution had to prove that the action which was the subject of complaint was both intended to stir up hatred and likely to have this effect. By the Public Order Act 1986 this was changed to make it possible for an offender to be convicted if either intent *or* likely effect was proven. Between 1987 and 1995 fifteen prosecutions had been commenced under the new law, fewer than the use of the corresponding provisions in France.

Research findings do not yet support any claim that the Act has reduced the overall incidence of discrimination in employment, even if it has had an effect in particular companies and trades. One measure has been derived from research into the responses of employers who have advertised vacancies, when they receive similar applications from persons who appear English and persons reporting a foreign birthplace or with a foreign-sounding name. A study in 1984–5 found no significant change since a similar study eleven years earlier. Another study described a continuous scale with least discrimination against Australians, then French, Africans, West Indians, Indians and Pakistanis in that order. A dark complexion is a strongly negative factor, but there is no clear break in the scale of preferences.

Measurement of changes in the incidence of discrimination is made the more problematic by changes in expectations. In the past many members of racial minorities did not apply for certain kinds of position, either because they lacked the qualifications or because they thought there was little chance that their applications would be considered seriously. Now their qualifications and expectations are higher so they more frequently enter situations in which discrimination is possible. Something similar can be said about discrimination against women because women's expectations of equal treatment have also increased.

The successive Race Relations Acts seem to have succeeded in influencing public opinion in a manner comparable to the restrictions upon drinking and driving. Over the years 1982–93 alcohol-related road deaths in Britain were reduced by almost two-thirds, not because of police checks but because of changes in the attitudes and behaviour of young people. To mix drink and driving had become much less socially acceptable. In similar fashion, many more people now accept that appointing others to jobs or admitting them to housing are not matters of private preference, and that in taking such decisions it is wrong to act on racial grounds. The boundary between what is private and what is public has been moved, so that the duty that people owe to their neighbours is now accepted to a much greater extent as a duty owing irrespective of the other person's race or colour.

Government policy has been supported by a variety of institutions. At the centre, the Commonwealth Immigrants Advisory Committee of 1962 gave way to the Community Relations Commission and then to the Commission for Racial Equality (CRE). In the areas where the immigrants had settled, a large number of local racial equality councils were funded partly by the local authorities and partly by the central body. All the various departments of the central government were expected to take action within their own spheres to prevent discrimination and promote harmonious relations.

Over the period since 1948 relations between the majority and the minorities have got better in some respects and worse in others. What constitutes 'better' is a complicated question, and much depends upon the standpoint of the person asking it. Social research contributes findings which can assist people to come to their own conclusions.

Starting in the 1960s, white Britons came slowly to perceive first blacks and then Asians as potential neighbours. Because most of the incomers were of low socio-economic status, native attitudes reflected considerations of class as well as colour, but the rising generation of young whites were quicker to accept new social patterns than were their elders. Changes occurred first in the more public sectors of social life. Gallup Poll data show that the expression of social distance by white towards non-white people declined substantially over the period 1964 to 1981 (Table 8.1). The percentage of respondents saying that they would accept coloured people as neighbours went up from 49 to 59 per cent; as friends from 49 to 78 per cent; as schoolfellows to their children from 54 to 78 per cent; as fellow-workers from 61 to 82 per cent; as a principal or employer from 35 to 63 per cent; as son-in-law from 15 to 35 per cent; as daughter-in-law from 16 to 37 per cent. It is important to note that social distance towards minority residents was declining at the same time as hostility towards further non-white immigration

Table 8.1 Changes in social distance expressed by whites

Which of these four phrases best describes how you would feel about having coloured people . . .

	November 1964				May 1981			
	Pleased	*Not mind*	*Rather not*	*Strongly dislike*	*Pleased*	*Not mind*	*Rather not*	*Strongly dislike*
(a) as neighbours?	5	44	26	17	2	57	28	10
(b) as friends?	5	40	21	12	10	68	13	5
(c) as schoolfellows to your children?	4	50	16	11	6	72	11	4
(d) as fellow workers?	4	57	16	13	6	76	10	4
(e) as your principal or employer?	2	33	22	28	3	60	16	13
(f) as your son-in-law?	2	13	27	44	3	32	25	33
(g) as your daughter-in-law	2	14	26	44	3	34	24	33

Source: Gallup poll

was rising to the high plateau on which it has remained. A small minority of whites have thought that opposition to further immigration justified the discriminatory treatment of settled immigrants, but the figures show that they are quite unrepresentative and that it is misleading to use attitudes towards immigration as an index of racism.

Opinion polls up to 1995 continued to show that the great majority of white people acknowledged that there was much prejudice against black people, but they thought that its incidence was declining, while more claimed that they themselves were not prejudiced. An ICM poll (*Guardian* 20 March 1995) found that men were more likely to describe themselves as prejudiced than were women, Conservatives rather more than Labour supporters, and older rather more than younger people. When asked 'How prejudiced are people in your street?', the answers showed a consistent discrepancy. The 3 per cent of respondents who said that they themselves were 'very prejudiced' considered 9 per cent of people in their street to be very prejudiced. The 16 per cent who said that they were 'a little prejudiced' attributed the same attitude to 32 per cent of their neighbours. The 80 per cent who said that they were 'not prejudiced at all' attributed the same freedom from prejudice to 59 per cent of their neighbours. This tendency is known in psychology as 'pluralistic ignorance' (Banton 1986), and has been noted in studies of racial attitudes in a variety of countries. What causes it is still far from clear: there may be elements of selective perception and of risk-avoidance (i.e. in thinking it better not to risk the disapproval of peers); there may be a tendency for respondents to project negative feelings onto others; and the findings may reflect images obtained from the mass media.

Messages received from the mass media may also help account for the findings of surveys in which whites have expressed a belief that racial prejudice is increasing. The respondents may not have been reporting on anything of which they had personal knowledge. Those who are responsible for the preparation of television programmes and those who write for the newspapers may see white prejudice as a problem which, if unchecked, is likely to cause increasing social conflict and economic cost in the future. If so, they may try to persuade their audiences of the seriousness of the situation: to do so they may highlight instances of conflict, prejudice and discrimination; thereby they will build an image of relations being worse than might appear from a statistical measure of their frequency. This would explain why some people believe that relations have got worse. If at the same time white people's own sentiments have become more positive it would not be surprising if they concluded that the decline must have been caused by an increase in prejudice among other people. Certainly, and as already explained in the Chapter 7, there has been a great change in the white British public's conception of its own behaviour.

Levels of ethnic or racial consciousness are reflected in the rates of intermarriage, or the frequency with which someone lives with a partner conventionally assigned to another group. In the USA 3 per cent of blacks marry someone of a different race or ethnicity, compared to 8 per cent of whites and 20 per cent of Asians (Edmonston *et al.*, 1996: 32). In Britain blacks are ten times more likely to marry or live with a white, while such unions are contracted much more often by persons who consider themselves partly black in their origins. In the United States there has been little increase in the frequency of black–white marriage whereas in Britain it has been increasing significantly. This can be seen firstly from Table 8.2, which presents estimates of the numbers of children in Great Britain according to the ethnic group in which their mothers classify themselves. These numbers can be compared with those reported for 1984 which were reproduced as Table 6.3 in the first edition of this book. They are based on information from a sample of 60,000 households used for the Labour Force Survey. This is a relatively

Table 8.2 **Ethnic group of children by mother's ethnic group and country of birth, Great Britain 1995 (thousands)**

Child's ethnic group	Age of child (years)			All children
	0–4	5–9	10–4	
White, UK-born	3303	3312	3134	9755
Overseas-born	264	253	238	756
Black-Caribbean, UK-born	38	32	24	94
Overseas-born	17	14	18	45
Black-African, UK-born	8	5	3	16
Overseas-born	32	22	20	74
Black-other, UK-born	12	7	4	25
Overseas-born	8	7	7	23
Black-mixed, UK-born	36	25	21	82
Overseas-born	12	8	8	29
Indian, UK-born	24	9	5	38
Overseas-born	60	66	77	203
Pakistani, UK-born	18	12	3	33
Overseas-born	64	68	66	198
Bangladeshi, UK-born	2	1	1	4
Overseas-born	24	22	21	67
Chinese, UK-born		1		2
Overseas-born	3	6	10	19
Other Asian, UK-born	2	2	1	5
Overseas-born	14	12	11	36
Other, UK-born	3	3	3	9
Overseas-born	14	9	8	31
Mixed, UK-born	32	32	21	85
Overseas-born	15	18	19	53

Source: Labour Force Survey, 1995, Crown Copyright, reproduction authorized.

large sample, but, like any sample, it is subject to a degree of error. Though any figure of less than 10 in Tables 8.2 and 8.3 is therefore to be regarded as unreliable, these smaller figures confirm a more general pattern.

The categories used in such a survey have to be ones that ordinary members of the public can use to classify themselves. To avoid confusion, those who designed the survey labelled the fourth and fifth categories 'Black – Other (non-mixed)' and 'Black – Mixed'. Everyone's ethnic origins are to some degree mixed, but not everyone identifies himself or herself as being of mixed origin. A person with a black African and a black Caribbean parent might have identified themself as 'Black – Other', while someone with a black African and a white parent might have chosen 'Black – Mixed'. The tenth category was labelled 'Other – Asian (non-mixed)', the eleventh 'Other – Other (non-mixed)' and the twelfth 'Other – Mixed'. A person from Japan or Sri Lanka might have chosen the tenth category, while someone from, say, Brazil of partly Japanese origin, might have chosen either the eleventh or the twelfth. There will have been some variation from one respondent to another since some people will not count as 'mixing' the unions that occurred several generations back.

The number of children whose mothers assign themselves to non-white ethnic groups increased over the period 1984–95, the increases being greater for Pakistanis and Bangladeshis because they are more recent immigrants, and greater for the mixed groups. As can be seen from Table 8.2, the process of settlement is reflected in the proportion of mothers born in the UK and, to a lesser extent, in the age of their children.

Compared with the figures for 1984, Table 8.3 shows that while most marriages, or unions, are between persons who assign themselves to the same ethnic group, the proportion of interethnic unions has been increasing in a patterned fashion. By 1995 the survey classifications had become more elaborate, but they still permit some measuring of the changes. Taking first the most recently settled group, that of Pakistanis and Bangladeshis, over the eleven year period the percentage of males living with a white partner rose from 6 to 16, while the percentage of females living with a white partner remained at one per cent. Among Indians, the percentage of males with a white partner rose from 5 to 7, and that of females from 2 to 7. The percentage of West Indian males with a white partner rose from 20 to 38, and that for females from 13 to 21. The percentages of persons of mixed ethnic origins living with a white partner rose for males from 46 to 63 per cent and for females from 50 to 67. These figures demonstrate a clear and strong trend.

In the United States a concept of race is employed which counts as black persons with only small proportions of African ancestry. The trend displayed in Tables 8.2 and 8.3 suggests that ethnic or racial classification in Britain may develop differently. This

Table 8.3 Ethnic group of husband by ethnic group of wife, Great Britain 1995 (thousands)

Ethnic group of husband	Ethnic group of wife											
	White	Black – Caribbean	Black – African	Black – Other	Black – Mixed	I*	P*	B*	C*	Other Asian	O*	Other Mixed
White	13,406	12	5	3	7	15	1		10	17	9	16
Black – Caribbean	31	42	2	2	2							
Black – African	8	3	31	2	1							
Black – Other	5									1		
Black – Mixed	5	2									1	
Indian	16					203	4			2		
Pakistani	8				1	2	100					1
Bangladeshi	1							35				
Chinese	7								20			
Other Asian	5									25	1	
Other	12									2	14	1
Other–Mixed	13									2		4

Key: I = Indian; P = Pakistani; B = Bangladeshi; C = Chinese; O = Other.
Source: Labour Force Survey, 1995. Crown Copyright, reproduction authorized.

inference is strengthened by the findings of research into conceptions of identity among children of mixed ethnic origins and young
people adopted or fostered by parents belonging to the ethnic
majority.

Against such figures suggesting that racial consciousness in
Britain has been declining should be set the evidence of dissatisfaction manifested in a series of urban riots. The first was in Bristol in
1980; then in the following year there were riots in Brixton (south
London) and a variety of other locations which attracted much media
attention and debate about their causes. There have been sporadic
riots since, mostly in reaction to occasions when black people have
died in police custody. In the 1970s disquiet grew about the
incidence of racially motivated attacks, primarily upon blacks and
Asians. The central government issued advice intended to improve
coordination between the various agencies involved in preventing
and reacting to such attacks, but seems not to have been able to
reduce their incidence. A Home Office calculation in 1994, based
upon responses from the general public in the course of a survey of
their experiences of crime, concluded that each year there were
between 89,000 and 171,000 racially motivated incidents, such as
assault, the making of threats, or vandalism, directed against Asians
or Afro-Caribbeans.

A comparison of the occupational status of groups in Britain over
the period 1966–91 found that, despite the persistence of discrimination, the black and Asian groups had made considerable progress
(Iganski and Payne 1996). The findings suggest some grounds for
optimism, but social mobility is a complicated process and a
comparison based on census-style information cannot tap some
important variables. Others have pointed to a growth in 'credential-
ism', a tendency for employers, faced with plenty of job applicants
to select on the basis of paper qualifications beyond what the job
actually requires. A young person who did not obtain the right
qualifications early on may have difficulty making up for this later.
In some sectors, the opportunities for upward mobility within a
career may be diminishing.

Some ethnic groups overcome their disadvantages more quickly
than others, possibly because they obtain jobs which allow more
individual mobility. By 1990 well-qualified Indian, African-Asian
and Chinese men were as likely as white men to be employed in
professional posts. The African-Asians were mostly the 29,500
Asians expelled from Uganda in 1972; over the years 1981–91 the
proportion of the men recorded as managers increased from 25 to 37
per cent (white men having increased from 23 to 28 per cent); the
proportion of female managers went from 6 to 24 per cent (whites
from 21 to 25). Some of the establishments managed will have been
shops. Though these groups' rates of unemployment were higher
than the comparable figure for whites, the difference was much
smaller than it was for West Indians, Pakistanis and Bangladeshis.

The progress of the three leading groups could be attributed to the shift in the economy from manufacturing towards the service sector, to the success of the named groups in extending their education and in developing business networks, and to skill shortages in the south-east of Britain in the preceding years. Afro-Caribbean women were employed at job levels comparable to those of white women (Jones 1993). In general, the differences reflected differences in the human capital brought by the groups and the length and location of their settlement.

The group consciousness of members of ethnic minorities in Britain varies with the generations. The first-generation settlers had self-conceptions, or identities, rooted in their socialization in the sending societies. Their children grew up in a very different kind of society, one in which the individual is not dependent in the same way upon the support of a family group. Modern British society is permeated by the values of consumption; it is a society in which many males cultivate a self-perception as the supporter of a sports team, and many young people define themselves as the fans of particular 'pop' musicians. The stress on self-expression led some observers to label the young people of the 1980s as 'the me generation'. For the second generation, influences which they can share with their white English classmates compete as sources of personal identity with those they share with their parents. According to the authors of a special study of these questions (Modood *et al.* 1994)

In the second generation of every group studied here there is a strong sense of ethnic pride, of wanting to know about or at least to affirm one's roots in the face of a history and a contemporary society in which one's ethnicity has been suppressed or tainted with inferiority. This pride is not necessarily primarily located in a community religion, for this varies from group to group. Its significance here is that even those young Asians who do not practice their religion nevertheless recognise that religion as part of their distinctive heritage and ethnic identity and state that they wish to pass it on to their children in at least that form.

(Modood *et al.* 1994: 59–60)

Language can play a special part in maintaining a distinctive consciousness. One young Asian spoke for many others in telling the researchers 'To be in touch with one's roots, it's vital we are able to speak the language'. Yet some of those who agreed with this could not speak their language well enough to be able to pass it on in turn to their own children. As language use changes, so will group consciousness.

The UK report as a case study

In 1993, reporting to the General Assembly on its examination of the Twelfth periodic report of the UK, the Committee on the Elimination of Racial Discrimination welcomed the attempts of the government to improve the protection of the country's ethnic minorities and to remedy outstanding problems. Among other many things, it observed more critically that

By not prohibiting the British National Party and other groups and organizations of a racist nature, and by allowing them to pursue their activities, the State party was failing to implement article 4, which called for condemnation of all organizations attempting to justify or promote racial hatred and discrimination.

Additionally, the Committee considered that, in the light of the increase in the manifestation of racist ideas and of racially motivated attacks, the restrictive interpretation of article 4 violated the purpose and objective of the Convention.

In its Thirteenth report the UK responded robustly to this observation, declaring that

It is the considered view of the Government that to ban extremist organizations, or to try to curtail their activities, on the grounds of their political principles would not be seen as in keeping with the long traditions of freedom of speech enjoyed in the United Kingdom and would, almost certainly, be counterproductive. The Government believes that such action is likely to lead to greater publicity and support for the groups in question. The Government has therefore concluded that the effects of banning groups like the British National Party would run counter to the object and purpose of the Convention.

There was much else in the report, which consisted of twenty-six tightly packed pages and twenty-three annexes setting out the texts of legislation and related statistics.

The Thirteenth report began with the declaration that

It is a fundamental objective of the UK Government to enable members of ethnic minorities to participate freely and fully in the economic, social and public life of the nation, with all the benefits and responsibilities which that entails, while still being able to maintain their own culture, traditions, language and values. Government action is directed towards addressing problems of discrimination and disadvantage which prevent members of ethnic minorities from fulfilling their potential as full members of British society.

It should be noted that this formulation refers to 'members of ethnic minorities' as individuals. Persons who were of ethnic minority descent but did not consider themselves as members of such a minority would therefore not be included within it. Nor does it recognize ethnic minority communities as units, though associations representing particular religions or interests are consulted from time to time.

The report went on to explain that its commitment to eliminating the barriers to full participation was expressed in legislation and in programmes to regenerate the vitality of life in inner cities. It stated that 'research suggests that the majority of the population supports race relations policies and shows that racial prejudice is diminishing within the white population generally and within the younger age group in particular'. It described the ethnic breakdown of the population and the legislation against incitement to racial hatred. Responding to the demand for a new law against racially motivated assault, it quoted the declaration of the Court of Appeal that 'where there is a racial element in an offence of violence, that is a gravely aggravating feature' to be taken into account in the determination of sentence. Discussing the exercise of political rights, it furnished calculations of the varying percentages of persons who had avoided being registered to vote. Among whites 6 per cent were not registered; among blacks, 24 per cent; among South Asians, 15 per cent; among all other minorities (including Chinese), 24 per cent. Advertising campaigns had improved awareness among under-represented groups of the need to register.

With respect to employment, surveys showed that the proportion of males working in managerial and professional jobs reached 40 per cent among whites, 50 per cent among Indians, 28 per cent among blacks and 20 per cent among Pakistanis and Bangladeshis. Male unemployment was running at 12 per cent for whites, 14 per cent for Indians, 31 per cent for Pakistanis and Bangladeshis, and 34 per cent for blacks. Female unemployment rates were for whites 7 per cent, Indians 11 per cent, blacks 20 per cent and Pakistanis and Bangladeshis 29 per cent. Surveys also showed 'evidence of remarkable entrepreneurship' in that 21 per cent of all Asians were self-employed compared with 12 per cent of whites.

With regard to housing, the 1991 census had shown a high proportion of owner-occupation among persons of Indian or Pakistani origin. Bangladeshis made up one of the youngest immigrant groups, many of them being concentrated in local authority rented property in inner London boroughs where the cost of housing was relatively high. Local authorities were said to be making greater use of their new powers to repossess the properties of tenants (usually white) who engaged in the racial harassment of other tenants.

The report discussed briefly actions taken to see that the personal social services, including health services, were responsive to the needs of all ethnic groups and worked towards the fair representation of the minorities at all levels among the staff. Educational programmes were described, together with advice to schools concerning action against racial harassment. The report concluded with the statement that the government had no plans to make the declaration that would permit persons in Britain to appeal to the Committee in Geneva if they believed that their rights under the Convention had not been adequately protected.

CERD's reception of the UK's Thirteenth report

In March 1996 a UK delegation attended a meeting of CERD to present the government's report. The delegation was led by an Assistant Secretary from the Home Office, who was there to speak for that part of the report which dealt with the metropolitan territory, and a legal adviser to the Foreign and Commonwealth Office to speak on matters relating to dependent territories, and in particular, on Hong Kong. Other members of the delegation came from three departments within the Home Office (police, immigration and research) and from the Hong Kong government. The imminence of the return of that colony to Chinese sovereignty had raised anxieties about the future protection of human rights there. The occasion was also notable for the abundance of additional material submitted by non-governmental organizations (NGOs). Members received a joint submission supported by twenty-two organizations in the UK, plus seven further separate submissions, together with a further set of documents from the Hong Kong Legislative Council and NGOs in that territory; all these submissions were set out systematically in relation to the Convention's articles.

The delegation explained that legislative proposals to prohibit racial discrimination in Northern Ireland would soon be published. New measures were being introduced to enable all sections of society, including the ethnic minority communities, to have full confidence in the criminal justice system. Since fair and effective immigration control was a necessary condition for maintaining good race relations, the procedures for dealing with asylum-seekers were being revised to prevent abuse. A Housing Bill currently before Parliament provided for a power of arrest and other measures to make it easier for local authorities to deal with racial harassment. In Hong Kong, all English-language legislation had been translated into Chinese. All legislation was being brought into line with the colony's Bill of Rights. The Sino-British Joint Declaration of December 1984 and the Basic Law of the Hong Kong Special Administrative Region provided for the continuance of the provisions of the International Covenant on Economic, Social and Cultural Rights and the International Covenant on Civil and Political Rights.

The Committee's consideration of the report was opened by the 'country rapporteur', Professor Theodoor van Boven (Netherlands). He welcomed the interest which the report had evoked and the commitment which the UK had displayed to the elimination of racial discrimination. He drew attention to several reports suggesting a growth of anti-Muslim sentiment in Britain and to some recommendations of the Commission for Racial Equality which the government had so far been unwilling to accept. In his view, the statistics indicated that there was much racial bias in the immigration controls. Among other things, he noted that Irish people living in

Britain experienced substantial disadvantages. They were reported to have the highest rate of mortality of any ethnic minority in Britain and to be over-represented among homeless and unemployed people. Turning to Hong Kong, he noted the vulnerability of foreign household-workers, of Vietnamese asylum-seekers, and of the South Asian ethnic minorities whose citizenship status would soon be uncertain.

Mrs Sadiq Ali (India) asked what the government had done to ease the situation in Bradford following the riots there in June 1995. She asked about the protection of Indians from racial attacks in Leicester, and the 'one year' rule under which Asian women marrying men in Britain must remain within the marriage for one year before becoming eligible for permanent residence. This had forced some of them into total dependence upon spouses who had abused the power conferred on them by the rule. Mr Chigovera (Zimbabwe) observed that while Article 4(b) of the Convention prohibited both the activity and membership of organizations that incited racial discrimination, UK legislation prohibited only the former. He also asked about the differential treatment of visitors, notably the action taken against passengers on a charter flight from Jamaica in December 1933.

Mr de Gouttes (France) remarked that the UK's reports testified to the exemplary efforts being made to tackle racial discrimination; they built on an abundance of documentation that was supplemented by evidence from NGOs. Yet the government's unwillingness to fully implement Article 4 was the more regrettable because the Convention's provisions could not be invoked in British courts. Mr Rechetov (Russian Federation) shared this view. While he could agree that it was the states' parties who were the main interpreters of the Convention, and not the Committee, he thought that the conflict of interpretations should be resolved. Mr Valencia Rodriguez (Ecuador) observed that the submissions from NGOs cast doubt on the some of the government's claims. They questioned whether public officials, especially the police, discharged their duties sufficiently conscientiously. Nevertheless the compilation of statistics on racial incidents was to be welcomed. Mr Lechuga Hevia (Cuba) was unpersuaded by the arguments for not banning racist organizations. He regretted the evidence pointing to the poorer living standards of certain ethnic minorities and their greater difficulties in obtaining employment. Mr Garvalov (Bulgaria) favoured adoption of the CRE's proposal for a specific offence of racial assault, and asked about appeals from industrial tribunals. Mr Diaconu (Romania) regretted the lack of information on measures to permit members of ethnic minorities to preserve their cultural and linguistic identity.

Mrs Zou (China) noted that the UK government had refused to grant to the 2,000 to 3,000 persons of Indian or Pakistani origin in Hong Kong the kind of citizenship that would allow them to move to the UK. The white inhabitants of Gibraltar and the Falkland

Islands had been treated more favourably. Mr Yutzis (Argentina) referred to the government's claim that research findings suggested a diminution of racial prejudice, concluding that it was thrown into doubt by other research showing that only one black person in twelve expressed confidence in the system of justice. Mr Sherifis (Cyprus) asked what the government was doing to increase the proportion of ethnic minority members registered to vote, and wanted more information about educational measures. Mr Ferrero Costa (Peru) expressed appreciation for the constructive attitude of the delegation but regretted that the legislation against racial discrimination should not yet have been extended to Northern Ireland.

The members of the delegation then took it in turns to reply to the questions falling within their spheres of special competence. After some responses to these replies and the withdrawal of the delegation, the Committee passed to the next report (one from Hungary). Later in the session the Committee agreed its 'concluding observations' expressing a collective view for transmittal to the UN General Assembly. These welcomed the plan to move permit the CRE to accept legally binding undertakings as an alternative to a formal investigation under the Race Relations Act. They commended attempts to increase representation of ethnic minorities in the police and the attention paid to collecting data on and investigating racially motivated crimes, deaths in detention and complaints of police brutality (though it went on to express 'serious concern' about possible discrimination in these areas). The Committee stated:

Note is taken of the fact that the 1976 Race Relations Act, by which many of the provisions of the Convention are given effect in domestic law, is subordinate to a wide range of rules and may be superseded by new rules or laws. The legal framework is further weakened by the non-incorporation of the Convention into domestic legislation, the absence of a bill of rights espousing the principle of equality before the law and non-discrimination, and the lack of recourse of individuals to petition an international body such as the Committee. In addition, concern is expressed that the laws relevant to the implementation of the Convention do not appear to be uniformly applied throughout the territory of the United Kingdom; specifically, the Race Relations Act does not extend to Northern Ireland and some provisions of the Criminal Justice Act do not apply to Scotland.

The Committee recommended that the UK reconsider its interpretation of Article 4 of the Convention (none of the many NGOs which commented on the government's report had advocated the banning of such organizations, but this seems not to have impressed the Committee).

Other subjects of concern mentioned were discrimination against Muslims, disproportionate unemployment, the exclusion of black children from schools, and the likely consequences should the Asylum and Immigration Bill be enacted without alteration. A variety of concerns about the situation in Hong Kong were specified. The Committee recommended

that effective programmes be established to care for the health and educational needs of the Irish Traveller community in Great Britain and Northern Ireland [and] that the Government regularly collect and analyse data relating to the academic progress of children, broken down by ethnicity, to develop policies and programmes with a view to eliminating disadvantages based on race.

Conclusion

Comments such as these seem sometimes to influence governments, though often they have little discernible impact. Sometimes delegations conclude that Committee members understand too little about circumstances in their countries. At other times, Committee members are able to persuade delegations that the Convention does require legislation or other action of a kind that would be appropriate to the state in question, and the delegates are able to persuade the responsible ministers to take that action. This process of persuasion may take many years. If the Committee is acting on its own, its influence is limited, but when it presses a view that is in line with well-supported proposals inside the country, there is a much better chance that the state will come into line. Publicity in the mass media can play an important part, but treaty bodies like CERD have difficulty catching media attention. Since they have to treat all states equally, they have to be careful about criticizing one state if they have not criticized all other states which are equally in default. The constraints upon them as monitors of a legal instrument, plus the sometimes delicate political considerations, often oblige them to express their views in a cautious form of language that may need reinterpretation if it is to become newsworthy.

CERD has struck out in new directions since the ending of the Cold War, fashioning for itself a role in the prevention of racial discrimination. It has called for special reports when it has seen reason to fear a deterioration in a situation, and has examined developments in certain states without any report from the government. It has expressed a readiness to call for intervention from the Security Council, something that would have been unthinkable only a few years earlier. Many readers may still be unimpressed, but progress is bound to be slow when so many states deny that the UN has any right to intervene even when there are reliable reports of massive and persistent violations of human rights. The history of conflict in Rwanda demonstrates that the right time for the UN and the OAU to have intervened was in 1993, but other states did not understand the dangers. Nor were the journalists who covered African affairs alert to the possibilities. There is still a major task in educating public opinion, especially since political decisions are so often taken on a calculation of short-term advantage. The lesson that is being so slowly learned about environmental pollution applies also to inter-group relations: a short time-perspective in political affairs means that an unfair burden is passed to future generations.

CHAPTER 9

Collective action

The period following the end of the Cold War has been a time of hope and frustration. The easing of tension between East and West permitted a substantial disarmament and the dismantling or destruction of huge quantities of terrible weapons. Authoritarian regimes have been yielding to democratic forces and some have been replaced by responsible governments. It was a time of opportunity for the great powers to cooperate in tackling the world's problems. For years the UN had been rendered incapable of responding to many crises by vetoes cast in the Security Council. Up to the end of May 1990 there had been 279 such vetoes. Thereafter there was a lull. As demands on the UN multiplied, the Security Council invited the Secretary-General to prepare an assessment which was then published under the title *An Agenda for Peace*.

In it, Mr Boutros Boutros-Ghali defined the processes of preventive diplomacy, peace-making and peace-keeping, and the part that the UN might play in them. He stated:

The foundation-stone of this work is and must remain the State. Respect for its fundamental sovereignty and integrity are crucial to any common international progress. The time of absolute and exclusive sovereignty, however, has passed; its theory was never matched by reality.

The Secretary-General also noted that

fierce new assertions of nationalism and sovereignty spring up, and the cohesion of States is threatened by brutal ethnic, religious, social, cultural or linguistic strife.

Ethnic strife headed his list. If the recent period has been one of frustration, this has been in part because the UN and its member states failed so dismally to respond to the crises presented by the breakup of the former Yugoslavia and the conflicts in Somalia, Rwanda and Burundi.

Nationalist leaders, or would-be leaders, are inclined to represent changes such as those in Serbia, Croatia and Bosnia as caused by the welling up of some previously suppressed national identity. This has been described earlier in this book as a primordialist conception of ethnic consciousness. Earlier chapters have maintained that before accepting any such interpretation the reader should reflect on the language in which such events are described. The words in popular use do not always correspond very closely with what has actually been observed. A practical language has been developed which helps the journalists get on with their task of reporting, but it is far from perfect. Social scientists should be modest in view of the rudimentary state of knowledge in their field, but they have started assembling a theoretical language that should open the way to a more sophisticated understanding of what has been going on.

Humans belong to many groups other than nations and ethnic groups. Their sense of belonging in nations is not a constant, but a variable that goes up and down with variations in circumstance. The internal and the external relations of the national, ethnic or racial group are both important. The key to the internal relations is the extent to which the individual needs to cooperate with other group members to attain his or her ends. External relations are important because opposition from other groups can make internal cooperation the more important, while the form taken by that opposition influences the nature of group consciousness. Chapter 4 discussed the relation between ends and means, but it is time to relate that discussion to the larger social groups and the ways in which they interact.

Morale

When individuals try to attain the same ends, and can agree about the means to be used in seeking them, collective action is possible. Yet there are great variations in the cooperation that results. It was the generals, apparently, who first identified morale as a factor which helped explain why sometimes small armies defeated larger ones. Today, every player or follower of a team sport recognizes the importance of team-spirit to success in competition. Morale appears to have played a part in the rise and fall of civilizations; it can influence the productivity of industries, the examination results of schools, and the recovery rates of patients in hospital wards. Sports teams do better when every member performs to the limit of his or her ability.

This would look like an argument in favour of democracy were it not for the counter-example of Nazi Germany. Hitler and his associates were able to mobilize the German *Volk* to such a degree that they mastered most of Europe while fighting wars to both West and East. The *Volk* was not the same as the citizenry, because Jews, Gypsies and others considered degenerate were excluded from it. Though most of the German people did not join in the persecution and then the genocide of these minorities, they were persuaded to ignore it. Nazism was an astonishing example of what can be achieved by political engineering, and the dangers inherent in it. It showed that a high level of team-spirit can be attained without regard for, and perhaps even at the expense of, minorities.

At the end of the twentieth century there are many countries where state power is used in ways that divide citizens from one another. Military rulers may have known team-spirit in their armies and believe, wrongly, that by adopting military methods they can evoke a similar spirit in the nation. They fail, as communist rule failed, because the speed and complexity of change is too great for central control to be effective. The options recall those described by Sir Henry Maine in 1861 when, in his book *Ancient Law*, he observed that of the great number of societies known to history, only a few had proved progressive. In some the political structures had been too restrictive and they had stagnated. In others the structures had been too loose and the societies had disintegrated. Many Third World countries today are ruled for the benefit of the rulers and national morale is low. Rigid governmental structures hinder economic growth. In countries like Somalia, Liberia, Rwanda and Burundi, the structures have been unable to contain the tensions; the machinery of government has collapsed and international oversight has failed to prevent massive violations of human rights. The tensions can arise from a country's relations with the world outside. For example, the relative ease of cultivating illegal drugs in countries as different as Afghanistan and Colombia, and of selling them for great profit, leads to the formation of criminal gangs and the corruption of the persons expected to prevent drug-trafficking. Governments may have great difficulty exerting control.

In all the continents, governments are faced with new problems. If they are democratic they have to satisfy electors whose expectations have been built up over the years. In Europe the electors expect welfare benefits for elderly people, needy and unemployed people. But the ratio of pensioners to persons of working age has increased while technological changes have reduced the demand for labour. Improved transportation and the mobility of capital have moved production to low-wage countries, so that the new international division of labour has made it more difficult for governments to finance welfare states at the same level as before. Trying to balance internal expectations against the need to respond to external changes, some governments behave as if they were under seige.

The nation-state

The key institution for integrating individual aspirations and energies is now the nation-state. It has not always been so, for in earlier eras empires sprawled across large swathes of the globe. Popes and religious leaders were princes exercising political power. Many ethnic groups were untouched by either, but led independent lives trading with their neighbours, unaffected by the world outside. In the nineteenth century the map of Europe was changed by the rise of nationalism, a new consciousness which assumed that everyone had a nationality (expressed in language and culture but often identified with what people of that period thought to be race). From this assumption the conclusion was drawn that everyone had the right to be governed with others of the same nationality as citizens of a distinctive state. The state became an expression of primary ethnicity. The effect of the twentieth century's two world wars was to divide the world into some 180 states so that almost every bit of land belonged to some state. Formerly colonial territories, sometimes quite tiny ones, had like others to model themselves on the European conception of the nation-state.

As a form of economic organization, the nation-state is more efficient than the empire. The nation-state sweeps every person within its boundaries into a common scheme for cooperation. It leaves only small niches in which minorities can come together and maintain a cultural distinctiveness. When the state is democratic, its institutions have to respond to the votes of the electors, who may be unsympathetic to minority claims. By improving cooperation, the nation-state both generates power and centralizes its exercise in the central government. Some governments use this power to support international measures for the protection of human rights and their observance within the country in question; other governments use their power to try to force the assimilation of ethnic minorities. Local groups within the majority population tend to put their own short-term interests first and often resist the granting of rights to immigrants unless they are sure that this will be to their advantage.

Leading figures in Japan have attributed the economic success and low crime rates of their society to its ethnic homogeneity, contrasting it favourably with the heterogeneity of the crime-ridden United States. There is a powerful argument that it is easier to develop team-spirit among a group of players who can easily identify with one another and who associate as friends when they are not playing together. Does this apply to nations? Sociologists have long contrasted community and association as forms of cooperation. Small communities have many positive features, but when faced with economic competition they cannot adapt as efficiently as business corporations. Nations are conceived as imagined communities, but need to combine the feelings of community with some of the qualities of corporations. Their team-spirit can be fractured by internal differences (especially those between Christianity and Islam, and between black and white), so governments seek to mitigate their effects by political rhetoric. The Canadian government, for example, has attempted to change the way Canadians think of themselves, exhorting them to take pride in Canada's multiculturalism as something distinctive which enables different groups to make complementary contributions to the life of the whole. It is a way of influencing national and ethnic consciousness.

The need to organize and defend a common territory gives rise to a whole series of state institutions: to govern, to regulate an economy tied to a national currency, and to promote cooperation. These institutions maintain national distinctiveness even when nations resemble their neighbours. It is difficult to think of any three states which are closer to each other than Denmark, Norway and Sweden. In international politics they form the core of the Nordic bloc. The peoples of the three feel strong bonds of alliance and at times an identity of interest, and yet in many other circumstances, like sport, they are great rivals, and they tell bitter jokes about one another. Their languages, like their state churches, are similar, but still different. Their children learn to identify with the histories of their own countries. Their economic interests (e.g. in relation to the European Union) are different. Danes, Norwegians and Swedes will remain distinctive peoples as long as present international patterns continue.

Other groups seem set to retain their ethnic or national distinctiveness even though they do not control the states in which they live. In the area in which the French and Dutch cultures meet and sometimes overlap, the state of Belgium was created in 1830. The southern area, now called Walloonia, is French-speaking. In the northern area of Flanders a dialect of Dutch, called Flemish, is spoken, although for centuries the middle class in the north was French-speaking. In the 1920s class tensions in Flanders were expressed in a struggle over language use. Then after 1945 the economic development of Flanders was more rapid so that the Walloons felt left behind. Both groups felt threatened and aggrieved, and some politicians played upon this. Under the constitution of 1994 Belgium became a federal state comprising three ethnic communities (French, Flemish and German-speaking), three territorial and four linguistic regions. The Council of Ministers has to observe the principle of parity and include as many French-speaking as Flemish-speaking members. The three communities have their own governments. At the federal level there is an 'alarm bell' procedure to prevent the adoption of any measures which might seriously affect relations between communities. These arrangements ensure a political equilibrium, but they lock citizens into a structure which maintains their ethnic distinctiveness.

Switzerland is a federation in which citizenship derives from membership in one of the twenty-five cantons or local communities. The cantons have the ultimate responsibility for the relief and welfare of those individuals who are on their registers. They have little incentive to add to their lists the names of migrant workers or their children. Within the same cantons political animosities can run deep. Protestant and Catholic families often keep well apart. There are four national languages – German, French, Italian and Romansch. Two-thirds of the Swiss speak *Schwyzerdütsch*, a dialect which turns them into a minority within the German-speaking world and gives them many of the touchy attitudes of the speakers of minority languages. So nearly everyone in Switzerland feels a member of a minority group. The country carries its commitment to democracy through to the local level. All legislation, whether federal or cantonal, can be altered if citizens demand a referendum. Since the political balance can change at central or local elections Swiss voters are always conscious of their group allegiances. There are also some striking contrasts between Switzerland and Sweden, though they are countries of similar size and high living standards. Whereas Sweden is highly centralized, in Switzerland much of the power is retained at local level. For example, it is only the cantons which keep statistics of crime. There seems to be much less crime in Switzerland, where the informal controls of the local community are much tighter, but the same factors make it a much more conservative country.

Political structures can also operate to reduce ethnic distinctiveness, as when national identification gains importance at the expense of secondary ethnicity. An example is provided by the Swedish-speaking group in western Finland. For some six centuries Finland was ruled by Swedes. Swedish language and culture dominated government, business, education and the courts. Then in 1809 Sweden was forced to cede the territory to Russia, though the country continued to be administered by Swedish-speakers. A few weeks after the Bolshevik revolution of 1917 the Finns declared their independence. Finnish and Swedish were proclaimed national languages and the administration made bilingual. Nevertheless there has been a steady decline in Swedish. According to the census of 1880, 14.3 per cent of the population were Swedish-Finns; by 1920 it was 11.0 per cent and by 1975 6.4 per cent. The higher birth-rate of the Finnish-speakers is partly responsible for this. At present forty-four communes are Swedish-speaking and forty-seven bilingual. Communes are obliged to provide primary schooling in the minority's language wherever there are at least eighteen pupils. In 1978 6.3 per cent of a national sample stated that Swedish was their mother-tongue, but 5.8 per cent gave it as their main language and only 4.8 per cent said that the language was used at their place of work. Though every facility has been given to the maintenance of the Swedish language and culture, its use is declining because ethnic differences are not part of a competitive structure as in Belgium and Quebec. The one locality which differs is that of the Åland Islands in the Gulf of Bothnia between the two states. There Swedish is dominant and the islanders have a special regional citizenship. Only people with this citizenship can acquire land or vote in communal or provincial elections. The islanders have special interests to preserve and, helped by their geographical isolation, they maintain their Swedishness.

Religion

The only rival to the state as an institution able to coordinate the actions of large numbers of people is that of organized religion. Each such religion teaches its adherents to identify with others who share their faith and tells them how to behave towards those who do not. Some, like Judaism and Hinduism, are particularistic: their doctrines and practices are directed towards those who are born into the faith. Others, like Christianity and Islam, are proselytizing religions which seek to spread their faith. Some religious people regard their religious beliefs as personal, as belonging to a realm which should be free of state interference or regulation. It was to secure religious freedom that the earliest settlers sailed to North America, and they have been followed by others who wanted the same freedom. In the United States the organs of government are formally separate from matters of religion. They take no part in deciding who shall speak on behalf of a faith or what demands may be made in its name. Seen from an international standpoint, this is an unusual position for a government to adopt. Elsewhere people of strong religious belief have demanded that their governments act to support and extend the true faith. Several states now proclaim themselves Islamic republics. Others have state churches. Not all states can agree that the right to freedom of religion includes a person's right to change his or her religion.

The suggestion that only organized religion can teach people what their ends should be is contested vigorously by those who maintain only nominal connections with it, or none at all, and whose philosophy may be described as humanist. Their contributions to the human rights movement have often been outstanding, but within states they have not been very successful in recruiting the masses to their outlook. The Indian state was founded in 1947 as a socialist and secular republic with an equal regard for all religions and an insistence that the languages of religion be kept out of the affairs of state. This has been challenged by the rise of the Hindu nationalist Bharatiya Janata Party (BJP), which can itself be seen as a reaction to what has been perceived as Muslim assertiveness. The BJP's demolition of the mosque at Ayodhya in 1992 is seen by some as marking a new phase in Indian politics. Yet organized religion is increasingly challenged from another direction. Over much of the world one of the major movements teaching people what their ends should be is that of mass consumption. The media of mass communication, including advertising, hold out influential images of what is to be desired. Economic growth is driven by the desires for greater personal spending and goods for private and domestic consumption. While this is by no means incompatible with religious faith it gives greater support to materialistic outlooks.

Religion often serves as a basis for secondary ethnicity. As was mentioned in Chapter 4, one feature of the Ottoman empire was the *millet* system whereby the religious leaders of ethnic minorities were held responsible for their communities (an arrangement which survives in modern Israel). Though members of these communities had lived alongside one another in the *millet* system for centuries they retained their distinctiveness.

The power of religion to justify other kinds of differences is well illustrated in Northern Ireland, an area in which the British and Irish states meet and overlap. Catholic and Protestant leaders can agree in condemning terrorist actions. Nothing in either version of Christianity condones them, so in that sense the conflict is not religious. There is a political conflict over the division of resources within the province of Northern Ireland and over the relation of the province to Britain and Ireland. The parties to the conflict are interest groups which are identified by religious institutions. Their members have attended separate Catholic and Protestant schools. Their religious leaders can also agree in condemning secularism. In their view of the world a religious faith must be the foundation of a person's social being. So in Northern Ireland almost everyone is accounted either a Catholic or a Protestant regardless of whether he or she attends church or believes in the tenets of either faith. Everyone is shut into a religious classification which recognizes no half-way house.

The proportion of the white British population who attend church regularly or are more than nominally Christian has fallen dramatically during the twentieth century. The secularizing trend has been strengthened by the weakening of local communities, by the spread of scientific explanation, and by the market economy. In modern industrial society the major forces bringing about cultural change are those which derive from the opportunities for producers to extract profit from providing goods and services which consumers purchase. Other powerful pressures are generated by mass entertainment, popular music, spectator sports and similar activities in which the customer calls the tune. The mass is an aggregate of individuals who share common tastes in varying and changing degrees. Since many of these tastes are shared by people of different religion and different ethnic origin, the pursuit of consumer satisfaction can weaken the bonds of ethnic community.

In teaching believers about what their ends in life should be, organized religion has to take account of changes in social life. If religious functionaries are to offer proper leadership, they have to understand the pressures to which their followers are subject and the nature of the choices they have to make. This has posed particular problems for Muslim communities in Western Europe. Many of them have recruited *imams* from their homelands, or have been offered religious leaders by Muslim institutions in the Middle East which seek to propagate their own interpretations of Islam. Leaders recruited in this way can appeal to only a small minority of the young Muslims who have been born in Europe. Consequently the majority society has an interest in assisting the establishment of seminaries in Europe for the education of minority religious leaders and in seeing that their interpretations of religion do not conflict with the integration of their followers into the non-religious aspects of the life of the national society. Yet the stances which European governments adopt towards the religions of the ethnic majority restrict the positions they can take up with respect to the religions of the ethnic minorities.

Diversity

The ways in which people's ends may change over time is illustrated by migration. Individuals leave one country for another for many reasons. Often they hope to return soon but instead they remain in the country of immigration. There they are subject to processes of change as one generation succeeds the next. Studies in the United States of the settlement of immigrants from Europe have pointed to differences in the outlooks of the first three generations. The experience of the first generation includes special kinds of excitement and pain. On the one hand is the excitement of new opportunities that often stimulate members of the first generation to work particularly hard to provide security for themselves and their families. The pain arises because they have learned in their countries of origin values which are rejected in their new country. This is particularly relevant to relations between parents and children. The immigrants have frequently come from societies in which great respect is shown to elderly relatives, and they expect similar respect as they in turn grow older. Their children, however, have to make their way with their peers in the new society and they often spurn their parents' exhortations as old-fashioned and irrelevant. So in many immigrant communities there is a struggle, as parents seek to maintain central elements of their homeland culture and to resist what they see as the corrupting influence of the majority culture.

To judge from the American studies, the second generation is usually fairly successful in going its own way and forcing the parents to recognize that the customs of the new country must prevail. For this generation the school and the peer group have set the standards as to how a good American should behave. This must account for the tremendous pressure to conform to peer group expectations which all children still experience in United States schools. The pain of the second generation lies in the feeling of guilt that they have been too harsh in reacting against their parents' ideas. In the third generation this burden is lifted and young people often wish to return to their 'roots', finding out about their grandparents' origins and sometimes identifying with their ethnicity, secure that they are not the less American for doing so. This sequence led Marcus Lee Hansen, a historian of Swedish settlement in North America, to formulate what has been called 'Hansen's law': 'What the son wishes to forget, the grandson wishes to remember'. This proposition embodies a valuable insight, but it cannot be regarded as valid for all minorities. In some cities of the north-east of the United States, political parties have sought to ensure that their slate of candidates always included one name identifiable with each of the locally numerous minorities, so there might be one Irish, one Italian and one Jewish name. When ethnicity was built into the political structure in this way, and when relatively cheap air flights provided a means whereby groups could keep in touch with their communities of origin, there was less reason for the second generation to react against their parents' ideas.

The children of Irish and Italian settlers in the United States have often married fellow Catholics of a different ethnic parentage. An increasing proportion of young Jewish people have married Gentiles and ceased to observe the Jewish religion. So in successive generations individuals have had ancestors of varied ethnicity and could identify themselves with one or more ethnic groups, or with none at all. Distinctive ethnic communities have usually dissolved by the third generation. This experience may contain some lessons for those members of New Commonwealth minorities in Britain who hope that their cultural distinctiveness can be preserved. The evidence suggests that a group can maintain cultural distinctiveness for more than three generations when for religious reasons it follows a self-segregating way of life based upon agricultural production. The notable examples are the Amish communities of Pennsylvania and some similar groups in other parts of North America. About one in four of their children eventually leave these communities but, since their birth-rate is high, they have been expanding in population. Their way of life is based upon a rejection of modern technology, of schooling beyond the eighth grade (about 14 years) and of the materialistic values of an industrial culture. Their distinctive costume means that if they take a horse and buggy to drive to a neighbouring town, they stand out as very different from the majority. Many features combine to reinforce the division between them and others. Another group which has maintained its distinctiveness for an even longer period is that of the Gypsies, or Roma. Though they have distinctive beliefs about sources of pollution, their culture is not so very different from that of non-Gypsies, except (in Western Europe) for their moving from place to place; this restricts their children's schooling, and because of circumstances in which it is done, attracts the hostility of the non-Gypsies. That hostility is not 100-per-cent unwelcome to Gypsy parents because it helps bind their children to the group's way of life and discourages them from seeking opportunities in the wider society. In the West they live on the fringes of industrial society, collecting scrap metal, laying tarmac and undertaking seasonal work like berry-picking.

Hitherto only Jews have sustained an ethnic distinctiveness while living in the heart of such societies. Their success is attributable in part to a religion which tells them that they are the chosen people, and in part to a distinctive language which was for long a purely religious language but has now become a state language. For nearly two thousand years Jews were a people without a homeland, who, if they were to follow the dictates of their religion, had to do so as a minority wherever they found themselves. The foundation of the state of Israel in 1948 changed that. In every generation Jewish communities have lost some of their members who have ceased to identify themselves as Jews. In the United States and in Western

Europe those who wish to identify as Jews may now feel under more pressure to move to Israel to feel fully Jewish, and in such circumstances their identity will acquire a more strongly national character. It was estimated that in 1990 52 per cent of Jewish males in the United States were marrying non-Jewish females; under Jewish law their children would not count as Jews. In 1996 it was calculated that 44 per cent of Jewish men in Britain under the age of 40 were married to or were living with non-Jewish partners. The Director of the Institute of Jewish Affairs was reported as saying that British Jews were becoming more of an ethnic as opposed to a religious community. To judge from the views of some young British Hindus, Sikhs and Muslims described in the study quoted in Chapter 8, these other groups are moving in the same direction.

A review of the history of minorities therefore suggests that no ethnic group can maintain its cultural distinctiveness for more than three generations unless it has several distinctive characteristics, e.g.

- it controls its own territory
- it enjoys rights protected by the state's constitution
- it is so large that it can prevent any other group enforcing upon it an unacceptable policy
- its members are content not to claim all the rights of citizenship in the state in which they live
- its members are committed to a distinctive religion, preferably one which requires worship in a language peculiar to the group.

This does not mean, however, that it may not be desirable to assist minorities to retain their cultures by providing financial assistance to community enterprises, or by arranging extra tuition in minority languages. Multicultural policies in education can help all pupils better appreciate that peoples in other cultures see international affairs from a different standpoint. They can ease the pressures upon ethnic minority children to conform to majority expectations. Such policies can be justified by short-term considerations and do not depend upon any particular assumptions about long-term change.

Conclusion

This book opened with a question: why was the fall of the Berlin wall followed by a series of ethnic conflicts in the East but not in the West? My answer has been that people choose the means appropriate to the ends they seek. For all people in certain circumstances (like national defence), it is necessary to combine with others to pursue their ends. There are ends which may be pursued collectively in some societies and by individual action in others. In the people's democracies of Eastern Europe the public had been accustomed to collective action and citizens had little in the way of private property or private interests. Their voices at the end of the 1980s suggested that they had changed the priorities they attached to some of their ends and had changed their views about the best ways to pursue them. They had to undergo a peaceful revolution, but it has been proving almost as painful as a bloody one because the task of creating the requisite new institutions is so difficult. In the resulting popular discontent of the 1990s, a would-be leader could most easily build up a following by appealing to nationalist sentiment.

In the West, as was said in Chapter 1, the citizens had far more in the way of private property and interests. Many had to repay mortgages on the houses they had purchased, loans on the cars they were using, to save for their family holidays, and so on. Most of the opposition to Western governments was the opposition of political parties who wanted office to make relatively small changes to the political system. There was less pressure for collective action in any form and therefore less inclination to exploit ethnic consciousness in the service of political campaigns. That could change.

Practically all the states of the world are now faced with some sort of ethnic problem, and in most cases there is no obvious solution. There are some minorities whose members are discontented with the policies of the state within which they have to live and would like to see a revision of state boundaries. Such changes are now virtually impossible except in the aftermath of a war, so other means have to be found for addressing desires for ethnically homogeneous political units. In some Western states, like France, there are now political parties which can attract many votes from electors who would like certain immigrant minorities to be repatriated to the countries from which they originate. The possibilities for implementing any such action without breaching international law are very restricted. So most states are obliged to be multi-ethnic. If they are to integrate all groups within the life of the nation they are obliged to combat discrimination on grounds of race and national or ethnic origin.

The ethnic problems of the future will, of course, be political, expressed as contests between states or groups within states, but the prime causes may well be the pressures generated by inequality. As has been noted, many of the diplomats at the UN in 1965 who proposed the adoption of the International Convention on the Elimination of All Forms of Racial Discrimination maintained that colonialism was the chief cause of such discrimination. It would have been more accurate to blame it on unequal development. When some regions of the world were developing rapidly and others were stationary, it was inevitable that individuals and institutions from the former would establish themselves in the latter and that the differences in the resources at their command would create relations of unequal power. This happened irrespective of the political structures within which contact took place. When persons from economically developed and undeveloped societies were not of the same skin colour, physical differences were bound to be taken as signs of status differences. Such equations are the more potent because differences of colour and economic advantage are both transmitted from one generation to the next. These processes which operated in the Third World, in Soviet Central Asia and in Latin America will be just as relevant to developments in West European societies in the twenty-first century.

In an illuminating discussion, the French sociologist Michel Wieviorka (1994a) has maintained that in Western Europe during the 1950s and 1960s, nation and state achieved an unprecedently high level of integration. This was based on industrial production, particularly in manufacturing, with a large proletariat and a political life structured round the opposition between capital and labour. The welfare state was a vehicle for a redistribution of resources. In the 1970s this model started to break down because of changes in production. The opposition between the forces of organized labour and the employers no longer provided an adequate principle for political organization. Whereas industrial society had offered everyone a dominant or inferior position in society, post-industrial society separated two or three sections with different relations to employment, health care, education and participation in social life. The welfare state had to contract. New social movements centring on opposition to nuclear weapons, women's rights and concern for the environment reoriented political debate. These changes then affected popular attitudes towards immigration and immigrants, evoking increases in racism and xenophobia. The dislocation of the European integration model and the decomposition of national societies signalled a crisis of modernity. Racism was an expression of this crisis.

To this interpretation of recent history can be added the prediction that the increased competition from the newly industrializing societies of the Pacific has not yet reached its peak. Competition, beneficial as it may be to production, generates personal and social stress. In organizing to meet it, Western societies have to increase the incentives they offer for restructuring. Those who succeed benefit to an extent that seems disproportionate to the less successful. The low morale of the socially excluded increases the attractions to them of extremist political movements.

Social inequalities within and between countries will acquire an ethnic or racial dimension. As national boundaries are weakened by the mass media, by increased trade, and by the growth of consumer markets, disparities will be more noticeable. Over the period 1990 to 2025 the proportion of the world's population resident in the industrialized countries is set to fall from 22.8 to 15.9 per cent. As can be seen from Table 9.1, whites are becoming a smaller proportion of the world's population and their relative wealth will become even more noticeable. Other disparities, within as well as between continents, are likely to grow and to stimulate the kinds of group consciousness that are called ethnic and racial. This will make

Table 9.1 **World population: estimated and projected population size by region, 1950–2025**

	1950	1970	1990	2000	2025
Total (billion)	2.516	3.698	5.292	6.261	8.504
Percentages					
Africa	8.8	9.8	12.1	13.8	18.8
North America	6.6	6.1	5.2	4.7	3.9
Latin America	6.6	7.7	8.5	8.6	8.9
Asia	54.7	56.8	58.8	59.3	57.8
Europe	15.6	12.4	9.4	8.1	6.1
Oceania	0.5	0.5	0.5	0.5	0.4
USSR/CIS	7.2	6.6	5.5	4.9	4.1

Source: UN World Population Prospects, 1990 (New York 1991)

it the more important to comprehend the nature and causes of such forms of consciousness.

Popular discussions in this field often look for an explanation in what the commentators believe to be the nature of ethnicity or of race as a social grouping. This book has stated a case for concentrating instead upon what is common to the formation and continuation of groups. It has not sought to offer a full demonstration of how collective action can result in ethnic and racial consciousness, but simply to indicate the possibilities by bringing together in a common framework a wide range of observations. These have been chosen to illustrate the potential of a relatively new theoretical approach that is of interest to research workers in all the social sciences. Its aspiration can be illustrated by a further claim. One of the sources of recent frustration in international politics has been the difficulty of getting different states, either in the UN or in Europe (where it should be easier) to come together in collective action to address shared problems. The theoretical approach from which this book has drawn aspires not only to account for the formation of groups within societies but also to explain why it is difficult for states to cooperate.

1 Introduction

Culturally diverse societies are sometimes described as polyethnic, on the grounds that since ethnic is a word of Greek origin it should be combined with the Greek form 'poly' rather than the Latin 'multi'. Since the name 'sociology' is a mixture of Latin and Greek roots, its practitioners are not well placed to argue against the use of 'multi-ethnic', which seems to be the more used.

2 Naming groups

A reading of Chapter 2 should lead you to reflect upon the circumstances in which you are most and least conscious of group differences, and what it is that triggers off your awareness. It should also lead you to notice what words the people around you use to designate those they assign to other groups. Is there any difference between older and younger generations? Is there any difference between the words used in your locality and those employed in television programmes? Are people of other groups identified by their colour, their nationality, or the locality in which they reside?

You should be able to say how you would set about drafting a question concerning ethnic and racial identification for use in a census; or for use in a form for monitoring appointments to see if the proportion of persons in the various categories appointed to particular kinds of jobs corresponds to their proportion in the wider society. A good discussion is to be found in *Ethnic and Racial Questions in the Census* (HC 33) plus the two volumes of evidence. This is a report to the Parliament of the House of Commons Home Affairs Committee, Subcommittee on Race Relations and Immigration, for the session 1982–3.

A reading of Chapter 2 should also have led you to conclude that some apparent disagreements about group relations derive from a failure to define the terms that are being used. Since these relations are complex they require a complex vocabulary if they are to be properly described. One way of reducing potential disagreements is to get maximum clarity about the reasons for raising a topic. The *Race Relations Act 1976* (in section 43) requires the Commission for Racial Equality 'to promote ... good relations between persons of different racial groups'. How can 'better' relations be defined? What implications would 'improvement' have for the nature of the groups? These questions can give rise to lengthy discussion without coming to any definite conclusion, yet everyone might agree upon what in practice would constitute an improvement to a particular situation.

It is possible that a sociologist's view will differ from the views of people for whom inter-racial contacts are a matter of daily experience. A Dutch anthropologist who lived in Southall for over seven years remarks, in the course of a somewhat technical article (Baumann 1995: 738), that when he uses the words 'ethnic' and 'community' they should be placed in inverted commas to represent notions he quotes from others, including people in the locality. He adds:

My work in Southall has left me quite unconvinced of their analytical usefulness. What is interesting about urban 'ethnicity', and in particular its discursive devices of 'ethnic' and 'community', is its capacity to hide the very multiplicity of linguistic, regional, national and other cultural cleavages that cut across each other. Any of these cross-cutting cleavages, and several others such as religion and caste, can take on the significance of 'ethnic' or 'community' boundaries, depending on context.

You should be able to appreciate the tension between a social scientist's desire for linguistic precision and the wish to communicate to a wider readership in terms which will be understood. It is also worthwhile pausing over the way in which conflict may be differentiated from other forms of struggle, the distinction between constructive and destructive conflict, and the idea of positive-sum, negative-sum and zero-sum games; game theory is now being used in all the social sciences.

3 Accounting for differences

Chapter 2 drew attention to the problems of classifying people in everyday life and the names given to the resulting categories. Chapter 3 has taken one of those words and shown how its meaning has changed and diversified over the past 400 years. The best way to understand the many sense of the word 'race' is to learn how and why it has been used in new ways. For Britain, a useful book is Walvin (1971) which reprints some documents that are difficult to locate in their original form. There is widespread misunderstanding about the influence of the slave trade upon British ideas of race; by far the best treatment of this subject is to be found in Barker (1978), but it is a dense and detailed study that deserves to be read slowly. For the nineteenth century, Lorimer (1978) can be recommended, but this, too, is a book based on a doctoral thesis and is not an introductory work.

You should understand the historical contexts within which ideas about race took shape, while appreciating that there was an independent growth in scientific knowledge about the causes of phenotypical variation. There were three main phases. In the eighteenth century the dominant view was that all humans were descended from Adam and Eve; environmental differences were thought to account for the appearance of racial differences. The second phase, in which racial differences were considered permanent, culminated in the doctrine of racial typology. The third phase, inaugurated by Darwin, has led to the creation of genetics and to a revolution in the understanding of biology. Banton and Harwood (1975) offer an elementary account both of the history and of contemporary scientific knowledge concerning differences in culture, behaviour and measured intelligence. For blood groups, Mourant (1983) is useful, but you may prefer to look for an introductory account in a textbook of human biology.

The reader will doubtless reflect upon the significance of new words. Were there racial relations in the period before there was a word 'race'? What difference might the availability of the word have made to interpersonal relations? Was 'race' actually used, or did people designate groups by colour, country of origin or religion? Unfortunately, the historical evidence is scanty. The development of racial consciousness depends upon there being words to evoke and mould that consciousness. Words that are introduced by scholars and scientists have to be popularized if they are to affect that consciousness. This is also true of the word 'racism'. You should be able to differentiate the use of this word in any sociological context in which it is given a technical meaning, from its meaning in popular argument. Sometimes 'racism' is used as a concept, and sometimes as an epithet to disparage and stigmatize something or someone. The art and language of persuasive speaking is called rhetoric, and there is a rhetoric of racial relations in which people use those words which best enable them to project their interpretations. This rhetoric takes different forms depending upon the viewpoint advanced, but a common feature is that of concealing the assumptions which underlie the words chosen. Consider again the different definitions in the UN debate about Zionism. Whether Zionism is or is not a form of racism depends upon the definition of the key terms. On occasion racism has been defined in such a way that only white people can display it. One of sociology's contributions is to clarify the vocabulary of discussion about the various kinds of social relations. In this it resembles John Locke's conception of the philosopher as an 'underlabourer' who clears the ground and brings the tools for the craftsman who has to do the job.

Chapter 3 maintained that while the words 'racism' and 'anti-semitism' are much used in the practical language of everyday life, the emergent theoretical language of social science does better without them. The same argument applies to the words 'nation' and 'nationalism'. The sense of belonging to a nation is important to many individuals but does not have a consistent meaning. A political scientist (Gallagher 1995) asked 'How many nations are there in Ireland?' Whether the Unionists in Northern Ireland regard themselves as members of a British nation, and whether they are so regarded either by mainland Britons or by other groups in Ireland, are matters of political significance. Since they influence the parties' conceptions of their inter-relations, they also influence the prospects for reducing group consciousness. However, as was asserted at the end of Chapter 2, social scientists are not obliged to take over the perceptions of the parties to a conflict. They should examine the circumstances in which a person perceives someone else as a fellow group-member and the extent of the sacrifice he or she is willing to make on account of this identification. Choosing the best name for the identification should come later. Discussions about the nature of nationalism soon pass the point of diminishing returns and become disputes about the meaning which the word has for one set of people in a particular time when using a particular language.

4 Groups and individuals

Chapter 3 introduced the idea of variation. This one explains the difference between continuous and discontinuous variation. When you read Chapters 2 and 3 did you assume that racial variation was discontinuous? Does your understanding of continuous variation cause you to modify any ideas you may have held about race? Can you use it to explain the frequency of blood group B in Europe?

For further information on the different kinds of classifications that developed in North, Central and South America, see Banton (1983: 15-31). A helpful account of the way in which the concept of equilibrium can be used in sociology is to be found in Homans (1950: 281-312).

The distortion of the concept of assimilation has given it a bad name, so that those who are concerned to describe a goal for social policy more frequently write of integration as 'a process by which diverse elements are combined into a unity while retaining their basic identity', or of pluralism as one which 'aims at uniting different ethnic groups in a relation of mutual interdependence'. These are quotations from a UN special study in 1971 which also stated 'based on the idea of the superiority of the dominant culture, assimilation aims at the achievement of homogeneity within the State by ensuring that groups discard their cultures in favour of the dominant culture'. The rhetorical component in these statements should be obvious. In this book, assimilation is used to mean 'becoming similar' without any assumption of superiority and without equating it with absorption. It is also worth noting that UN bodies have been trying since 1950 to agree upon a definition of 'minority', so far without success. The difficulty is that minorities are assumed to be populations which deserve special treatment from the state, whereas governments, for political reasons, do not wish to acknowledge any special obligations to them. The simplest solution is to use the word in a numerical sense and regard any set of persons who are less than half the population as a minority. This can then be qualified by saying whether it is a political or a religious or a linguistic minority, etc.

After studying Chapter 4 you should have an understanding of group consciousness as something that is manifested by individuals because they are members of groups and subject to group influences. One of sociology's major problems is to account for the interaction between the individual and society. You should now be able to show how group consciousness is a product of that interaction. Individual change (as by the learning of a new language or the loss of an old one) is usually the result of a series of small decisions, but they are made in a social context. Group changes (like those which occur when the members of one group try to establish a new inter-group equilibrium) are possible only because of pressure from individuals. If one group fails to initiate change, or loses ground because the other succeeds, that shows how the social structure restricts the alternatives available to individuals.

5 Peoples and states

The writer who pioneered the analysis of the processes discussed in Chapter 5 was Leo Kuper. Writing at times in collaboration with M.G. Smith, he propounded a conception of the plural society as one in which political relations influence relations to the means of production more than any influence in the opposite direction (for a summary, see pp. 179–80). Kuper applied this to the analysis of revolutions in Zanzibar, Rwanda, Burundi and Algeria, sometimes drawing parallels with South Africa (Kuper 1977). He then went on to the analysis of the processes which lead to and make possible genocide (Kuper 1982) and cast a spotlight on the relative ineffectiveness of the United Nations and other international organizations in preventing abuses by member states (Kuper 1985). Students of racial relations have been slow to see the significance for their studies of international organizations and the development of international law. A useful digest of Kuper's later work is available in his 1985 report (published by the Minority Rights Group, 379 Brixton Road, London SW9 7DE). While much has been written recently about Rwanda and Burundi, a convenient summary regarding Burundi is to be found in another publication from the same organization, Reyntjens (1995). Also see Lemarchand (1983).

Chapter 5 has given further examples of the ways in which large-scale social processes (in particular the material superiority of European states associated with their adoption of a capitalist economy) can structure the kinds of relations possible between people assigned to different racial groups. It has shown that a desire for political dominance can transform the relations between groups of people of the same colour into bitter and bloody conflict. It should stimulate you to think what relation, if any, there has been between racial ideology and imperialism. How might you have set about determining the racial consciousness of whites in Zimbabwe prior to its independence? How might it have differed from Nigeria, where whites were so much smaller a minority? It is important to consider what kind of information is needed to answer questions like these before looking to see if that information is available, or what is the next best method of approach. Sometimes novels and autobiographies cast more light on everyday relations than any academic studies. Remember, too, that imperial rule often entailed the introduction of people of a third racial group – Indians in Africa, Chinese in Malaysia, Indians in Fiji, for example – and that there were individuals who did not fit neatly in any particular category.

Such questions can be linked with the discussion of constitutional engineering at the end of Chapter 5. It is constitutions which prescribe who may vote, what the legislature may do (whether, for example, it may pass laws that prevent an immigrant minority purchasing land, as in Fiji). Constitutions regulate citizenship (in independent Sierra Leone, for example, citizenship was restricted 'to persons of Negro African descent'). The constitution and the law determine the kinds of relations which people from different groups may enter. They may prevent conflict and they may provoke it. They attempt to secure an equilibrium.

6 Increasing group consciousness

Readers should have no difficulty locating histories of the United States and South Africa to fill out what is written here. Encyclopedia articles can also be helpful. For chapter-length summaries which concentrate upon the aspects most relevant to racial relations, and indicate the sources used here, refer to Banton (1983: 209-84). After reading Chapter 6 you should be in a position to draw up a balance sheet with respect to the first three steps for maintaining a caste-like structure (classification, segregation, sanctions) to show the antici-pated benefits that led to their adoption and the costs that were entailed. For the proposition that when people compete as individuals this dissolves racial boundaries, whereas when they compete as groups this reinforces them, see pp. 180–1. The inter-generational transmission of inequality is discussed in many sociology textbooks. The question to consider is how ethnic and racial group relations are affected by social patterns which structure the whole society.

After studying Chapter 6 you should be able to explain why the steps taken by the superordinate racial group increase racial consciousness in the subordinated group. The people in the B group feel deprived relative to those in the P group once they come to appreciate that the differences are not facts of nature but the outcome of social (including political and economic) relations. Religion may be important to this awakening if it stresses the moral equality possible in an alternative kind of society. Read the Old Testament book of *Daniel* 11: 11–15, and think how these verses might have appeared to African-Americans before the Civil War between North and South.

For a summary review of the trends resulting in ethnic conflict Brogan (1989) may be of help; it draws substantially on reports of the Minority Rights Group. With respect to Africa, Davidson (1992) has much to recommend it; his blind spots regarding Rwanda are noted in Pottier (1996).

7 Decreasing group consciousness

Publications about developments in the countries discussed in Chapter 7 come thick and fast. For up-to-date information, a useful source is *Keesings Contemporary Archives*, which summarizes press reports.

On the USA, Massey and Denton (1993: chapters 1–2 and 6–8) are warmly recommended as an account of the increase in residential segregation and its consequences.

There may be well be major changes in South Africa, but they will not detract from the value of Nelson Mandela's (1994) autobiography *Long Walk to Freedom* which could serve anyone as an introduction to the developments in that country.

It is far from easy to compare the position of ethnic minorities in the various countries of Western Europe systematically, but one important perspective is that from migrant labour, on which see Cohen (1987).

8 International oversight

For a general introduction to human rights law, Sieghart (1986) can be recommended with confidence. For a more substantial account of UN action against racial discrimination, see Banton (1996). An account of the development of British policy concerning the immigration and settlement of immigrants from the New Commonwealth can be found in Banton (1985); alternative views can be found in Solomos (1989) and Miles and Phizacklea (1984).

The first of the decennial censuses of England and Wales to include a question on the racial or ethnic origins of residents was that of 1991. Useful information can be derived from sample surveys like the *Labour Force Survey* and the *National Dwelling and Household Survey*. In the former, subjects are given a card and asked 'To which of the groups on the card do you consider that you belong?'; the question is repeated for other members of the household. Statistics deriving from such studies are brought up-to-date in government publications like *Key Data, Social Trends* and *Population Trends*. Periodic summaries are published in *The Runneymede Bulletin* (Runneymede Trust, 133 Aldersgate Street, London EC1A 4JA).

There is much popular misunderstanding of the meaning of the term 'racial discrimination'. Individuals who make a long series of decisions about people may sincerely believe that they have treated everyone equally regardless of race, ethnic or national origin, sex, etc. Only by systematically collecting information on these decisions is it possible to ascertain, after the event, whether persons belonging in one category have been treated more or less favourably than others. The difference may be one of only a few percentage points, and it can be established only after allowance has been made for the influence of other possible variables. For example, as from 1996, the processing of cases in the criminal justice system of England and Wales is being subjected to ethnic monitoring. The ethnic origin of persons arrested is recorded, and then this is to be tracked through the sequence of granting or withholding bail, decisions as to trial, verdicts and sentences. It will then be possible to identify discrepancies at any stage after allowing for the seriousness of the charge, the accused person's record of previous offences, and so on.

An alternative measure of possible discrimination is the experimental procedure of situation testing, exemplified in Daniel (1968). This study seems to have been the first of its kind carried out anywhere in the world (see pp. 135–6). It has been followed by similar studies carried out from the same institute (earlier known as Political and Economic Planning, now the Policy Studies Institute). The second was Smith (1977), the third in Brown (1984) and the fourth is Berthoud and Modood (1996). There have been other studies of discrimination in the recruitment to jobs, the allocation of council houses, the price paid for housing in the private sector, the operation of housing agencies, etc., using situation-testing, correspondence-testing or the statistical analysis of outcomes. Some results are summarized in Banton (1994), which also offers an introductory discussion of the concept of discrimination in relation to national and international law.

Recently the International Labour Organization has embarked upon a research programme which attempts to compare racial and ethnic discrimination in access to employment in a variety of countries. One report in this series is that of Bendick (1996) concerning the USA. It summarizes findings which indicate that when equally well-qualified black and white applicants applied for the same kinds of posts, in 19.4 per cent of cases the black applicant was rejected but the white applicant was offered a post. When Hispanic and white applicants applied for the same kinds of posts, the Hispanic candidates experienced a 33.2 per cent net rate of discrimination. When both whites and blacks were offered jobs, white applicants were sometimes 'steered' towards posts with higher wage rates and blacks towards ones with lower rates. For example, applying for a position in automobile sales, a black tester was advised to start as a porter/car-washer, whereas his white testing partner, who arrived shortly afterwards, presenting identical credentials, was immediately interviewed for the sales position that had been advertised. This study recorded an average differential of 30 per cent in the wages offered to white and black applicants. Applicants were treated with equal courtesy, which

reflects the behaviour of employers who, although they know ahead of time that they would never hire a minority candidate, feel forced by social pressure or potential legal penalties to 'go through the motions' of interviewing minority applicants.

In a US study using correspondence testing, applications were submitted by post from dummy applicants. One of the pair could be identified as Hispanic but had higher qualifications (e.g. a typing speed of 60 words per minute instead of 45 words per minute). In 12.4 per cent of cases the employer pursued the application from the white applicant despite the weaker qualification. The test showed that discrimination might have occurred in 61.6 per cent of cases. Since it is sometimes suggested that racial or ethnic consciousness leads minority members to overestimate the incidence of discrimination, it is of some importance to note that one conclusion of empirical testing is that they underestimate it.

For current information on racial and ethnic discrimination in Britain the annual reports of the Commission for Racial Equality contain summaries of cases brought under the 1976 Act. For information on some of the main ethnic minorities in Britain of South Asian origin, Ballard (1994) can be recommended. The annual volume *British Social Attitudes* prepared and published by Social and Community Planning Research periodically includes special studies on racial and ethnic attitudes (e.g. Young 1992: 181–7). On the particular question of pluralistic ignorance a convenient starting point is Banton (1986), while Tizard and Phoenix (1993) offers an interesting account of the views of young people of mixed parentage.

9 Collective action

By now you will be aware both of the importance of group consciousness and of the difficulty of studying it systematically. The ethnic and/or racial component can never be abstracted completely from other features of a person's outlook. One way to approach the problem is through cross-identification. A class of pupils in a London school could be asked to imagine that they are watching a boxing match between a white boxer from Glasgow and a black boxer from London. How many of the pupils would identify with the boxer from Glasgow because he is white? Using this sort of technique it is possible to vary identities and situations in order to test the strength of one kind of identification compared to other kinds.

You should also by now be alert to elements of majority–minority relations that are common to several countries, and to some of the contrasts. For the comparison of Belgium, Switzerland and Finland, see Palley *et al.* (1986), and for Northern Ireland, O'Duffy (1993). Marshall Clinard's (1978) *Cities with Little Crime* brings out in a stimulating way the contrasts between Sweden and Switzerland in respect of general crime. A fuller discussion of the Amish, Gypsies and Jews as resisting assimilation is in Banton (1983: 153–64). A film entitled *Witness!* gives an impression of life inside an Amish community. How the Japanese have prevented their minorities assimilating can be learned from De Vos and Wetherall (1983). Common features in the social psychology of minorities are brought out in Tajfel (1978).

The pressures that bear upon second and third generation members of ethnic and racial minorities in Britain differ from the pressures which, in the United States, affected the immigrants from Europe and led to the formulation of Hansen's law (which is critically reviewed in Lyman 1994: 105–47). You should be able to work out the main differences. For an entertaining novel which shows how West Indian men recently arrived in London could find their new opportunities exciting and pleasurable, see Selvon (1956). Discussion of the appropriate policies for majority–minority relations in Britain usually turn upon not only measures to reduce discrimination and promote equality, but also the extent to which minorities should be recognized as distinct groups requiring their own representation. Chapter 9 has cast doubt upon the chances of such groups maintaining their distinctiveness for more than three generations. You should now be able to discuss the issues in terms of consciousness, structure and process; the variables of territory, constitutional rights and relative size are structural features; the commitment of minority members to their own groups and their adoption or rejection of the majority's values can be discussed in terms of process, since they change more rapidly than the structural features. You should understand relations in contemporary Britain the better for having formed a view of the long-term possibilities.

Further reading on sociological theories

All writing on the subject of ethnic and racial consciousness is shot
through with assumptions of a theoretical character. Because there is
so much loose generalization about sociological theory in this field,
it can be salutary to try to enumerate the number of theories, for,
after all, that number must be finite. It should also be possible (and
it is certainly instructive) to formulate them as sets of propositions.
In an earlier work (Banton 1983) I identified eight.

The first was the Typological Theory, a pre-Darwinian theory
which greatly influenced popular thought in Europe and North
America and which underlay Nazi ideology. This theory held that:

1   Variations in the constitution and behaviour of individuals are
    the expression of differences between underlying types of a
    relatively permanent kind, each one of which is suited to a
    particular continent or zoological province.
2   Social categories in the long run reflect and are aligned with the
    natural categories which produce them.
3   Individuals belonging to a particular racial type display an
    innate antagonism towards individuals belonging to other types,
    the degree of antagonism depending upon the relationship
    between the two types.

The Typological Theory has sometimes been called 'scientific
racism', but that description can equally well be applied to the post-
Darwinian theory which represented racial prejudice as the product
of natural selection, and which can therefore be called the Selection-
ist Theory. It holds that:

1   Evolution may be assisted if interbreeding populations are kept
    separate so that they can develop their special capacities (as in
    animal breeding).
2   Racial prejudice serves this function and in so doing reinforces
    racial categories in social life.
3   Therefore racial categories are determined by evolutionary
    processes of inheritance and selection.

These were biological theories, the first maintaining that pure races
had existed in the past, the second that they would be created in the
future. The first truly sociological theory was the Ecological Theory
of the 1920s inspired by Robert E. Park, which held that:

1   Migration brings together, in unequal relations, people who are
    phenotypically distinct.
2   In relations of competition, individuals become conscious of the
    features by which their statuses are differentiated.
3   People of superior status are unwilling to compete on equal
    terms with those of inferior status; they represent the latter as
    belonging to naturally distinct categories and as therefore suited
    to a different place in the division of labour.

4 Prejudice is an expression of the group consciousness of the privileged people; it protects their interests and reinforces the structure of categories.

This was followed by the Freudian Theory, which can also be expressed in four propositions:

1 Social life causes a build-up of frustration in the individual's psychological make-up.
2 The frustration can be eased by being released as aggression.
3 (a) Aggression is more easily released by displacement upon suitable targets.
   (b) For white peoples, blackness is associated with repressed feelings and desires.
   (c) The more defenceless a minority, the more suitable it is as a target.
4 Whenever direct aggression is released it is accompanied by displaced aggression, adding an irrational element to the rational attack.

Chronologically, the Freudian Theory was followed by the approach which became known as structural-functionalism. It represented societies as founded upon the sharing of common ultimate ends, and individuals as using available means to try to attain their ends, but since each society was unique there was no prospect of a general theory. The clearest alternative approach at the time was one deriving from Marxism which also does not lend itself to generalization across societies, but from which can be derived something that may reasonably be called the Class Theory of Racial and Ethnic Relations. This then states:

1 As European capitalism expanded into territories where natural resources were abundant, there were advantages in securing a source of labour power which, being distinctive, could easily be kept in a servile state.
2 Within this unequal relationship beliefs justifying the inequality were developed. These have been built into the structure of capitalist societies, dividing white workers from black.
3 Racial categories exist in the social life of capitalist societies because (a) they serve the interests of the ruling classes, and (b) the contradictions in these societies have not yet reached the point at which the true nature of the social system is apparent to the workers.

Two later theories built upon the class theory. The first was what Leo Kuper would have called a Theory of Racial Relations in Plural Societies, running as follows:

1 Societies composed of status groups or estates that are phenotypically distinguished, have different positions in the economic order, and are differentially incorporated into the political

structure, are to be called plural societies and differentiated from class societies. In plural societies political relations influence relations to the means of production more than any influence in the reverse direction.

2   When conflicts develop in plural societies they follow the lines of racial cleavage more closely than those of class.

3   Racial categories in plural societies are historically conditioned; they are shaped by inter-group competition and conflict.

The second was the Split Labour Market Theory developed by Edna Bonacich:

1   Some labour markets are split along ethnic lines, so that higher-paid groups of workers are distinguished from cheaper labour by their ethnic characteristics (in which racial features may be included).

2   The three key classes have different interests:
(a) Members of the business class want as cheap and docile a labour force as possible in order to compete with other businesses.
(b) Members of the higher-paid labour class are threatened by the introduction of cheaper labour.
(c) The very weakness of the class of cheaper labour makes it threatening to the higher-paid since it can so easily be controlled by the business class.

3   The higher-paid class will seek to defend its position by either
(a) pressing for the exclusion of the cheaper class from the territory, or
(b) resorting to a caste arrangement which restricts the cheaper group to a particular set of jobs paid at lower rates.

4   Ethnic antagonism is produced by the competition that arises from a differential price for labour; it does not necessarily emanate from a dominant group but may be the product of interaction. Ethnic antagonism in large measure expresses class conflict between the higher and lower-paid groups within the labour force.

I proposed a quite different theory in the same book, and called it the Rational Choice Theory of Racial and Ethnic Relations. This name has led some readers to infer that it is a theory of rational choices only, whereas it claims to be a theory of all kinds of choices and to indicate that when people make irrational or suboptimal decisions they incur an additional cost. In its current version, the theory presupposes that

1   Individuals act so as to obtain maximum net advantage.

2   Actions at one moment in time influence and modify the alternatives between which individuals will have to choose at subsequent moments.

3   Socialization causes humans to recognize their dependence

upon others and the need to forgo selfish gratification at times. Humans can develop their potential only if they are brought up in social groups. They learn that they have obligations (debts) to those who are defined as fellow group-members.

4 To attain their ends, individuals will at times be obliged to join with others in collective action or to follow strategies that assume that others will engage in such action. Social groups result from and are maintained by the goal-seeking actions of individuals, but each individual has many goals with different priorities.

The theory then divides into (a) a theory of discrimination, which, among other things, holds that

1 Individuals use physical and cultural differences to create groups and categories by processes of inclusion and exclusion. Ethnic groups result from inclusion and racial groups from exclusive processes.

2 When groups interact, processes of change affect their boundaries in ways determined by the form and intensity of competition. In particular, when people compete as individuals, this tends to dissolve the boundaries that define the groups; when they compete as groups, this reinforces those boundaries.

There is then (b) a theory of collective action which is concerned to explain when individuals combine with others in collective action and when they prefer to 'go it alone'; and (c) a theory of intergroup bargaining concerned with strategies of collective action (Banton 1995). An account of the theory of collective action is given in Hardin (1982) while Hechter (1987) is strong on its application to political activity.

It should be noted that these theories all seek to cover ethnic as well as racial relations, but they address slightly different aspects of the data and therefore it is difficult to find situations in which the explanatory power of two theories can be compared. The reader who is interested in the improvement of sociological theory should consider which of the available theories seems least unsatisfactory, and then set about improving it.

GLOSSARY

Assimilation The process of becoming similar.

Colour tax The price differential paid by persons of a different colour to obtain services of a quality similar to those obtained by persons not subject to discrimination.

Confederation An association of sovereign states in which the association does not have direct power over the citizens of the states. Switzerland calls itself a confederation but is more accurately described as a federation. The European Union is a confederation because the association's power over citizens is mediated through the states which compose it.

Ethnic group A category of persons constituted by self-identification in terms of common descent and culture.

Ethnic relations Relations in which behaviour is motivated by the assignment of the parties to ethnic roles.

Ethnicity, primary The shared self-identification as members of a group based upon common descent and culture which coincides with membership of a nation.

Ethnicity, secondary The shared self-identification as members of a group based upon common descent and culture within a state containing other groups.

Ethnocentrism The tendency to evaluate matters by reference to the values shared in the subject's own ethnic group as if that group were the centre of everything.

Ethnogenesis The genesis of a new ethnic group.

Federation A political unit composed of smaller units which entrust specified powers over themselves and their citizens (e.g. with respect to the conduct of foreign affairs) to a federal government.

Genocide Action intended to destroy, in whole or in part, a national, ethnic, racial or religious group as such.

Incitement to racial hatred Publication (in speech or writing) of words threatening, abusive or insulting to members of a racial group with either the intention or the likely effect of stirring up hatred against them.

Multiculturalism
1 An ideology favouring respect for cultural differences between groups enjoying a common citizenship.
2 A policy implementing this ideology, as by encouraging group retention of distinctive languages.

The expression was introduced in 1971 by Canada's Prime Minister Trudeau when he promoted a policy of 'multiculturalism within a bilingual framework', and taken up two years later in Australia. Its use then spread to Britain to designate school curricula designed to reflect the cultural diversity of the groups from which the pupils in the classroom originated.

Phenotype The phenotype is the outward appearance of an organism (such as a human being). It may be paired with a concept of genotype, denoting the underlying genetic constitution of the organism.

Plural society

1 Societies made up of culturally distinctive groups which combine only when, and to the extent that, it is in their interest to do so (J.S. Furnival).

2 Societies in which the political relations between ethnic groups influence their relations to the means of production more than any influence in the reverse direction (Leo Kuper).

Pluralism

1 The philosophy or practice of distributing political power between different institutions, as notably in the United States between the executive, the legislature and the judiciary.

2 The philosophy or practice of encouraging groups to maintain their distinctiveness in the private sphere while sharing common institutions in the public sphere.

Positive action (miscalled positive discrimination) A British designation for legally permitted action to assist members of disadvantaged groups. For example, where applicants for positions have to sit a qualifying examination, applicants from underrepresented groups may be given additional tuition to improve their chances of passing the examination.

Prejudice An emotional and rigidly unfavourable attitude towards persons assigned to a given category.

Race

1 A set of persons of common descent (race as lineage) (from 1570).

2 A set of persons with a distinctive nature (race as type) (from about 1820).

3 A set of persons with common characters (race as subspecies) (from 1959).

4 A set of persons distinguished by the frequency of one or more genes (race as population) (1950).

5 A set of persons who identify with, or are assigned to, a category called a race in everyday speech (race as a social construct) (difficult to date, but has become more significant with the better popular understanding of biological inheritance).

Racial category A set defined by a popular assumption that persons of a particular appearance belong together, are likely to behave in distinctive ways, and in some circumstances should be treated differently.

Racial disadvantage Any form of handicap associated with assignment to a racial category.

Racial discrimination The less favourable treatment of persons on racial grounds. Discrimination is not necessarily unlawful or necessarily immoral. Discrimination occurs when all members of a category are treated as if they shared the characteristics which evoke discrimination, but the underlying motivations may vary. Categorical discrimination derives from negative views about the whole category; statistical discrimination derives from a belief that a high proportion of persons in a category share a characteristic (e.g. that young female workers are more likely to give up their jobs to start a family). In law, racial discrimination and sex discrimination can both be either direct or indirect. Direct discrimination is categorical and intentional. Indirect racial discrimination may be intentional or unintentional; it occurs when someone imposes on another a condition which (a) is such that the proportion of persons of the same racial group as that other who can comply with it is considerably smaller than the proportion of persons not of that racial group who can comply with it: *and* (b) he or she cannot show to be justifiable irrespective of the colour, race, nationality, or ethnic or national origin of the person to whom it is applied; *and* (c) it is to the detriment of that other because he or she cannot comply with it. This definition covers statistical discrimination.

Racial equality This may be defined either factually (as an absence of racial disadvantage) or morally (as a belief that no one shall be treated less favourably on the grounds of race or colour).

Racial group A category of persons defined in racial terms by non-members (it may in practice be a category rather than a group).

Racial relations Relations in which behaviour is racially motivated. When individuals define someone as belonging in a racial category other than their own, they regard that person as having rights and obligations in some way different from those of a person belonging to the same racial category as themselves.

Racialization The representation of group differences as caused by the biological determinants postulated in racial theories.

Racism
1   The doctrine that race determines culture (1933).
2   The use of racial beliefs and attitudes to subordinate and control a category of people defined in racial terms (1967).
3   A historical complex, generated within capitalism, facilitating the exploitation of categories of people defined in racial terms (1970).
4   Anything connected with racial discrimination (1980).

Relations The behaviour between two individuals, who may interact in accordance with one or more sets of role-expectations.

Relationship The behaviour expected of persons occupying two paired roles (e.g. landlord and tenant).

Role The expected behaviour associated with a social position. The concept is usually employed in circumstances in which one role is paired with another (e.g. father–daughter) or related to others in an organization (e.g. manager–foreman–machinist).

Social distance Social acceptability in relationships of varying intimacy.

Underclass A class of persons who, because of the effects of cumulated disadvantage, are excluded from mainstream working-class opportunities and institutions.

Xenophobia Fear of strangers. The word is coming into use in Europe to denote negative attitudes towards immigrant groups on account of their cultural difference; sometimes these feelings are distinguished from racism.

Aberbach, Joel D. and Walker, Jack L. (1970) 'The meanings of Black Power: a comparison of white and black interpretations of a political slogan', *American Political Science Review* 64: 367–88.

Adam, Heribert (1995) 'The politics of ethnic identity: comparing South Africa', *Ethnic and Racial Studies* 18: 457–75.

Ballard, Roger (ed.) (1994) *Desh Pardesh: The South Asian Presence in Britain*, London: Hurst.

Banton, Michael (1976) 'On the use of the adjective "black"', *Network* 6: 2–3, reprinted (1977) *New Community* 5: 480–3.

——— (1983) *Racial and Ethnic Competition*, Cambridge: Cambridge University Press, reprinted 1992, Aldershot: Gregg Revivals.

——— (1985) *Promoting Racial Harmony*, Cambridge: Cambridge University Press.

——— (1986) 'Pluralistic ignorance as a factor in racial attitudes', *New Community* 14: 18–26, and 'Correction', *New Community* 14: 313.

——— (1994) *Discrimination*, Buckingham: Open University Press.

——— (1995) 'Rational choice theories', *American Behavioural Scientist* 38: 478–97.

——— (1996) *International Action against Racial Discrimination*, Oxford: Clarendon Press.

Banton, Michael, and Harwood, Jonathan (1975) *The Race Concept*, Newton Abbott: David & Charles.

Barker, Anthony J. (1978) *The African Link: British Attitudes to the Negro in the Era of the African Slave Trade, 1550–1807*, London: Frank Cass.

Baumann, Gerd (1995) 'Managing a polyethnic milieu: kinship and interaction in a London suburb', *Journal of the Royal Anthropological Institute (NS)* 1: 725–41.

Bendick, M., Jr (1996) *Discrimination against Racial/Ethnic Minorities in Access to Employment in the United States: Empirical Findings from Situation Testing*, International Migration Papers 12, Geneva: International Labour Office.

Berthoud, Richard and Modood, Tariq with others (1996) *The Fourth National Survey of Ethnic Minorities*, London: Policy Studies Institute.

Blumenbach, Johann Friedrich (1865) *The Anthropological Treatises of Johann Friedrich Blumenbach*, London: Anthropological Society of London.

Bonney, Norman (1996) 'The black ghetto and mainstream America' (review article), *Ethnic and Racial Studies* 19: 193–200.

Boutros-Ghali, Boutros (1992) *An Agenda for Peace: Preventive Diplomacy, Peacemaking and Peace-keeping*, New York: United Nations.

Boyd, William C. (1950) *Genetics and the Races of Man*, Boston, MA: Little, Brown.

Brogan, Patrick (1989) *World Conflicts: Why and Where They are Happening*, London: Bloomsbury.

Brown, Colin (1984) *Black and White Britain: The Third PSI Survey*, London: Heinemann.

Brown, Colin and Gay, Pat (1985) *Racial Discrimination: 17 Years after the Act*, Report 646, London: Policy Studies Institute.

Bryce, James (1912) *South America: Observations and Impressions*, New York: Macmillan.

Cashmore, Ernest (1996) *Dictionary of Race and Ethnic Relations*, 4th edn, London: Routledge.

Clinard, Marshall (1978) *Cities with Little Crime: The Case of Switzerland*, Cambridge: Cambridge University Press.

Cohen, Robin (1987) *The New Helots: Migrants in the International Division of Labour*, Aldershot: Gower.

Connor, Walter (ed.) (1985) *Mexican-Americans in Comparative Perspective*, Washington, DC: The Urban Institute.

Covell, Maureen (1993) 'Belgium: the variability of ethnic relations', pp. 275–95 in McGarry and O'Leary (1993).

Daniel, W.W. (1968) *Racial Discrimination in England*, Harmondsworth: Penguin.

Davidson, Basil (1992) *The Black Man's Burden: Africa and the Curse of the Nation-State*, London: James Currey.

Davis, Allison, Gardner, Burleigh B. and Gardner, Mary (1941) *Deep South: A Social Anthropological Study of Caste and Class*, Chicago: Chicago University Press.

De Vos, George and Wetherall, William O. (1983) *Japan's Minorities: Burakumin, Koreans, Ainu and Okinawans*, Report 3, London: Minority Rights Group.

Edmonston, Barry, Goldstein, Joshua and Lott, Juanita Tamayo (eds) (1996) *Spotlight on Heterogeneity. The Federal Standards for Racial and Ethnic Classification*, Washington DC: National Academy Press.

Ehn, Billy (1986) *Det otydliga kulturmötet: Om invandrare och svenskar på ett daghem*, Malmö: Liber Förlag.

Foner, Nancy (1979) 'West Indians in New York City and London: a comparative analysis', *International Migration Review* 13: 284–97.

Gallagher, Michael (1995) 'How many nations are there in Ireland?', *Ethnic and Racial Studies* 18: 715–39.

Glenny, Mischa (1992) *The Fall of Yugoslavia*, Harmondsworth: Penguin.

Grebler, Leo, Moore, Joan W. and Guzman, Ralph C. (1970) *The Mexican-American People: The Nation's Second Largest Minority*, New York: Free Press.

Guillaumin, Colette (1972) *L'Idéologie raciste: genèse et language actuel*, Paris: Mouton.

Hardin, Russell (1982) *Collective Action*, Baltimore, MD: Johns Hopkins University Press.

Haut Conseil à l'Intégration (1993) *L'Intégration à la Française*, Paris: La Documentation Française.

Hechter, Michael (1987) *Principles of Group Solidarity*, Berkeley: University of California Press.

Hinnells, John R. (1994) 'Parsi Zoroastrians in London', pp. 251–71 in Roger Ballard (ed.) *Desh Pardesh: The South Asian Presence in Britain*, London: Hurst.

Hjarnø, Jan (1988) *Invandrere fra Turkiet i Stockhom og København*, Esbjerg: Sydjysk Universitetsforlag.

Homans, George Caspar (1950) *The Human Group*, London: Routledge.

Horowitz, Donald L. (1991) *A Democratic South Africa? Constitutional Engineering in a Divided Society*, Berkeley: University of California Press.

Hughes, Everett C. and Hughes, Helen M. (1952) *Where Peoples Meet: Racial and Ethnic Frontiers*, Glencoe, IL: Free Press.

Huxley, Julian S. and Haddon, A.C. (1935) *We Europeans: A Survey of Racial Problems*, London: Jonathan Cape.

Iganski, Paul, and Payne, Geoff (1996) 'Declining racial disadvantage in the British labour market', *Ethnic and Racial Studies* 19: 113–34.

Jenkins, Roy (1966) 'Address to a meeting of Voluntary Liaison Committees', London: National Committee for Commonwealth Immigrants.

Johnson, R.W. (1977) *How Long will South Africa Survive?*, London: Macmillan.

Jones, Trevor (1993) *Britain's Ethnic Minorities*, London: Policy Studies Institute.

Kuper, Leo (1960) 'The heightening of racial tension', *Race* 2: 24–32.

―――― (1977) *The Pity of it All: Polarization of Racial and Ethnic Relations*, London: Duckworth.

―――― (1982) *Genocide: Its Political Use in the Twentieth Century*, New Haven, CT: Yale University Press.

―――― (1985) *International Action against Genocide*, Report 53, London: Minority Rights Group.

Lemarchand, René (1993) 'Burundi in comparative perspective: dimensions of ethnic strife', pp. 151–71 in McGarry and O'Leary, (1993).

Lijphart, Arend (1994) 'Prospects for power-sharing in the new South Africa', pp. 231–31 in Reynolds (1994).

Lorimer, Douglas, A. (1978) *Colour, Class and the Victorians: English Attitudes towards the Negro in the Mid-Nineteenth Century*, Leicester: Leicester University Press.

Lyman, Stanford M. (1994) *Colour, Culture, Civilization*, Urbana: University of Illinois.

Mandela, Nelson (1994) *Long Walk to Freedom*, London: Little, Brown.

Massey, Douglas S. and Denton, Nancy A. (1993) *American Apartheid: Segregation and the Making of the Underclass*, Cambridge, MA: Harvard University Press.

McGarry, John, and O'Leary, Brendan (eds) (1993) *The Politics of Ethnic Conflict Regulation: Case Studies of Protracted Ethnic Conflicts*, London: Routledge.

Miles, Robert (1989) *Racism*, London: Routledge.

Miles, Robert, and Phizacklea, Annie (1984) *White Man's Country: Racism in British Politics*, London: Pluto Press.

Modood, Tariq (1988) '"Black", racial equality and Asian identity', *New Community* 14: 397–404.

——— (1994) 'Establishment, multiculturalism and British citizenship', *Political Quarterly*, 65: 53–73.

Modood, Tariq, Beishon, Sharon, and Virdee, Satnam (1994) *Changing Ethnic Identities*, London: Policy Studies Institute.

Mörner, Magnus (1967) *Race Mixture in the History of Latin America*, Boston, MA: Little, Brown.

Mourant, A.E. (1983) *Blood Relations: Blood Groups and Anthropology*, Oxford: Oxford University Press.

O'Duffy, Brendan (1993) 'Containment or regulation? The British approach to ethnic conflict in Northern Ireland', pp. 128–50 in McGarry and O'Leary (1993).

Palley, Claire (1974) *Constitutional Law and Minorities*, Report 36, London: Minority Rights Group.

Palley, Claire, Alcock, Antony, Bossuyt, Marc, *et al.* (1986) *Coexistence in some Plural European Societies*, Report 72, London: Minority Rights Group.

Pottier, Johan (1996) 'Representations of ethnicity in post-genocide writings on Rwanda', pp. 53–76 in Obi, Igwara (ed.) *Ethnic Hatred: Genocide in Rwanda*, London: Association for the Study of Ethnicity and Nationalism.

Reynolds, Andrew (ed.) (1994) *Election '94 South Africa*, London: James Currey.

Reyntjens, Filip (1995) *Burundi: Breaking the Cycle of Violence*, London: Minority Rights Group.

Sartre, Jean-Paul (1948) 'Orphée Noir', preface to L. Sédar-Senghor (ed.) *Anthologie de la nouvelle poésie nègre et malgache*, Paris: Presses Universitaires de France.

Selvon, Samuel (1956) *The Lonely Londoners*, London: Wingate.

Sieghart, Paul (1986) *The Lawful Rights of Mankind*, Oxford: Oxford University Press.

Silber, Laura and Little, Allan (1995) *The Death of Yugoslavia*, London: Penguin and BBC.

Smith, David J. (1977) *Racial Disadvantage in Britain: The PEP Report*, Harmondsworth: Penguin.

Solomos, John (1989) *Race and Racism in Contemporary Britain*, London: Macmillan.

Stymeist, David H. (1975) *Ethnics and Indians: Social Relationships in a Northwestern Ontario Town*, Toronto: Peter Martin Associates.

Taguieff, Pierre-André (1988) *La Force du préjugé: essais sur le racisme et ses doubles*, Paris: La Découverte.

Tajfel, Henri (1970) 'Experiments in intergroup discrimination' *Scientific American* 223(5): 96–102.

—— (1978) *The Social Psychology of Minorities*, Report 38, London: Minority Rights Group.

Thornberry, Patrick (1991) *Minorities and Human Rights Law*, London: Minority Rights Group.

Tizard, Barbara and Phoenix, Anne (1993) *Black, White or Mixed Race? Race and Racism in the Lives of Young People of Mixed Parentage*, London: Routledge.

Tumin, Melvin M. (1961) *Social Class and Social Change in Puerto Rico*, Princeton, NJ: Princeton University Press.

Walvin, James (1971) *The Black Presence: A Documentary History of the Negro in England*, London: Orbach & Chambers.

Wieviorka, Michel (1994a) *Racisme et xénophobie en Europe*, Paris: La Découverte.

—— (1994b) *The Arena of Racism*, London: Sage.

Young, Ken (1992) 'Race, class and opportunity', pp. 175–93 in Jowell, Roger, Brook, Lindsay, Prior, G. and Taylor, B. (eds) (1992) *British Social Attitudes: The 9th Report*, Aldershot: Dartmouth.

INDEX